50 ¢

From Dream to Reality

From scouting properties to making your investment, some of the [...] real estate investor include the following:

1. **Get ready:** Determine what you're looking for in a property, and which type of property best matches your personal and investment criteria.

2. **Get financing:** Determine the amount of mortgage financing for which you qualify, and whether or not you would be comfortable accepting that much financing and debt. Once you've figured out your mortgage preferences, obtain a pre-approved mortgage from a mortgage broker.

3. **Get focused, part 1:** Determine where you would like to invest and research the property possibilities in the geographic area of preference using both print and online sources such as local newspapers, online listings services, and other means. Don't forget to cruise the area by car, keeping your eyes open for sale signs.

4. **Get help:** Select a real estate agent to represent your interest in the purchase you're thinking about making. Depending on the purchase, you may also wish to enlist an accountant, financial planner, lawyer, appraiser, and other advisers. These advisers may also be able to identify properties worth your interest.

5. **Get focused, part 2:** Shortlist properties of interest in the area you've been researching, noting the pros and cons of each. Arrange for a viewing of each property.

6. **Get real:** View the property with an adviser and/or a trusted colleague, friend, or relative who will offer candid and honest feedback regarding the positive and negative aspects of your potential investment.

7. **Get coverage:** Select an insurance broker to insure your pending property purchase.

8. **Get busy:** Draft a purchase offer for the property with the assistance of your real estate agent and the lawyer you've engaged to oversee the transaction. With their advice, include appropriate conditions in your offer. Determine and budget for the potential costs of closing the deal.

9. **Get answers:** Proceed with due diligence and don't remove any conditions on the sale until you're fully satisfied with the purchase. This includes ensuring the property inspection is satisfactory and that all outstanding concerns with regards to title are clear. Obtain title insurance for additional security and peace of mind.

10. **Get out your wallet:** Proceed with the property purchase and mortgage documentation through your lawyer.

11. **Get settled:** Depending on the kind of property in which you've invested, hire a moving company and get set up, or introduce yourself to the current tenants.

Real Estate Investing For Canadians For Dummies®

Scouting Properties

Considering a few practical elements may help you choose between an adorable rental property in the middle of nowhere and a tear-down shack with long-term potential:

- ✔ **Price:** Compare the asking price of a property to the average sale price for the area. An under-valued property in a good neighbourhood stands a better chance of increasing in value than an overpriced home in a neighbourhood that's going nowhere.

- ✔ **Condition:** You may be getting a great deal on a property, but if you haven't counted on the cost of long-overdue maintenance, you may face a losing proposition. Though you may be able to make something of a property, if the improvements cancel the potential return, what's the point?

- ✔ **Cash flow:** Make sure you can attract tenants to a property if you're counting on cash flow, not just a rising price, from your investment. Remember to balance the projected cash flow against operating costs, to ensure your income stays ahead of expenses.

Finding Help

When you want help in a hurry, visit these sites:

- ✔ **Canada Mortgage and Housing Corp.** (www.cmhc.ca): Need to know how many homes are being built in your area or what rental rates are like? Need information on financing and incentives for renovations? You'll find it all, and much more, here.

- ✔ **Canadian Real Estate Association** (www.crea.ca): Get connected with your local real estate association, find property listings, and discover what it takes to sell real estate. Packed with useful information, this site is an online primer for home buyers and the residential properties.

- ✔ **Bank of Canada** (www.bankofcanada.ca): More useful than it sounds, the Bank of Canada site provides valuable information to investors and wannabes alike. Whether you're looking for interest rate trends, fiscal analyses, or calculators to figure out the impact of inflation on your investments, here are the resources you need to make sense of your dollars.

For Dummies: Bestselling Book Series for Beginners

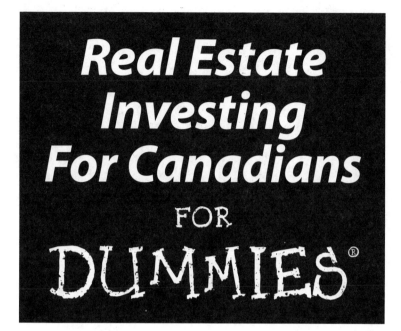

Real Estate Investing For Canadians

FOR DUMMIES®

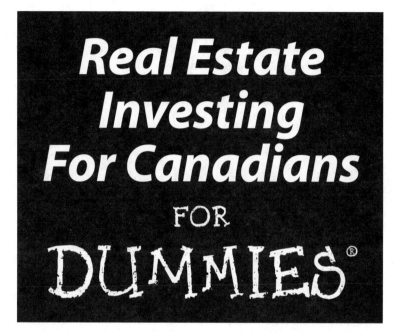

Real Estate Investing For Canadians

FOR DUMMIES®

by Douglas Gray and Peter Mitham

John Wiley & Sons Canada, Ltd.

Real Estate Investing For Canadians For Dummies®

Published by
John Wiley & Sons Canada, Ltd
6045 Freemont Boulevard
Mississauga, Ontario, L5R 4J3
www.wiley.com

Library and Archives Canada Catologuing in Publication

Gray, Douglas A.

    Real estate investing for Canadians for dummies / Douglas A. Gray, Peter

Mitham.

Includes index.

ISBN-13: 978-0-470-83418-3

ISBN-10: 0-470-83418-8

    1. Real estate investment–Canada. I. Mitham, Peter James, 1969-

II. Title.

HD316.G73 2006   332.63'240971   C2006-902219-4

Printed in Canada

1 2 3 4 5 TRI 10 09 08 07 06

Distributed in Canada by John Wiley & Sons Canada, Ltd.

For general information on John Wiley & Sons Canada, Ltd, including all books published by Wiley Publishing, Inc., please call our warehouse, Tel 1-800-567-4797. For reseller information, including discounts and premium sales, please call our sales department, Tel 416-646-7992. For press review copies, author interviews, or other publicity information, please contact our marketing department, Tel 416-646-4584, Fax 416-236-4448.

For authorization to photocopy items for corporate, personal, or educational use, please contact in writing The Canadian Copyright Licensing Agency (Access Copyright). For an Access Copyright license, visit www.accesscopyright.ca or call toll free, 1-800-893-5777.

WILEY

About the Authors

Douglas Gray, LLB, is one of the foremost experts on real estate in Canada. He's written over 22 books on real estate and personal finance, all of them bestsellers. They include seven books on real estate, such as *Making Money in Real Estate, 101 Streetsmart Condo Buying Tips for Canadians,* and *Mortgages Made Easy.* He brings to this book 35 years of experience investing in residential properties, as well as many years as a lawyer representing buyers, sellers, lenders, borrowers, and developers. President of the National Real Estate Institute Inc., headquartered in Vancouver, British Columbia, Doug is a consultant and columnist, and regularly gives seminars on real estate across Canada for both professional Realtors and the public. His Web site is www.homebuyer.ca.

Peter Mitham is a prolific freelance contributor to newspapers and magazines who has written on Canadian real estate for publications in both Canada and abroad. He writes a weekly column of real estate news for *Business in Vancouver* (www.biv.com) and contributes regularly to *Western Investor* (www.westerninvestor.com), a sister publication focused on real estate investment opportunities in Western Canada. Peter's articles on real estate, renovations, and construction appear regularly in agricultural, trade, and consumer publications in Canada and the United States. Growing up in Quebec, he was fascinated with the catalogues of property listings and mortgage applications in the home office of his father, an appraiser (now retired). This is his second book.

Dedication

We dedicate this book to the current and potential property owners and landlords of Canada, for whom it was written, and from whose experiences and insights it evolved.

Authors' Acknowledgments

This book has been much more than a collaboration between two authors. The insights and advice of several readers, editors, and professionals has helped make this book what it is.

The steady encouragement of John Wiley & Sons Canada associate editor Robert Hickey allowed us to soldier on through the close reading given the text by developmental editor Kelli Howey, who provided much practical food for thought and impetus for improvement in the text. We would also like to thank Allyson Latta for her skilful copyediting.

Doug would like to express his appreciation to the many real estate–related clients he has enjoyed working with over the years. They include legal and consulting clients, as well as seminar participants. Doug would also like to express his appreciation to Don Loney, executive editor at John Wiley & Sons Canada. Don has been Doug's muse and mentor on real estate books for almost 15 years and is a consummate and talented professional in the publishing business.

Peter especially appreciates the landlords he's had across the country for more than a few insights that made it into the sections on property management. The opportunities he's had to cover real estate for Business in Vancouver Media Group also gave him invaluable insight into the acquisition, management and disposition of investment properties. He acknowledges his debt to those who have shared with him their real estate adventures, stories that have spurred many of the anecdotes and some of the advice offered in these pages (names have been changed to protect the innocent).

Finally, we thank our wives, Diana and May, for the support and understanding they've shown us through our various writing projects, this latest effort among them.

Publisher's Acknowledgments

We're proud of this book; please send us your comments at canadapt@wiley.com. Some of the people who helped bring this book to market include the following:

Acquisitions, Editorial, and Media Development

Editor: Robert Hickey

Developmental Editor: Kelli Howey

Copy Editor: Allyson Latta

Cartoons: Rich Tennant
(www.the5thwave.com)

Composition

Publishing Services Director: Karen Bryan

Publishing Services Manager: Ian Koo

Project Manager: Elizabeth McCurdy

Project Coordinator: Lindsay Humphreys

Layout and Graphics: Carl Byers, Andrea Dahl, Denny Hager, Barbara Moore, Heather Ryan, Alicia B. South

Proofreaders: Susan Moritz, Techbooks

Indexer: Andrea Battiston, Colborne Communications Inc.

John Wiley & Sons Canada, Ltd

    Bill Zerter, Chief Operating Officer

    Jennifer Smith, Publisher, Professional and Trade Division

Publishing and Editorial for Consumer Dummies

    Diane Graves Steele, Vice President and Publisher, Consumer Dummies

    Joyce Pepple, Acquisitions Director, Consumer Dummies

    Kristin A. Cocks, Product Development Director, Consumer Dummies

    Michael Spring, Vice President and Publisher, Travel

    Suzanne Jannetta, Editorial Director, Travel

Publishing for Technology Dummies

    Andy Cummings, Vice President and Publisher, Dummies Technology/General User

Composition Services

    Gerry Fahey, Vice President of Production Services

    Debbie Stailey, Director of Composition Service

Contents at a Glance

Table of Contents

Introduction

*I*f you've ever bought a home, you've invested in real estate, even if you didn't plan to use the property to finance your retirement. Chances are, like many people, you may not even have considered real estate from an investment perspective — it's simply been your own patch of ground, somewhere you can relax and call home.

But real estate is an important part of the personal investment strategies pursued by many people — and not just the Donald Trumps of the world. If you've picked up this book, you probably think real estate might be for you. Congratulations! No matter where you are in your journey, this book can get you started and see you through to the close of your first deal — and the beginning of your second!

Foolish Assumptions

This book is reader-focused, so by definition we've had to make a few assumptions about you. Although we've never had the pleasure of meeting, we expect that you're most likely a novice when it comes to investing in real estate. Perhaps you've never bought a property; perhaps you've bought only your own home. This book will be a primer for you.

We also want to make sure that you enjoy a fresh take on the art of investing in real estate, particularly if you do have some experience in the market. Although we can't offer an in-depth analysis of each topic, we do provide an excellent overview and some pointers for honing your strategy (watch for sidebars, vignettes drawn from real-life examples, and so forth).

Because you may be interested in more than just buying a property, we haven't neglected to track down other ways in which you can understand, participate in, and benefit from the real estate market even if you don't want to own your own acreage — yet.

Should any of these assumptions about yourself ring true, read on! We look forward to working with you.

How This Book Is Organized

We've organized this book into five parts and an appendix. We hope you'll find it easy to use, and a clear guide to investing in real estate. But for starters, here's a quick look at what you can expect to find in each part. The book is modular in format, allowing you to read chapters as you require the information. But that doesn't mean you can't read it through, beginning to end.

Part 1: Understanding Real Estate

No investment opportunity comes without risk, so we take some time in this part to discuss the options open to you as a real estate investor and the requirements for entering the market, as well as briefly cover the risks you'll face once you're involved. We take a look at how real estate can play a role in your long-term financial plan, and how the various kinds of real estate can work for you. We also introduce you to the concept of market cycles and some of the challenges joint ownership and government regulations can pose. Finally, we discuss investing strategies and how to formulate one that works for you.

Part 11: Preparing to Buy: Financing Real Estate Investments

A bit of cash and a fistful of dreams can work wonders, but you should also know how much property you're capable of buying. In this part, we cover financing of your investment and help you identify resources, and cultivate the relationships that can assist you in finding even more resources. We also talk about mortgages, and how to make the financing you've got go further (not to mention the limits of financing). Because the ownership structure you choose may help you achieve your investment goals, we discuss ways you can own real estate, such as personally, through a partnership or a company.

Part 111: Selecting Properties: Where to Look, What to Watch For

A prime location isn't the only thing that makes for a good real estate investment. Researching and identifying a property for purchase involves so much more, and we discuss the factors you need to consider as well as brief you on the basics of sizing up neighbourhoods. We also give you a heads-up on working with market cycles to improve your chances of being a successful investor. We try to make sense of complex topics like appraisals, cap rates, and operating expenses, and give tips on making the best of bad situations. We walk you through the due diligence process — one of the most important parts of selecting a property — and tip you off to the kinds of frauds that could rob you of your investment. Finally, we discuss closing the deal, and strategies that will help you get a deal that's to your liking — and the vendor's.

Part IV: Building Value: Managing Your Investment and Seeing a Return

Becoming an investor means knowing how to manage a property, not just buy it, and this part helps you make the most of your hard-won asset. We discuss property managers, tenant selection, and landlord-tenant relations. We offer tips on reducing your risks through sound management practices, and reducing your costs through regular maintenance. We also offer insights into strategies for managing expenses and deductions that can save you money, and what to do when it's your turn to become a seller.

Part V: The Part of Tens

There's always something more to say, and always something more to explore. This section points to places you can turn to, whether you're researching a purchase, preparing to renovate, or looking to sell. We also offer tips on building the value of your property, from doing upgrades to managing cash flow.

Icons Used in This Book

Several icons throughout this book flag information for you that you may want to record, remember, or read later. These include the following:

Why reinvent the wheel? Tips pass along useful information based on the experience of those who've gone before.

Knowing what *not* to do is key to managing your risks. Warnings convey information that can save you time, money, and frustration.

Some concepts deserve extra emphasis. Remembering these items may make your life as an investor easier and, we hope, more successful!

We aim to provide useful information, but sometimes it helps to have some background. Technical stuff is important, but feel free to read it later.

When the basic information we provide can benefit from more specifics, we encourage you to do your own research.

Where to Go from Here

Canada is a big country, and that means a lot of real estate. But because the real estate that makes up each province is governed by the laws in that province, much of what we talk about in this book may play out differently in different jurisdictions. But this book can get you started, and we hope you take time to read the whole thing (even if you don't read it in order). You should find it a good companion as you navigate through the idiosyncrasies of various provincial regimes and at the same time stay focused on the big picture. Consider us part of your research team, and let us back you up as you pursue deals and discuss the finer points of your own situation with your advisers.

Above all, enjoy the time you spend investing in real estate!

Part I
Understanding Real Estate

"I could rent you this one. It's got a pool in the backyard. Then I got a six bedroom with a fountain out front, but nothing right now with a moat."

In this part . . .

Wondering how real estate is going to fit into your life? Here's the best place to start! We demystify the basic concepts associated with real estate investing and give you the tools you need to start developing your investment strategy. We discuss the various challenges and opportunities and explore how you can prepare yourself to become a successful real estate investor.

Chapter 1

Identifying Opportunities

Some days, it seems like everyone wants to be a real estate tycoon. And why not? Land is a relatively stable investment and, hey, it's nice to *see* your investment once in a while, which you can do with land, unlike with other, intangible investments that are just figures on paper. Whether you have a handful of homes you rent to university students, renovate a run-down character house you can sell for a handsome profit, or buy the neighbourhood strip mall and make it a gathering point for the area, you've got opportunities for making money as well as making a contribution to your community.

Real estate is everywhere: the apartment or house you call home, the mall where you go shopping for groceries and clothes, and the office where you work. Even the park where you take your kids and walk your dog are properties with potential investment value. But like any other investment, real estate has its risks, too. Remember the old saying "land rich, cash poor"? The expression summarizes the very real wealth that exists in land but also the financial dangers land ownership poses if you don't have a strategy. What kind of real estate interests you most? Have you considered the skills — and weaknesses — you bring to your role as an investor? Successful investment in real estate means becoming land rich in order to become cash rich, too. You want to do it right!

In this chapter, we discuss the various opportunities awaiting you as an investor, and some of the risks real estate carries. We look at some of the considerations you should bear in mind as you're sizing up the different investment tools available. Finally, we investigate how real estate can fit into a long-term financial plan, and the implications that it can have for your retirement and your estate.

Investigating Real Estate Investing

So what's the big deal about real estate, anyhow? Why is everyone from the government honchos who manage the Canada Pension Plan right on down to your uncle Ed buying property? In this section, we check out the advantages of real estate and compare property relative to other kinds of investments you may consider as part of your portfolio.

Discovering the opportunities

Statistics from the Canadian Real Estate Association indicate that residential real estate has increased in value by an average of 5 percent annually over the past 30 years. Not every property will make the same gains in every year or from city to city, but the trend is unmistakable: The long-term potential for the appreciation of your real estate investment is tremendous. And several reasons bolster our argument that an investment in real estate makes sense. We outline them below.

Leverage opportunities

Leverage is all about using a small amount of your own money and letting someone else's cash do the rest of the work. Because real estate provides the loan's *security,* a guarantee of repayment if you're unable to pay off the loan, the risk is low. Should your *creditors,* the people who've loaned you cash, demand immediate repayment and call your loan, you could find your property the subject of proceedings that lead to its court-ordered sale.

We discuss some of the basics of setting your limits as an investor elsewhere in this chapter, and discuss financing at greater length in Chapter 5.

Equity opportunities

By paying down a mortgage, you're paying down the purchase value of the property and making its value your own. Real estate is unlike many other investments because it gives you a chance to build *equity* — your share of the property's net worth at the time of sale — over the course of the investment rather than put it in up front and hope for the best. Given the chance of appreciation in the value of real estate while you're making those payments, that's a significant advantage at the time of sale.

Return opportunities

That's return on money, not the chances you'll return alive from a property! But you'll probably do that, too, and get to enjoy the benefits of a net return of as much as 150 percent annually on your investment. How do we figure that?

Simply put, the return is calculated on your investment. If you buy a $200,000 property with a $20,000 down payment and the property doubles in value over five years, the increase in equity is $200,000. That amounts to approximately $150,000 after the government taxes the appreciation in the property's value, or *capital gain* (we discuss capital gains at greater length in Chapter 15). This would represent a return of 750 percent over five years, or at least 150 percent annually on your original investment of $20,000. Given that the debt you incurred to buy the property would have decreased over the course of the five years, and provided leasing allowed you to see income from the property, you would enjoy an even greater return on your investment.

Tax opportunities

Real estate offers several tax advantages for investors, especially if you have a strategy in place. Though taxes erode the return you'll see on investments that provide a fixed return, such as bank accounts, bonds and guaranteed investment certificates (GICs), and though stocks and other equities put your principal at risk, real estate investments often allow you a reduced tax rate. The tax advantages range from tax-free capital gains on your principal residence to savings as great as 50 percent on taxes levied on capital gains from investment properties. You'll also be able to deduct investment expenses and write off any depreciation in property values. We discuss taxes in greater detail in Chapter 15.

Hedge opportunities

No, we're not suggesting you hide from your creditors in a bush! The kind of hedging we're talking about means taking shelter from the effects of inflation, which works to erode your buying power. The rate of inflation varies from month to month, year to year and even country to country. But real estate typically appreciates at a rate three to five percentage points above the inflation rate. So if inflation is running at 3 percent, look for your investment in real estate to appreciate at 6 to 8 percent. If you choose wisely, your investment stands a good chance of increasing at a rate greater than that of inflation as Figure 1-1 shows.

You're paying off your mortgage in dollars that reflect inflation, also known as *real dollars.* So, although the value of your mortgage is going to diminish over time, you will be receiving more money thanks to salary increases or rental revenue increases that will make your mortgage more affordable.

Flexibility opportunities

Real estate offers a variety of investment options that give you flexibility in terms of how much attention they demand and the amount of risk you'll bear. By investing in just one property rather than several, or in partnership with family or friends, you can limit (or increase) your involvement to the level that suits you.

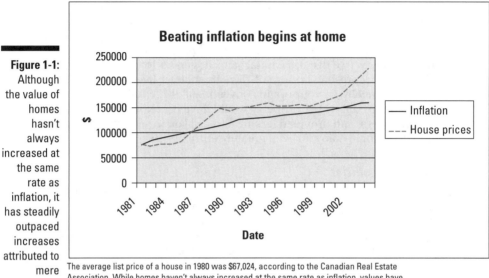

The average list price of a house in 1980 was $67,024, according to the Canadian Real Estate Association. While homes haven't always increased at the same rate as inflation, values have steadily outpaced any increases attributed to mere inflation.
Source: Canadian Real Estate Association

Learning opportunities

Most investments entail some sort of learning process. Real estate is no different. Prior involvement in buying property, such as a home, may make it easier, but don't underestimate the need to learn about the particular dynamics of investing in real property. Real estate investment also offers opportunities to learn about the community issues and economic trends at work in neighbourhoods. And, if you're game for the role of landlord, you'll also have a chance to improve your people-management skills.

Considering alternatives

But wait! Do you really want to buy a patch of dirt, or a stack of bricks? Why not let someone else worry about the paperwork associated with ownership and the hassles of managing an investment property? You have better things to do, and better places to put your money, right?

True enough — and if these are your nagging doubts, you will do well to consider other forms of investment. Fear not, though: Some investments even let you enjoy indirect benefits from the fortunes of the real estate business without direct exposure to the risks! The three main alternatives to investing in real estate include

✔ Fixed-term investments

✔ Equities

✔ Direct investment in businesses

Real estate typically stands out from other investments because of its stable and long-term nature, and the chance to derive a steady income from assets month by month. These three characteristics make it a preferred choice for many, but if you're not up for the risks inherent in real estate investments you might be safer with an alternative.

We're all for you making real estate your primary investment choice, but a mix of modesty and sheer prudence compels us to recommend a balanced portfolio. Because real estate carries its own measure of risk, having a diversified portfolio that includes a mix of investment vehicles is in your interest — just so your entire nest-egg isn't wiped out by, say, fire, flood, locusts, or a band of determined termites. If you need help, consult one of the many reference works available, such as *Investing for Canadians For Dummies* by Eric Tyson and Tony Martin (Wiley).

Fixed-term investments

Bank accounts, guaranteed investment certificates (GICs), and bonds are stable investments with minimal risk and a guaranteed return. Fixed-term investments are great if you don't have a lot of cash to play with or need readily accessible funds, but if you're holding a lot of them, consider real estate a step up to a more sophisticated form of investing.

The difference in return can be significant, with real estate often appreciating at a rate three to five percentage points above inflation. And unlike real estate earnings, interest received on term deposits and bonds is fully taxable as income and also subject to inflation. A GIC may offer a 4-percent return on your cash, but if inflation is 3 percent, you're seeing an effective return of just 1 percent on those dollars. Even if you're in the lowest tax bracket, you're probably just breaking even.

Equities

Not to be confused with the equity you build by paying down your mortgage, *equities* like stocks trade on the open market and expose investors to fluctuations in value on a per-share or per-unit basis. The return is never guaranteed, though depending on your portfolio you may do better at some points than others. The stock market can offer good returns to dedicated, savvy investors — everyone seemed to be investing in equities during the tech boom of the late 1990s — but it's also subject to downturns that can wipe out the value of your investment. The crash of tech stocks in the early 2000s was one of the reasons why the popularity of tangible, bricks-and-mortar real estate began to surge in the opening years of this decade.

Mutual funds, though not strictly speaking equities, also fluctuate in value in response to market conditions but tend to be more diversified, reducing exposure to market volatility and in turn minimizing risk.

Stocks, income trusts, and mutual funds all carry greater risk than real estate. The return on equities will fluctuate with daily market forces, but a good real estate investment typically delivers a steady cash flow as a result of consistent demand either from a series of short-term or long-term tenants.

Direct investment in businesses

Supporting a business venture you believe in by providing it with a start-up loan may be one of the most rewarding investments you make, but it also comes with the uncertainties associated with the company's business. Though the return isn't guaranteed, if the business succeeds, you can be paid back handsomely depending on the terms of the financing arrangement (which should be in your favour, because you get to have a hand in writing them).

Knowing Your Limits

Real estate, like other investment options, demands that you have a plan for building your portfolio. Just as you're careful not to contribute too much in a given month or year to your RRSP, you don't want to sink too much of your available cash resources into a real estate investment you may not be able to sell for several years. Why own a palace if you can't live like a king?

Knowing your financial limits is just one aspect of determining your capacity for investing in real estate. Assessing the appetite you have for risk is equally important.

Risks are both real and perceived. For example, buying a property when the market is at its peak entails a real risk that the property could fall in value, leaving you open to a loss. Or you may be tempted to buy a property in the hope that City Hall will let you renovate it, but do your homework ahead of time to ensure that local zoning will allow it. Equally important to successful investing is knowing yourself and how much confidence you have as an investor. Avoid situations that could undermine your confidence and cloud your decision-making abilities, such as buying or renovating properties for nostalgic or emotional reasons without first drafting a solid business plan.

If you're serious about real estate investing (and if you're reading this book, you probably are), the first thing you need to do is determine whether you and real estate are a good investment match. This determination is the key to your financial future. In the next section, we help you figure that out.

How much can you invest?

Getting a handle on your personal finances is an important part of financing your real estate investment (something we discuss at greater length in Part II). Financing the actual purchase is just one part of the picture. Costs that crop up every day — from necessities such as shoes for the kids, to luxuries like your gym membership or a night out on the town — determine how much cash you have available for investment. Don't forget to take into account unexpected expenses such as an interruption in employment income. These factors each affect the amount you can invest, and the amount of risk you're willing to take on.

 Conventional wisdom suggests you should put aside three months' worth of living expenses to draw on in case of emergency, and the same holds true for your real estate investments. In case of emergency, you'll not only have to service the mortgage, you'll have to service the property itself — that is, cover ongoing maintenance of your building or property.

How much risk is too much?

The risks associated with real estate stem from its disadvantages. Chances are you're attracted to real estate and the stability it offers; after all, land isn't about to get up and walk away, and they're not making a whole lot more of it. But land also has its own limitations that can affect how you can use it and its value to investors. Some common risks include

- ✔ **Changes to surrounding properties and the local neighbourhood:** We all know of houses where the grass has grown long and shaggy, curtains in the windows are faded, and newspapers are piling up by the front door. Now, imagine that house is right next door to the home of your dreams. Or perhaps a few of them stand in the neighbourhood where you're thinking of buying. Chances are you won't find the neighbourhood as appealing. Changes in the condition of other properties can seriously affect the value of your own real estate, and may prompt you to try selling a property earlier than you had intended. On the other hand, positive changes to nearby properties can cause the value of your property to appreciate, and even prompt you to make improvements that will keep up not only with the Joneses but also with the broader market.

- ✔ **Changes in the political climate and government policies:** Regardless of who forms the government, real estate investments may be subject to policy changes. A city council may need extra funding and pass a bylaw requiring owners of apartment buildings to pay significantly more for city services than homeowners. Imagine the effect this could have on the market for that apartment block you're looking to sell! It could also boost your interest in buying single-family residential homes to rent out. Or perhaps city staff are about to rezone the lot down the street for commercial development; depending on whether they allow a tea boutique or a bar with exotic dancers, your property is likely to see a change in value. Whether you can make the most of such changes will determine the success of your investment.

✔ **Changes in the local economy that can lead to property depreciation through lower demand:** The amount of risk you can accept and manage will determine not only the kind of property you purchase but also whether you purchase at all. Take a close look at your background and the skills you bring to the challenges of being an investor. Are you familiar with the risks you face, or will they be new challenges for you? They might help you to discover and develop new skills, but you don't want to jeopardize your investment in the process. Becoming familiar with the risks you face — and recognizing when you need assistance, or even when you should reject an opportunity — is key to a successful investment.

We discuss other forms of risk at length in Chapters 8 and 14.

Are you ready for the long haul?

Real estate isn't usually a form of investment that yields a quick profit, though some investors have been known to *flip* properties (selling them at a gain shortly after buying them). Instead, most investors hold real estate for at least one cycle of the real estate market. A *market cycle* is the period in which a market goes from high to low, from a buyer's market to a seller's market (we discuss this concept at length in Chapter 3). A standard cycle in the real estate market typically lasts as few as 5 and as many as 12 years. Some observers believe market cycles are actually lengthening, which means longer holding periods before you'll be able to realize a return.

Determining your readiness for a long-term investment and establishing realistic financial goals will help you select the kind of property that will suit your needs.

Are you ready for a soft market?

A *soft market* occurs when demand is slack for a product or service. Think of it as kind of like a soft-boiled egg: If you don't know what you're dealing with before you crack into it, you'll find yourself with a mess on your hands. As an investor, a soft market is an opportunity to pick up properties at a lower price than you might otherwise. If you've already got property, you may find yourself unable to sell when you want. The situation will force you to make some hard choices: Are you comfortable holding the property a bit longer, or are you willing to accept a slightly lower return in exchange for a quick sale?

This is worth thinking about, in case your financial circumstances change and you need to access the equity that's accumulated in your property since you bought it.

Soft markets are also periods during which you can invest in property with a view to preparing it for sale when markets improve. We suggest some strategies for building property value in Chapter 18.

Getting into Real Estate Investing

Now that you've examined the alternatives and determined your limits, and if you still think real estate investing is for you, you can consider where you're going to invest and the opportunities available in these areas.

Looking for locales

Before you even start looking at investment properties, you'll need to decide *where* to invest. Your motivation for investing will influence where you search, so be sure to prioritize the criteria you want in an investment property so you can focus your search and have a better view to what you're seeking. Your interests will also influence the goals you set in the financial plan supporting your investment strategy.

The locale that's right for you depends on several factors. For example:

- ✔ You want a property close to your current home so that you can address tenants' needs, or admire your purchase on a daily basis.

- ✔ You want a vacation getaway you can rent out when you're not there, or a home for your retirement.

- ✔ You want a property you can renovate and resell, a strategy that could take you into older communities or run-down neighborhoods poised for revival.

If you're new to real estate investing, you might have a hard time figuring out just what you're looking for in a property. The following questions should help you put your finger on it:

- ✔ What are demographic trends for the area you're looking at? Are people moving in or out, and why?

- ✔ What have land values been doing in the areas where you're looking?

✔ Is the kind of property you're buying in short supply in the area? Why or why not?

✔ What are observers, both inside and outside the real estate industry, saying about the prospects for the various areas where you're considering making an investment?

Once you determine whether you're seeking a straightforward investment property or one you can also use, and a general price range, you'll be able to narrow your search to a few prospective investment areas. Identify at least three locales; if your first choice falls through, you'll have a backup plan.

Your ability to afford a property, both the basic purchase price and the cost of the mortgage, will also factor into where you scout opportunities. If you're financing your purchase by selling off an acre of land in rural Saskatchewan, chances are that purchasing an acre of land in an industrial park on the outskirts of Edmonton won't be in the cards (unless you can obtain additional financing). But, if you trade in a summer home in the Laurentians with dreams of buying a seaside cottage in Nova Scotia, your potential investment options will probably be greater.

We discuss the search for a property at greater length in Chapter 9.

Sizing up opportunities

The areas you've chosen to consider for investment will have strengths and weaknesses, not unlike the specific property you're hoping to find. But it's important to assess the big picture.

Depending on where you live and where the property is, you'll probably want to factor in travel time for visiting and administering your prospective purchase. An investment shouldn't be a burden, so be sure you can effectively manage it without the task consuming too much of your time.

A standard rule for determining where to invest rules out properties located more than four hours' driving distance of where you live. This ensures you can easily reach the property if required to do so.

The long-term factors affecting the general area surrounding your favoured location are also important. What are the economic indicators for the region? Are the prospects for employment growth and residential development strong? Just as the immediate vicinity may affect the value of your investment, the fortunes of the region can affect your fortunes as an investor. A seemingly unfavourable region may offer investors some good opportunities, but such properties will be less obvious if you don't understand the local dynamic. And they could be more difficult to sell when the time comes for you to move on, because you'll have to attract the attention of a buyer and educate them on the property's merits and potential.

Any interest you have in using the property should mesh with your long-term goals. Don't move to a city just because you enjoyed a visit you once had. A recreational property may seem an attractive investment today but lose its appeal once the novelty of the locale wears off and your preferences change. In this case, even if the market where you've bought offers the best prospects for resale in the world, the property won't have lived up to at least one of your original expectations.

Say, for example, you live in Calgary but have dreams of retiring in 10 to 15 years. Vancouver Island, the Okanagan Valley, or the outskirts of Calgary are three areas that appeal to you as potential retirement locales. Although Vancouver Island and the Okanagan would require a significant amount of travel time to visit over the next 15 years, you're not that keen on staying in Calgary. Maybe you found a great deal on a property on Vancouver Island and your research indicates strong potential for an appreciation in its value. But wait — you have found an equally promising property in the Okanagan, and strong local demand for housing means you can rent the house to a local family until you're ready to take occupancy. Weighing the merits of each, you eventually decide on the Okanagan: You've set your heart on eventually leaving Calgary, the Okanagan is closer than Vancouver Island, and you're certain cash flow from the Okanagan property will be steady.

Cross-border investing

U.S. real estate investing isn't a focus of this book, but we can't ignore the fact that about 90 percent of Canada's population lives within 160 kilometres of the U.S. border. That could make investing in real estate in our southern neighbour a tempting option. However, despite the fact that Canada and the United States share the world's longest undefended border, you can't count on being welcomed with open arms. Canadian citizens investing in U.S. real estate should bear in mind a few facts:

 ✔ The U.S. Department of Homeland Security continues to tighten its monitoring and control of cross-border traffic. Though regular visitors to the United States may enjoy faster passage across the line, you will still do well to consider how much inconvenience you are prepared to handle in managing an investment in another country.

✔ Private property rights tend to be more vigorously defended in the United States than in Canada. Becoming a property owner in the United States will also subject you to U.S. tax laws at the municipal level, if not the state and federal levels. You'll also have to comply with U.S. legislation affecting your property, as well as any policies or measures that may determine how you use and dispose of real estate.

✔ The U.S. Internal Revenue Service withholds 10 percent of the proceeds from the sale of foreign-owned properties. This is an important consideration, limiting the cash you are able to reinvest on the close of the sale.

Canada taxes residents' worldwide income, meaning that personal income you derive from investment properties outside Canada is subject to taxes in this country. But holding the property through a corporate entity in the United States will subject it to U.S. tax laws, which could significantly complicate matters.

Mexico is another country that enjoys significant interest from property investors, especially in the wake of the 1994 North American Free Trade Agreement and reforms to Mexico's property ownership and land tenure legislation. Make absolutely certain to review any Mexican property investments you're considering with a lawyer and other advisers who can coach you on the unique complexities of Mexican real estate.

Because we are not experts regarding real estate investing in the United States or Mexico, we invite you to take a look at what other authors have written on the topic. Researching the tax policies of the jurisdiction where you hope to invest — be it the United States or anywhere else — is also imperative. In addition to books such as Doug's own *The Canadian Snowbird Guide* (McGraw-Hill), seek professional advice from lawyers and accountants familiar with the implications of cross-border and overseas investing.

Fitting Real Estate into a Financial Plan

So you've weighed the alternatives, looked deep into your soul, and are still keen to get into real estate investing? Great. But before you charge ahead, make a plan, because the day will likely come when you want to retire, relaxing with a cool beverage on a beach instead of talking to your real estate agent. A financial plan is about how you'll *get* to that beach with a drink in your hand. Financial planning includes five basic steps:

1. Select your professional advisors (see Chapter 4).

2. Assess your current and future financial situation (see Chapter 5).

3. Establish your goals and priorities.

4. Develop a financial plan.

5. Evaluate your progress toward your goals.

An objective plan, prepared with the assistance of professional advisers, will equip you to develop a portfolio of real estate that will ultimately see you sipping umbrella drinks in the sand (see Chapter 4 for all you need to know about assembling your crack team of advisers). The plan should address the following:

✔ Personal insurance coverage

✔ Your entire investment portfolio

✔ Debts

✔ Tax considerations of your particular situation

✔ Your retirement strategy

✔ Estate plans

The next sections focus on the latter two aspects, which will have a direct impact on how you manage your real estate investments.

Considering when to sell

An investment not only helps you to make more of your resources in the present, it promises to help you do more in the future. Many people invest with a view to funding their retirement, so drafting a strategy for the sale of your portfolio that helps achieve your financial goals should be integral to the financial plan you develop.

Major reasons for disposing of assets include rebalancing your portfolio in favour of more liquid or higher yielding investments, or securing funds for retirement or in accordance with your estate plan. Knowing when to sell is discussed in Chapter 16.

Regular renewal of your portfolio, either through maintenance of the existing assets or trading up to new or higher yielding properties is a standard strategy. Consider the strategy of pyramiding. Not to be confused with pyramid schemes, *pyramiding* involves the purchase of one or two select assets on a regular basis, and the sale of others, ensuring that your portfolio constantly renews itself and doesn't become stale.

Pyramiding also provides an opportunity to review your investments and assess how your financial plan is helping you achieve the goals you've established.

Planning for retirement

With an average life expectancy of just over 78 years, Canadians are living longer and enjoying healthier retirements than ever before. Planning for increased life expectancy will affect how quickly you divest your real estate portfolio. Fortunately, real estate isn't like your Registered Retirement Savings Plan (RRSP), which must be converted to a Registered Retirement Income Fund (RRIF) by the time you turn 69. Other means exist to ensure real estate provides the stable retirement income that will make your golden years golden in fact as well as in name.

Common options, discussed in Chapter 16, include the following:

- ✔ Reverse mortgage
- ✔ Line of credit
- ✔ Sale and lease-back arrangement
- ✔ Living trust

Wills and (real) estate planning

Don't kid yourself — you're not immortal. You will need a will, if only to preserve the good memories people have of you. Not having a will invites frustration for the administrators of your estate, and could result in your paying a lot more tax, essentially defeating your best efforts to be a successful real estate investor. A will ensures that your investments are efficiently and promptly distributed as you wish, not by a government formula.

A will isn't the only tool available to manage your estate. Powers of attorney also help facilitate the orderly management and transfer of your investments prior to your death.

We discuss the essential role wills play in the management and divestment of your real estate assets in Chapter 16.

Chapter 2

Exploring Real Estate Investments

*I*f you're new to the world of real estate investing, you're in the right place. In this chapter, we introduce you to the various kinds of real estate on the market — residential, commercial and industrial, condos, recreational, and raw land — as well as alternatives such as syndicates and real estate investment trusts (REITs).

If you're a more seasoned investor, fear not. There's something here for you, too. You'll find good, solid information that not only will show you how one investment stacks up against another, but also may spark new ideas for developing a diversified portfolio with limited risk and maximum potential to deliver a return. You'll be inspired to consider how less common options, like industrial real estate or retail units in the latest condo development, can work for you.

Homing In on Residential

Buying a home is typically the first major real estate purchase you'll make. But if you've never considered your home as the starting point for an investment portfolio, why not? Even tycoons need somewhere to lay their heads, and finding a home for yourself is a convenient way to explore and hone the skills you'll need to tackle more complex deals as an investor.

Home-buying is a chance to practise the basic acquisition skills you'll need to select and secure properties. If you decide to rent out a suite in your house, you'll be able to test your management and human relations skills, as well as other joys of being a landlord. And of course, home ownership brings regular opportunities to familiarize yourself with the hands-on maintenance that makes up the practical side of managing a real estate investment.

Investing begins at home

For many, the family home has a venerable position worth more than its weight in gold. Making money on it is the last thing some people consider doing — but more than one homeowner has been delighted to find that his home has appreciated in value, bringing him a sizable nest-egg just in time for retirement. For families who have occupied the same house for several decades, the original investment can deliver a return in both happy memories and hard cash.

Go into any bookstore or library and you'll find several guides to advise you on the purchase of your first home. Many of the steps you'll go through and features you're looking for in your own home are equally important when you're buying a house as an investment property. Buying a home with the added motive of seeing it double as an investment property will intensify the importance of many of these issues. You'll be scouting features that not only are desirable to your family as occupants but also could appeal to potential tenants. You'll also be conscious of points that could help the house fetch a higher resale value when it comes time to sell.

Rent out a suite, pay down a mortgage

Tenants aren't called "mortgage-helpers" for nothing. Homeowners looking to build equity in their property can do so far faster if they have rental income feeding into their cash flow than by going it alone. Tenants also help a mortgage out in another way: Most mortgage companies will factor rental revenue into the value of a home when calculating the amount of a mortgage you can obtain when you're buying.

Tenants can help you pay off a mortgage faster, whether it's for your primary residence or a full-fledged rental property. Figure 2-1 shows why tenants can give you something to rave about — at least from a financial perspective.

Take the example of a $125,000 bungalow with a finished basement (separate entrance, of course) in Charlottetown. Renting the basement to a student at University of Prince Edward Island for $500 a month would give you enough to add an extra $100 a week to your mortgage payments. Assuming an interest rate of 6 percent over a 25-year term, those extra payments could reduce the length of your mortgage by 11 years and save you just over $37,300 in interest.

Figure 2-1:
A mortgage-helper can shorten the standard life of a $100,000 mortgage significantly.

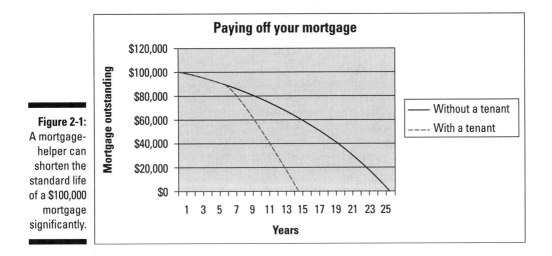

Paying off your mortgage

Mortgage outstanding
$120,000
$100,000
$80,000
$60,000
$40,000
$20,000
$0

1 3 5 7 9 11 13 15 17 19 21 23 25

Years

—— Without a tenant
---- With a tenant

Being a landlord isn't for everyone, however. Renting a suite in your home to a tenant, even temporarily, not only gives you some extra cash to put toward the mortgage, but also gives you a good idea of whether you want to become a full-time landlord on a larger property or multiple properties.

On the plus side, being a landlord gives you:

✔ Rental income

✔ Opportunities for tax deductions related to business expenses (see Chapter 15)

✔ Opportunities to indulge your penchant for home improvements

Points that might make you think twice about renting out a suite in your house are more numerous and include

✔ Reduced privacy and round-the-clock availability

✔ Having to live with someone else's idiosyncrasies

✔ Increased exposure to liability

✔ More maintenance

✔ Greater responsibility for the management and upkeep of your property

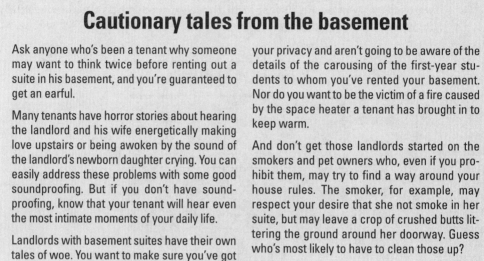

Cautionary tales from the basement

Ask anyone who's been a tenant why someone may want to think twice before renting out a suite in his basement, and you're guaranteed to get an earful.

Many tenants have horror stories about hearing the landlord and his wife energetically making love upstairs or being awoken by the sound of the landlord's newborn daughter crying. You can easily address these problems with some good soundproofing. But if you don't have sound-proofing, know that your tenant will hear even the most intimate moments of your daily life.

Landlords with basement suites have their own tales of woe. You want to make sure you've got your privacy and aren't going to be aware of the details of the carousing of the first-year students to whom you've rented your basement. Nor do you want to be the victim of a fire caused by the space heater a tenant has brought in to keep warm.

And don't get those landlords started on the smokers and pet owners who, even if you prohibit them, may try to find a way around your house rules. The smoker, for example, may respect your desire that she not smoke in her suite, but may leave a crop of crushed butts littering the ground around her doorway. Guess who's most likely to have to clean those up?

Managing tenants

Even the best tenants and properties require attention. From maintenance you might otherwise ignore, to keeping track of and collecting rent, you have to keep on top of issues that you wouldn't have to watch if you were just counting on your property to rise in value rather than generate revenue. Knowing some of the scenarios that could arise will help you prepare and be a more confident landlord — and a more successful investor! (We discuss the risks of being a landlord in Chapter 14.) Right now it's worth emphasizing the importance of having a rental agreement, especially if you're renting a suite in your primary residence.

Some people rent a part of their home on an informal basis, but this could cause problems. If you need to terminate a tenancy, for example, you will have less legal recourse if things go sour than if you have a formal lease agreement. Some provinces provide a standard form of lease, or you can consult a real estate lawyer who will prepare and approve a lease agreement for your tenants. This will help ensure that in the case of a dispute, the contract is (more or less) bulletproof.

Rental contracts include the number of permanent residents allowed in the unit and the term of the lease — whether month-to-month, renewable after a year, or reverting to month-to-month after an initial term (usually a year). A contract should also cover whether or not pets and smoking are allowed, as well as outline obligations to other tenants, including curfews on parties. The agreement should also stipulate the damage deposit and grounds for its return or retention. It's also important to obtain a tenancy application form soliciting information such as rental history, names of previous landlords and other references, and the right to do a credit bureau investigation.

A shifting rental market is one of the major risks to renting a suite in your home. This is particularly true in smaller college or university towns, where you may be able to count on only eight months of rental income a year. Should demand for rental accommodation slacken, you may lose your ability to levy rents adequate to service your mortgage.

Managing property

Your ability to attract tenants and charge a higher rent will increase with the quality of the suite you offer. Be prepared to make modest, ongoing investments in the suite that will allow you to maximize the rent you can reasonably expect a tenant to pay. Painting the suite may enable you to charge a higher rent that will more than pay for the paint job over the course of the tenancy. Getting in the habit of investing in regular maintenance and upgrades in your own home will prepare you for the economics of managing a stand-alone residential investment. We discuss the joys of landlording and property management in Part IV.

Modifying your home for rental purposes will affect your insurance coverage, so for peace of mind, make sure the policy you have protects you with additional coverage. Insist that tenants obtain their own home insurance and provide you with a copy. You need to be sure you're covered in case a fire starts in the rental suite and your own property is consumed.

Renovating for fun and profit

Making over a home can be a lot of fun and pay off in a property worth more than straight *appreciation,* or increase in market value, would allow. Renovating also allows you to build a home that you'll enjoy living in, at least until you sell it. Though this can be fun and satisfying, the major drawback is that this requires a lot of hard work.

For those willing to make the effort, homes suitable for renovation generally come for a better price than homes with the latest features and finishes. Buying a fixer-upper is a savvy way to enter an up-and-coming market earlier than other buyers. The fixing up you do allows you to offer a finished home to buyers who probably wouldn't have looked twice at the place before you worked your magic.

TIP

Hunting commercial properties

What the Multiple Listing Service (www.mls.ca) is for residential real estate, ICX (www.icx.ca) is for non-residential properties. It is one of several services that can help you locate commercial and industrial properties. The larger commercial brokerage firms also publish their listings, not all of which are necessarily linked to the MLS system. Don't forget to check out the various media that publish real estate listings, whether targeted specifically to real estate investors, such as Western Investor (www.westerninvestor.com), or trade publications for specific industries. A wide range of print and electronic resources exist to help you uncover opportunities.

Second homes and cottages

Nearly one-tenth of Canadians have a second residence, with a condo or cottage being among the most popular choices. As well as giving you an alternative place to hang your hat, a second home is yet another simple means of developing a successful real estate portfolio.

Second residences

A second house, a condo for the kids while they go to university, or even your own future retirement home can each be a practical answer to your personal needs and desires as well as work as an investment. Consider how a second (or third, or fourth) home can serve your current needs *and* those of your investment strategy.

For example, if you're shopping for a condo for the kids to use while they're studying at university, you'll probably be scouting neighbourhoods that will allow you to rent to other students when your kids graduate. Research the market and see if you can serve a need for student housing in a desirable neighbourhood that's currently undersupplied. Perhaps you want to be in a certain neighbourhood when you retire; finding someone to rent the house or apartment you buy until you're ready to move in will help reduce your retirement costs.

Cottages

Chances are you can't spend every day in cottage country, however appealing that sounds. But if local bylaws allow it, you may be able to derive a small amount of income from leasing your cottage to others for a few days or weeks at a time. It's a sensible way of making sure your property is occupied, and allows you to recover some of the purchase cost.

You may need to substantially upgrade the property, however, to make it appealing to renters. We've all heard the stories of rustic cottages in such poor repair that the vacation became a nightmare — you don't want to be *that* landlord. As with other rental properties, make sure what you're offering is in good repair. Also, confirm that the renovations you have in mind are allowed. Limitations exist in many areas regarding the type of upgrades permitted, especially for waterfront properties.

Some communities with large numbers of cottages limit the use of properties by anyone other than the owners. Short-term rentals to vacationers may sound like a good idea, but it may also invite the wrath of locals. The potential for more intensive use by people other than the owners lies at the heart of most local concerns; common issues include raucous parties, and greater demand on the water table by people unfamiliar with the vagaries of ground water.

Another common concern is that absentee landlords could contribute to a hollowing out of the local community. The last thing many year-round residents of any community want is to live in a neighbourhood where a significant portion of homes are vacant most of the year. If you intend to rent out the cottage you're buying, check what local regulations allow.

Securing Commercial and Industrial Properties

Commercial and industrial properties are not the most glamorous investments, but if they pass muster with the Canada Pension Plan and other institutional investors, why not with you? Buying an office building or warehouse is more complex than buying the average home, but with leases typically running for years at a time, you stand a good chance of enjoying a more stable cash flow than you would from residential properties. The trick is finding the opportunities, especially if you're just starting out. Although anyone can relate to residential housing, investing in commercial and industrial properties requires preparation and the help of experienced advisers.

However high the standards you have for residential real estate, houses are relatively simple propositions when it comes to market influences. By contrast, commercial and industrial properties are subject to diverse factors and influences rooted in economic trends. People shop in only so many places, and there's only so much office space required in each community. And warehouses? They're not quite as numerous as coffee shops.

Still, opportunities exist for even a small investor to do well by commercial and industrial properties, which are home to the businesses that can be the lifeblood of communities.

Assessing classes

Several classes of commercial and industrial real estate exist, with the most recognizable being retail, office, and industrial. Each has a different level of liquidity, based on the performance of the local economy and the shifting measure known as investor confidence. With several large players involved in these types of real estate, however, you stand a good chance of eventually being able to sell.

Retail

The humble shopfront is a mainstay of main streets everywhere. But not every merchant owns the shop, let alone the building where the shop is located. Often, a private landlord will own the building, which may or may not have some residential units above. Indeed, a mixed-use building in a smaller town can provide your portfolio with a measure of diversity by giving you a stake in two asset classes at once. Many large urban centres feature retail units within condo developments. The retail units are sold off like the apartments above, and at comparable prices. Providing you can find a tenant who will meet the needs of the surrounding neighbourhood — this often requires some skill, rooted in a knowledge of the neighbourhood and an ability to devise a lease package that will attract the right tenants — you will be able to reap the benefits of their success.

Small community-oriented plazas with just a few shops can also provide a steady income and, in the right location, appreciation in value if resold for redevelopment.

Retail units also work well if you need premises for your own business. Just as you buy a home rather than rent an apartment so you can build equity in your own property rather than someone else's, buying commercial space can be a good long-term investment. Car dealerships are typical examples; some auto dealers make more money off the lots from which they sell cars than from the cars themselves. Depending on your business, you may be able to operate out of a piece of property that will make you more money than your business ever does.

Office

Whether it's for the local newspaper or an ambitious entrepreneur, office space is a type of real estate few businesses can do without. Similar to residential, it's available in both stand-alone buildings and larger developments ranging from condo developments to business parks.

Despite exposure to shifts in the economy, office properties generally allow you to implement longer term leases than are typically possible on other forms of real estate. Businesses value long-term arrangements to ensure the stability of their own operations, and you can use that fact to stabilize your investment portfolio.

Although it's worth noting that vacancies are often higher than for residential real estate, remember that you'll also be able to charge a higher rent, and contract for increases over the life of a lease.

Industrial

The workhorses of the real estate sector, industrial properties are probably the least glamorous assets you'll encounter. Bare-bones construction makes them functional rather than fashionable, designed as they are to serve the needs of manufacturers, distributors, or any grab-bag of blue-collar uses. But the basic service they provide also makes them stable investments with a good potential for return.

Know what your tenants are doing with the industrial space you're leasing! The activities of some tenants raise the risk of soil contamination, which could negate any return rents hand you and even land you in debt or, worse, legal trouble. For example, a large industrial complex outside of Toronto previously home to a well-known brewery became the centre for a sophisticated marijuana grow-op. The operation was finally busted, but not without great embarrassment to the owners. To ensure better control over the activities on the land, invest in a building that will draw specific kinds of users because of its historical uses or location. You might also consider purchasing a parcel of industrial land and developing a simple building tailored for specific users. Researching the market will indicate sectors in particular need of industrial space, and some may eventually purchase the property from you when it comes time for you to sell.

Assessing liquidity

A property's *liquidity* — its ability to be sold — is more important in assessing the long-term potential of non-residential assets than homes and apartments. But it is also more complex to determine, depending on your familiarity with the several factors at play. Most residential buyers, for example, don't examine trends in a specific industry to determine where to buy a home. But you'll want to study the demand for retail space in a community if you're buying a strip mall, or examine commodity price trends if you've been offered a warehouse previously used by the forest sector. Are you up for the challenge?

Competitors, or potential purchasers?

Because some forms of real estate are in stronger demand than others, you're bound to run into competition at some point. Competition isn't necessarily bad, however. The relationships you build with other investors may lead to opportunities in the future. It pays to respect your competitors.

Respect for your competitors is a particularly important attribute in the close-knit world of commercial real estate investment. Relationships you develop now may help you sell a property in the future. Rather than see yourself in competition with other purchasers, consider them future business partners. The people you trump today may in future be interested in buying the asset you won.

Many large investors looking to develop their holdings won't enter a new market unless they can find a sizable portfolio that makes entry worth their while. You may have two or three properties, but if you can form partnerships with other small owners there's the potential you can attract the interest of a larger buyer.

An asset's liquidity is a function of its attractiveness and appeal to investors, perhaps even more than market cycles (which we discuss in Chapter 3). An asset in Montreal, for example, will tend to have greater liquidity than a property in Cornerbrook — not because Cornerbrook is a bad place to invest, but because Montreal is a larger centre with a more diverse economy and, in short, more opportunities for the use of the property. Properties that can deliver a greater return than more expensive assets will also enjoy healthy liquidity, regardless of how the broader market is faring.

The greater the future demand for a property, the better your chance of seeing a return when the time comes to sell — whether that's next year or five years away. Factors to take into account include

- The property's proximity to properties used by similar or complementary businesses
- Prospects for the growth of the sector the property serves
- The economic strength of the community in which the property is located
- The property's proximity to transportation networks that may enhance its appeal to users in a sector other than that of the current user

For example, a port is a good location for a warehouse, but an office building located nowhere near other offices might be a hard sell to potential tenants and therefore future buyers.

Laying into Condos

Condos, also known as strata-titled units in British Columbia and co-proprietorships in Quebec, are more than just apartments. Although residential condos (both apartments and townhomes) are the best-known form of this type of real estate, it also encompasses commercial and hotel properties. Residential condos are the primary form, however, with commercial and hotel units available in smaller quantities. When people talk of condos, they almost always mean residential.

All about condominiums

Condos are organized very differently from other types of property. Residential condominiums include apartments as well as single-detached, semi-detached, and row homes; stack town houses and duplexes. Building sites, subdivisions, and mobile home parks also fall into the condo class. Primary elements of the condo are the residential unit and the common elements. Common elements generally include walkways, driveways, lawns and gardens, lobbies, elevators, parking areas, recreational facilities, storage areas, laundry rooms, stairways, plumbing, electrical systems and portions of walls, ceilings, floors, and other items.

Ownership of the common elements is typically distributed equally among the unit owners. The exact description of the common elements, and what you own as part of your unit, may differ from development to development, but the documents you receive when you buy your unit will state these clearly. Some unit owners may have exclusive rights to some of the common elements. Typical examples of so-called limited common elements include parking spaces, storage lockers, roof gardens, balconies, patios, and front and back yards.

Residential condominiums occur in both urban and suburban settings. Urban condos typically take the following forms:

- A high-rise apartment building

- A three- to five-storey new mid-rise building

- An older building converted from rental apartments

- A building where unit owners own the street-level floor, which is leased to retailers to help offset the common maintenance fees of the residential condominiums in the rest of the building

Suburban condominiums maximize their use of the available land while affording attractive views, private driveways, and common recreational facilities such as swimming pools, tennis courts, saunas, and even playgrounds. Some of the most common formats include

- Cluster housing consisting of multi-unit structures of two or four units apiece, each with its own private entranceway

- Town-house-type single-family homes distributed in rows

- Garden apartments consisting of a group of apartment buildings surrounding a common green, frequently with each of the floors held by separate condo owners

- Duplexes, triplexes, or fourplexes

- A series of detached single-family homes in a subdivision format, all using the same land and parking areas.

Because condo units are generally subject to the building council's regulations, condos carry some of the perils of joint ownership (we discuss joint ownership and other ownership structures at length in Chapter 3). Condo bylaws occasionally limit activities allowed in suites, including the ability to rent units. Condo fees have the potential to vary, with special levies possible for maintenance and repairs. Just because a problem didn't affect your suite, the mere fact that it happened in the building at all may subject you to these levies and diminish the value of your unit.

Investing in residential condos

Residential condos are popular investments. Vancouver, which boasts one of Canada's most active condo markets, has seen as many as half the units in some new buildings sold to investors. That's an important statistic, but not great news if you're planning to rent a unit in that kind of situation. Investors who purchase a unit with the intention of renting it out want to know they have a reasonable hope of finding tenants, something that's more difficult to do when several landlords are competing for the same limited number of prospects.

On the other hand, condos can be an attractive alternative to standard rental accommodation. And this raises the potential for them to command a higher rent than other forms of residential rentals. Barring a glut of similar product, and providing your unit is in an appropriate neighbourhood, condos can be an affordable means for you to claim a slice of the rental market.

Because condos are run by a council of unit owners, make sure you know what the rules allow before you buy. Some buildings limit suites available for rental, others limit the kinds of improvements that can be made or whether pets are allowed. Other issues to consider include management fees and the potential for upcoming expenses, which are usually shared among the owners. Ask to see the minutes of the council meetings and view other records associated with the building's operation and management. (We discuss this further in Chapter 11.)

Investing in commercial condos

Retail, office and industrial condos are relatively few in number. The usual precautions regarding investment in the condo class aside, guidelines for investing in these properties are similar to those for other forms of commercial property.

Taking a hit

When terrorists hit the World Trade Center in New York in September 2001, the aftershocks rocked the global tourism trade. Vacancies at hotels rose and profits fell. For some owners of condo hotel suites in Canada, the result was under-performing real estate and a dramatic drop in the value of their investments.

At one hotel, the situation was made worse by the fact that the owners paid too high a price for the suites. Moreover, the return promised wasn't realistic given the volatile nature of the hotel business.

Although the original promise was for a 10-percent return, many of the investors saw no more than 3 percent on their suites. Some investors held out until better times returned, but many sold at a discount that ran anywhere from 20 to 40 percent.

Owner-occupiers reap the most advantages of owning a commercial condo, however. Some of the benefits include

- ✔ **Fixed business costs:** Because you own the commercial space, you aren't subject to rising rents. Although operating costs may fluctuate based on condo fees, as a member of the building council you have some input into what those fees will be.

- ✔ **Tax advantages:** The standard business-related advantages of occupying property you own hold true for condo units, including opportunities to deduct depreciation and business expenses associated with the unit.

- ✔ **Appreciation in value:** Like any other investment, you also reap the benefit from any appreciation in property value — the reason you became an investor in the first place!

Investing in hotel condos

Hotels developed on a condominium model have not been the best bets for investors. Units are typically sold to buyers who in turn contract with a management company to oversee the operation of the hotel. Proceeds from hotel operations then flow back to the suite owners. Disappointment may await investors who expect a certain return on their units.

Real estate is not without risk, and this goes double for hotel investments. Being subject to the vagaries of the tourist trade, a hotel condo suite may actually *cost* you money. Poor cash flow at the property and paltry returns will diminish your chances of selling your unit, so buy wisely. Select a property that has demonstrated its success in the market.

Some hotel condo units may come with a guarantee that they will return a specific amount to you as an investor. Beware of these properties, because the variable nature of the hotel market and operating costs makes this a difficult guarantee to keep and could lead to costly and stressful litigation.

Dreaming of Recreational Properties

Recreational properties are more than a cottage at the lake for an investor. From fractional ownership to islands with development potential, the opportunities available are wide-ranging and far-flung. Recreational properties are especially popular right now, and the aging baby-boom generation is a major catalyst for this interest.

Many boomers seek a balanced lifestyle and improved quality of life. Others want a retreat where they can enjoy that lifestyle as well as entertain friends and extended and blended families. They often have considerable disposable income, substantial equity in their principal residences, and inherited wealth. Many see recreational properties as the home to which they'll retire.

The Canada Mortgage and Housing Corp. (CMHC) encourages investment in recreational properties through high-ratio mortgage financing. This move makes buying a recreational property a more affordable proposition than it once was, and reflects the fact that many people are making recreational properties their primary homes. In the past, a purchaser would frequently have to provide a large down payment for what was once a discretionary purchase.

Should you have the chance to sell either your principal residence or recreational property, you have the option of naming one of the two properties as your principal residence. Generally, this is the one with the largest capital gain; as your principal residence it would not be subject to capital gains tax. The other property would be subject to capital gains tax. Talk to your accountant!

Cottages

Cottages are a simple form of recreational property with the same potential to appreciate in value as any other residential asset. Renovations and the possible renting out of cottages provides the opportunity to boost value and provide cash flow on an ongoing basis. When compared to other forms of recreational real estate, this is probably the one most familiar to people and easily understood.

Many cottages come with an acreage that provides recreational opportunities. The acreage itself may be good investment if you have the foresight (and good fortune) to buy in the path of urban development. Calgary is a good example of a city that has swallowed up many smaller communities in the course of its growth, turning countless former retreats from city life into part of the city itself — and handing the former owners of the properties a windfall to boot.

Fractional ownership

Fractional ownership, as the name implies, gives you an equity share in a property — usually a resort-style development — with rights to access it in proportion to your share. For example, if you own 10 to 25 percent of a property, you have rights to use it 10 to 25 percent of the time.

Unlike a time share, in which you purchase only rights to use the property in proportion to your interest, a fractional ownership purchase puts your name on the title deed, along with those of the other owners. The owners generally have an agreement outlining the procedure for selling interest in the property. To avoid any misunderstandings or conflict, make sure you have a proper legal structure and appropriate documentation of the arrangement.

One of the draws of fractional ownership is that your unit is often in a rental pool when you're not using it. Even if that option isn't offered, you may be able to rent it yourself. Either way, you'll get to enjoy some income in addition to having a getaway for your own use.

Resorts by the suite

Earlier in this chapter we talk about condo developments in the context of hotels. Many resort properties offer similar investment opportunities. Like fractional ownership arrangements, these allow owners to acquire stake in a property that's more affordable than if they had full ownership.

Developers have pursued these types of developments because they reduce the risk of proceeding with construction. You benefit from access to the suite for set periods of time each year, as well as proceeds from the net profits of the suite's operation.

Developing a Taste for Raw Land

Just because something hasn't been built on a piece of property doesn't mean the property's worthless. Sometimes the value has yet to be realized. As a *land banker,* someone who buys up properties for the value of the land alone, you can be the first to realize a value from property that will be in demand in the future. The future purchaser may be another investor, an individual who wants to build a home, or even a developer with visions of a subdivision. The land you bank doesn't have to be in the city, either; it can just as easily be in a rural community with a growing residential population.

Raw land is good if you're an investor with a long-term plan. The downside of land banking is the chance you'll find yourself waiting a long time before the value of the land increases enough to make it worth selling.

Staking your claim

You may feel like an old-time prospector when you first buy a piece of raw land. It might not pan out for you, regardless of your gut feeling. But for the low price at which you can buy undeveloped land in many parts of Canada, raw land is frequently a gamble worth taking. Whether you're in the city or the countryside, several alternatives can help you make good on your investment.

Choosing a locale, as with every other real estate purchase, requires research into the area's current conditions and future prospects. Because the return you're looking for probably requires the development of the property into something new, your attitude should be similar to that of a renovator: Look for a site with the potential to be popular, and one that is showing signs of a turnaround. For a rural community, the clues might lie in proximity to an urban centre, and demographic trends such as an influx of retirees or younger couples.

Try to find the best fit between the land you purchase and what your research tells you is fuelling the long-term potential of the surrounding community. You want to be where the action is, so that you can benefit from the potential future interest in your site.

Raw land comes with just as many responsibilities as any other property. You have to make sure your property conforms to any local bylaws, especially with regards to appearance and cleanliness. You don't want it to become a liability, and you will be liable if hazards exist on it that could bring others to harm. You also want to ensure it meets environmental conditions, so that you don't find yourself with a nasty surprise when the time comes to sell (we discuss some of the issues to consider as part of the due diligence associated with buying properties in Chapter 11).

Goin' country or swingin' in the city?

Development often follows a relentless pace. The patch of grass where you played as a kid has become a block of town houses. As a real estate investor you may not want to lose what was, but you can't help thinking of what's to come.

This country wouldn't have any cities had someone not first put up a house and begun developing undeveloped land. Because the cost of urban property is often quite high, opportunities to secure vacant lots are sometimes most frequent in rural communities. British Columbia and Ontario considered the trend so significant that legislation in these two provinces limits the use of farmland.

Vacant lots in urban settings are subject to far more variables, including the use of surrounding properties, local zoning and carrying costs (especially property taxes). You must often be prepared to hold land for a long time before you see a return. Often, the payoff comes from having a property someone else needs to pursue a development. Through strategic buying, a small investment can deliver a decent return relative to the time spent managing it.

This is true in small towns as well as cities. A small town won't always be small, especially if it is adjacent to a growing city. Calgary is a good example of a city that's grown, absorbing smaller communities in its path. Had you owned a parcel of land in some of those communities when they were outside the city, you might be enjoying a wealthy retirement today.

Banking on land

Rather than holding a single lot, you may have the opportunity to acquire a large tract of land. As a *land banker* you may add to this tract, or wait patiently to sell it either in whole or in part to a developer. Although land bankers typically deal with residential land, some bank land for other uses.

The main risk to banking land is that you're not receiving any income from it, unless you've been able to lease it to a farmer for grazing purposes, or otherwise make use of it. At the same time, you have to pay taxes and other carrying costs until you see a return. Knowing how long you can afford to carry the property is key to planning its eventual sale.

Deciding to build

Because you won't see a significant return on your investment in raw land until it's developed, it's important to plan potential uses for the property. What kind of development promises the greatest payoff? Are you willing to do it yourself? If not, are you willing to *joint-venture*, or partner, with a fellow investor or developer? Perhaps, in rare cases, you will be able to see a return by merely holding the land and selling it at a profit.

Becoming a developer

You're not likely to become a developer with your first piece of property, unless you're undertaking renovations. But if you've got the cash to fund development, why not add value to part or all of the land you've been acquiring? This can include everything from a single building on a rural acreage to an urban in-fill project that takes a sliver of land to a higher and better use.

Partnering with others

Sometimes it can pay to enter into an arrangement with a partner that allows you to reap a return from the development of your land. Perhaps you supply the land alone, or commit to arranging the servicing; perhaps you do more. Whatever the arrangement, this can allow you to see a better return than you would by selling off the raw land to an eager developer.

A partnership could also speed the sale of the land if your hopes for the area where you bought haven't quite come true. One developer we know had a tract of land subdivided for sale as development lots for single-family homes. But the lots weren't selling. So the developer approached a home builder who designed custom homes on the lots. The partnership added value to the land, allowing the developer to sell the lots for much more than the market value of the bare land, and the home builder was able to make a few sales, too.

Holding out for a gain

Occasionally, the land you've assembled and patiently held will yield a return without any improvement at all. This can happen when development happens on surrounding properties and the prospects for your property become brighter by association. Or, perhaps the land itself is suitable for a particular use, such as growing grapes rather than apples, and the price of vineyard land is rising. You'll be able to take advantage of the shift.

Needless to say, if you're planning to hold land, you should have a long-term plan that supports that objective.

Howdy, Pardners: Buying into Syndicates

Syndicates, in which money from investors supports a property's acquisition for investment purposes, have a checkered past (see the sidebar "Acknowledging history"). Reforms to the regulations governing them have boosted their favour among investors who have an appetite for real estate but no desire to actually own or manage property themselves.

Syndicated properties offer several benefits, including a lower degree of risk, because the syndicator rigorously scrutinizes properties before investors join the syndicate. Syndicated properties also typically offer a higher return to investors than comparable properties investors manage themselves because they enjoy the attention of a dedicated management team.

Syndication generally occurs through investment firms charged with selling the investment to clients. The investment managers at such firms are similar to those who manage equities, insofar as they're alert to trends in the investment world and determined to manage assets for the best return possible.

Acknowledging history

During the 1970s and 1980s, developers in Canada could take advantage of the federal multi-unit residential building (MURB) program to solicit investment in their multi-family rental projects. Such investments were effectively *tax shelters*, places where investors could put money to defer or reduce tax payments. During the late 1980s, many of the old MURBs were converted to condos, nixing the cash flow on which investors depended. A lack of adequate federal oversight didn't protect some investors from receiving the short end of the stick in the course of some conversions, and ultimately gave the investments a bad name.

Similarly, several mortgage investment corporations failed investors in the 1990s. Like syndicates, the mortgage investment corporation (MIC) would invest in real estate, but on the mortgage side. Investors would take a share of the interest paid on the mortgages. Though investors believed the MICs were reliable investment vehicles with limited risks, many turned out to be quite the opposite.

Today, syndicates and their kin are subject to strict regulations established by the province in which they operate. They typically identify properties and solicit funds for the purchase of the asset from established investment firms. The investment firms in turn offer shares in the properties to their clients, who receive both dividends from the ongoing operation of the property and a share in the proceeds from the property when it's eventually sold. Shares can be priced from $5,000.

Strength in numbers

The benefit of syndicates is that you're not alone. The acquisition of the property is through a partnership, meaning your share is one of several.

You pay for the limited risk the investment entails because the syndicator takes a cut of the proceeds on the property's sale, and the profits are shared with other investors. Among the benefits you enjoy are capital appreciation and even deferred taxes. As with any service for which you pay, however, shop around and find an investment and management team with which you feel comfortable.

Knowing the risks

Syndicates aren't risk-free. You run the chance an investment may not work out. But the advantage is that you're not the one taking the initial hit. Thanks to securities regulations, even if you lose your shirt, you're not likely to lose your pants as well. The partnership syndicating investment in the property is legally bound to live up to its obligations to investors.

Before anteing up your hard-earned cash, however, speak with your tax accountant, financial planner or lawyer for their opinion on the investment and the safeguards it provides. (We discuss finding and adding these professionals to your team in Chapter 4.)

Researching Real Estate Investment Trusts

Real estate investment trusts (REITs) are relative newcomers to the investment scene in Canada. They've gained popularity in recent years for the regular dividends they promise from the ongoing operation of their assets — by definition, real estate. Like syndicates, they offer an efficient means of investing in real estate while avoiding direct ownership of property.

What's the excitement about?

Like public companies, *income trusts* are traded on the public markets. Shares in the company are known as *units,* which can fluctuate in value but which entitle their holders to a share in the distributable income flowing from the business of the trust. For real estate investment trusts (REITs), that business is the operation of the various buildings in its portfolio. These can include apartment buildings, seniors' care facilities, shopping centres, office buildings, hotels, or any other class of real estate in which the REIT chooses to invest.

Trust units trade on the public markets like stocks but are different. Although stocks represent an ownership stake in the company that issues them, trust units entitle holders to distributions from the business or businesses that deliver their profits to the trust.

The range of the existing REITs in Canada offers investors opportunities to invest in most classes of real estate. The low degree of risk (beyond fluctuations in market value) makes them a good choice for conservative investors who want a stake in the real estate market.

Choosing an asset type

The constraints of the trust structure eliminate some of the guesswork you'll have to do as you weigh the merits of the various REITs. Regardless of the asset classes in which REITs are invested, they're limited to paying unitholders out of their taxable earnings, and are accountable to their unitholders for distributions that aren't made.

Searching for the perfect trust is as simple as opening the business pages of your daily newspaper or browsing the Internet. Searching the terms *investment trust, REIT*, and even *income fund* and *income trust* presents you with several options. You can then investigate the trusts that interest you via more online searching, looking up financial statements on SEDAR (www. sedar.com), if they're Canadian, or consulting your investment broker.

Regardless of the trust structure, the assets managed by the operating business of the trust are subject to the same forces that apply to every other building in their class. Multi-family residential properties tend to have stable incomes, for example. Hotel REITs operate in a more volatile environment and will tend to see greater fluctuations in the returns they can deliver. Shopping centres also offer a measure of stability, but will provide a return that reflects the strength of the retail sector.

Don't take the word *trust* literally! The trust's assets are subject to the trends influencing the sector in which they operate. These trends will have an impact on their operations, profitability and, in turn, the amount of the distributions you receive. In extreme cases, if the operating business of the trust performs poorly, a distribution may not land in your lap at all.

Reading financial statements

To get a better grasp of what the trust in which you're considering investing is all about, one of the most important things you can do is crack open its books. Thanks to SEDAR (`www.sedar.com`), an electronic database handling the filings of all public companies in Canada, this is relatively easy to do. SEDAR, which stands for System for Electronic Document Analysis and Retrieval, logs quarterly financial statements, annual reports, and annual information forms and all other public documents issued by the various real estate investment trusts that operate in Canada.

Studying the statements SEDAR collects gives you some insight into the performance of a trust, any issues it may have faced and how its executives handled them. Don't neglect the notes to the financial statements, which can harbour extra information not expressly stated in the formal part of the quarterly and annual reports! Before you even glance at a trust's financial statements, have a look at the annual information form. It provides an overview of the trust's business, its development, and observations on the risks to the operating business from which it receives the profits.

Understanding the operation of a given trust can be invaluable in helping you decide whether to buy units in the trust, or to opt for one involved in an asset class more to your taste.

Chapter 3

Knowing the Challenges

· ·

· ·

*D*espite the opportunities real estate offers, hazards exist. As in a game of golf, no matter how good a player you are, or how well you know a course, you may encounter water hazards, sand traps, and other factors that can throw off your game.

When it comes to investing in real estate, the challenges are just as likely to come from a poor location and other tangible, concrete factors as from market cycles, buyer demand, business partners, and a host of unexpected concerns. We prime you on the basics in this chapter, covering some of the tougher scenarios you could face as an investor.

Studying Market Cycles

Though the *market cycle* isn't something that goes on in a washing machine, it's true that some cycles can take you to the cleaners. Market cycles are more like the life cycle of supply and demand. A cycle will see both supply and demand grow, mature, and eventually die. All markets are cyclical to some degree, whether by virtue of simple supply or demand, seasonal trends or the latest fashion. The property market is no different. Certain types of real estate regularly pass in and out of favour, home sales typically slump in winter and rebound in spring, and the balance between buyer and seller is constantly shifting.

Understanding market cycles is important to your success as an investor, both as a buyer and a seller. Purchasing a property for a good price when demand is weak improves chances of selling the property at a gain, if you're able to gauge which direction the market is heading! As a seller, a market with many buyers allows you to name a higher price for your property, especially if it is a unique property or one in which buyers have plenty of interest.

The real estate cycle

The typical length of a cycle in the real estate market is five years, though it can last as long as 12 years. Some observers argue that market cycles are lengthening under the influence of global investment trends and interest in real estate as an investment. The basic cycle itself hasn't changed, however.

Factors driving real estate markets include the following:

- Capital available for development and purchase
- Developer and investor (this means you!) confidence
- Supply and demand

When financing and credit are readily available, as they have been for most of this decade, developers will buy land and build, and investors will move in. When mortgage rates rise and capital flows tighten, activity cools. Confidence in the market reflects which way those involved believe the market is going to turn. That call is a judgment based on the amount of cash flowing through the market as well as the supply of and demand for available real estate.

The two main components of the cycle are supply and demand. It's basic economics — supply relieves demand, while demand will work to limit supply. Too much supply will reduce value, while strong demand will inflate prices. Within general market areas, variations in supply and demand might occur at the regional and neighbourhood levels that aren't necessarily consistent with the broader trend. For example, Manitoba might be seeing a lacklustre market generally while Winnipeg might be strong; within Winnipeg, some areas may be doing better than others, depending on what kind of properties are on offer.

Three types of real estate markets

The market goes through three stages in the course of a full cycle. These include the buyer's market, the seller's market, and the balanced market. A balanced market has is the most fleeting of the three, but we'll give each of them equal time here.

Meshing with markets

Jon and Joan had planned to buy a home for many years. They saved their money religiously, planning to use Jon's money for expenses and Joan's money towards a down payment on a house that would be close to where they worked. They were each planning on using some of their RRSPs for a first-home purchase. They did not like debt, so wanted to save at least 50 percent of the house price before they would buy.

At the time, interest rates were 4 percent. However, over the five years they were saving, home prices in their area of choice went up 10 percent a year, so were now worth 50 percent more than they had budgeted for. They now could only afford a 5-percent down payment,

and their employment income was not enough to quality for the 95-percent mortgage, as interest rates were now 7 percent.

Jon and Joan then decided that the only place that could afford was about a two-hour commute outside of town. It had nice rural ambience, but not work proximity. They therefore decided to start a home-based business using their computer skills as Web designers. Thanks to technology, they could run their business from home without ever seeing their clients. The moral of the story is that one has to have a clear sense of the reality of the real estate marketplace, supply and demand, interest rates, and affordability, and a realistic game plan.

Buyer's market

The *buyer's market* typically comes at the bottom of a cycle, when properties are plentiful in relation to the number of potential buyers. Properties take longer to sell, prompting vendors to offer incentives such as lower prices and the opportunity to negotiate concessions. You also have an opportunity to shop around for better properties or lower prices on comparable assets, and to leverage existing assets to make purchases with a better chance of appreciation than those already in your portfolio.

Seller's market

A *seller's market* is the opposite of a buyer's market. Many buyers mean good demand, shorter sales times, and fewer properties to go around. Sale prices typically rise, and in extreme cases competition between potential buyers can lead to rapid appreciation in market value. Less room for bargaining means that as a buyer, you have to know what you want, be prepared to pay for it, and expect conditional offers to come under closer scrutiny as vendors try to secure the best deal for themselves.

Balanced market

Don't expect to find an exact balance in the market, which usually tends more to one side of the spectrum than the other. When it happens, however, a balanced market provides a stable environment for both buyers and sellers. Properties tend to sell in a reasonable length of time that allows for relaxed negotiation, adequate due diligence, and reasonable offers. The various parties to the deal have the best chance under these conditions of reaching a mutually satisfying conclusion.

Bearing with the markets

Goldilocks used to break into abandoned houses in seedy neighbourhoods to find places to sleep. She decided that was not the quality of lifestyle that met her emotional and aesthetic needs. So, she decided to get her own place. In true fairy-tale form, she was fortunate enough, through the assistance of her unbearable family, to borrow enough money to buy a little house in a buyer's market. She worked hard renovating and decorating it over several years, in an area of "cute" starter homes on big lots.

The real estate market started to heat up and eventually became very hot. Goldilocks sold her home at the top end of a seller's market, as her neighbourhood was now trendy and in high demand. She kept the money in the bank, and looked around for a home near the woods. By the time she found her dream home, the real estate market was no longer in a frenzy, and normalcy reigned supreme — the market was now balanced. Goldilocks was able to buy her dream home mortgage-free with the large amount of money she had saved from her first home sale, invest the rest of her cash through a financial planner, and live happily ever after. The End.

Factors affecting market conditions

Supply and demand, capital available for investment, and confidence in the market may help define market conditions, but they're not the only elements at play. Several factors affect the market directly and indirectly, influencing when you decide to buy and sell.

Recycling the impact of other markets

Because real estate deals are part of the larger economy, they're subject not just to the forces rippling through the property market, but to those of the national, provincial and local economies. The four are interrelated, so pay attention not just to what's selling (or not), but why. A boom, for example, may lead to a surge in the housing market, new retail openings, and demand for commercial properties to serve the bustling sectors of the economy. A recession, by contrast, will see depressed prices for real estate and force you to take a closer look at the sectors showing the greatest long-term promise.

Recessions are typically the time to prepare for the next boom, however. You may be able to scoop up underperforming assets and transform them into the gems of your portfolio. Have a look at reports on the local market from your local real estate brokerages, as well as growth forecasts that the Bank of Canada and other major financial institutions release on a regular basis.

The economic fortunes of a particular community are also important. One-industry towns do well so long as their industry prospers, but economic diversity is better for a community's long-term prospects. Diversity offers some protection against national and regional fortunes, as well as trends affecting specific industries. That's not to say single-job towns can't transform themselves, but the risk of a prolonged downturn is greater. An investor typically won't want to wait that long to see a return.

Communities, especially smaller ones, are also more subject to demographic changes and other shifts in local character that can affect the prospects for real estate. These changes are sometimes sparked by events in the local economy (a plant closure, for example, or the creation of new jobs), while others reflect the age of the incoming (or outgoing) owners.

Many of Canada's small towns, especially resource-dependent ones, have seen their stars rise and fall on the back of changing circumstances and trends. The British Columbia ski resort of Whistler, for example, is a small village turned international four-season resort as investors developed properties and amenities that attracted skiers, hikers, and convention-goers.

In Thunder Bay, Ontario, the growth of Lakehead University has stabilized the city's economic core and provided ancillary economic activity. A similar transformation is underway in the resource town of Prince George, British Columbia, where the University of Northern B.C. has drawn in a younger population.

Buying real estate in St. John's, Newfoundland, mightn't have been a wise choice when the fishing business was going down the tubes, but oil and natural gas have replaced fish and the boom has helped reinvigorate real estate markets.

Cutting through the (not so) small stuff

The supply of capital and confidence in the market are two elements that help drive the real estate market through its regular cycle. But the supply of capital and confidence are influenced by the following:

- ✔ **Interest rates:** Because interest rates have a direct effect on the financing of both development and investment properties, real estate professionals keep a close eye on where rates are heading. Typically, high rates will help cool the market by prompting price reductions. Lower rates will spur the market by making more cash available to investors and developers. Low interest rates may also stimulate demand and result in heightened competition for assets.

✔ **Tax rates:** Property taxes vary by community and type of property. A high tax rate typically discourages purchasers, often pushing investors into municipalities where rates are more favourable. Taxes levied by higher levels of government, such as federal capital gains tax and provincial property purchasers' tax, may also have an influence over investors' decisions, but less so than property taxes.

✔ **Occupancy rates:** Tenants play a role in real estate markets by indicating demand for certain types of assets. High vacancy levels mean assets return less income to owners, narrowing margins and potentially lowering investor expectations for real estate in the neighbourhood and ultimately property prices. This could create opportunities for purchasers. High occupancies typically boost the perceived value of an asset.

✔ **Perceived value:** Public perception of any particular piece of real estate plays a key role in determining what buyers are willing to pay. Good neighbourhoods, or those whose potential for growth is strong, enjoy stronger pricing than those with less favourable characteristics.

Public perception of what constitutes strong prospects isn't necessarily rooted in scientific research, however. Marketing, fashion, and simple word-of-mouth may all contribute to some areas becoming phenomena while others fall into decline. Keep your ears open to find out what people are saying about particular areas, read the local papers to see which neighbourhoods are making the news (and more important, why), and generally become a student of local fortunes to know which areas may be worth your while to investigate — and which may not.

Growth

Opportunities for acquiring additional properties and zoning conducive to redevelopment of those properties are two factors that can help drive a particular market forward. Among the investors they favour are those concentrating in a particular area (say a local shopping neighbourhood) or those aiming to assemble properties for further development. A wealth of opportunities for property acquisition and favourable zoning are also indicators of future potential, drawing in investors who can help drive the revival of an area in exchange for appreciation in the value of the sites on which they've gambled.

Don't expect these factors to produce the same results every time they mix. Knowing the role they each play in the market, however, gives you an understanding that enables you to make the right choice for your portfolio.

Assessing Liquidity

Liquidity is a measure of a property's ability to be sold and to deliver a return (these days, bottled water has really high liquidity). A market that favours the seller heightens the liquidity of a property. But a property that's just one of several similar properties can have a tough time getting sold, because it's got nothing unique to recommend it to buyers. It will have poor liquidity. Few properties can ever claim zero liquidity, but the investor who can boost the liquidity of a hard-to-sell property has a true skill — and a shot at being successful.

A liquid asset is like the water running off a melting ice cube: Although some assets are fixed in place, a liquid asset has the opportunity to find its own level in the market.

You'll more than likely want — and need — a different amount of liquidity in your portfolio at different stages of your investing career. Determining just how much liquidity you want will come down to your available financial resources and how much you'll expect to need in the future. The less money you need immediately, the longer the term of the investment you want to locate. If you need some of the money right away, you want a relatively liquid investment.

Regularly review your investment strategy to make sure you have an appropriate level of liquid and non-liquid assets in your portfolio. Never invest money you can't afford to lose. Although this is always good sense, it is especially true in the context of liquidity. If you do need to liquidate assets, you don't want to sell at a loss.

To counter the challenges a hard-to-sell property faces, you should understand not just the concept of liquidity, but also the factors affecting it. We tell you how to make them work in your favour in Chapter 16.

Questioning saleability

If you're going to be able to liquidate your assets on *your* terms, they have to be saleable. Whether they are or not will depend on various factors — what stage the market is at, what people are saying about the market and the neighbourhood where the property is, and how you've positioned it for sale. Determining the ability of an asset to sell is as much about its intrinsic worth as the effort you're willing to put into helping it sell.

Gauging the market

Saleability of a given asset tends to rise as market conditions shift in the seller's favour. Though you probably won't be able to judge what kind of market awaits an asset's sale when you first buy it, it makes sense to review your portfolio on a regular basis and keep an eye on the market. By taking stock of both, you can gauge which of your properties has the best sales potential in the year ahead, and, if it suits your strategy, prepare to sell.

Selling and buying on a regular basis helps keep your portfolio fresh. The strategy of *pyramiding,* whereby you regularly turn over and enhance your portfolio (not when you stash all your belongings in a pyramid to take with you in the afterlife), will benefit from your ability to gauge the saleability of your properties.

Gauging perceptions

Regardless of what stage the market is at, public perception of an asset's value is important in its ultimate liquidity. Being aware of potential buyers' attitudes toward your property, and its location may play a key role in your ability to liquidate it. We've all heard stories of buildings whose *feng shui* — simply put, positioning and layout — limited their saleability. Even if you don't accept this traditional Chinese way of seeing the world, you don't want it, or any other perceptions, limiting the saleability of your property.

Public confidence in the market is another perception that could limit your ability to sell a property. Depending on where people see the market going, and any policies meant to stimulate or cool development, your property may face limited sales prospects. Responding to such perceptions is difficult, but may require you to make some concessions. On the other hand, as a buyer you may be able to play on the vendor's perception of the market to secure yourself a better deal.

Gauging your pitch

Arguing the saleability of your assets is part of savvy negotiating and helps improve the liquidity of your portfolio. Though some assets face a difficult ride in any market, being able to convince people that they're getting a deal is a skill worth learning. (And not just in real estate. We find it's a skill that's really worth having at garage sales. "Why yes, that Betamax VCR sure is a collectors' item...") (We explore negotiating from the vendor's point of view in Chapter 16.)

Determining pricing and timing

Patience is a virtue, and that may be especially true for an investor in a tough market. A property that refuses to sell may enjoy greater liquidity at a lower price. If lowering the price doesn't encourage a sale, you may have to wait a little longer until you can close a deal on terms that are acceptable to you.

Timing is one of the great risks of any investment, because you want to be able to sell for an amount that makes your waiting worthwhile. But at the same time, adjusting pricing to suit the market gives you access to the cash you've got tied up in a property. You may lower your return, but you also succeed in closing the deal. Knowing which is more important to you, securing your cash or getting a better return, helps you decide when to sell a property.

Understanding Joint Ownership

The basic adage of student real estate, never become your best friend's roommate, applies equally well to the question of joint ownership of property. Although investing with your pals often works, it can also lead to ruined friendships and disappointment. To prevent hard feelings, remember to establish a correct legal framework for the partnership. And when difficulties arise, deal with them promptly in a businesslike, professional manner.

Here we introduce you to partnerships and discusses some of the common challenges you face when you invest with others.

Considering partnerships

Many people love the idea of property ownership because of the connection it allows between them and their investment. Rather than having an abstract figure or sheet of paper detailing their wealth, they can see, feel, and put some sweat equity into a property. A partnership lessens that sense of power, and the challenge of balancing the interests of other investors with your own isn't for everyone.

Choosing partners

Joint ownership has its advantages, however. For a new investor, having the support of others in the purchase and management of a first property can be important. The benefits of pooling capital and expertise, and sharing responsibilities makes a partnership with one or several other investors attractive. You'll probably be able to consider investing in a wider range of properties, and spend less of your own time managing the assets you do purchase.

At the same time, don't fool yourself into thinking that partnerships with friends or family are going to be any easier than ones with mere acquaintances or even strangers. Take time to select your partners wisely, assessing the interests, skills, and expertise each member brings to the partnership and how those elements work together.

By determining the guiding principles of your investment group, and entrenching these in a formal partnership agreement, you can maximize the group's chances of succeeding in spite of individual partners' interests.

Working with Government

No matter who wins the next election, you always have to deal with the government. Becoming aware of the various ways federal, provincial, and municipal authorities can have an impact on your properties is just part of life for a real estate investor. You can avoid some government influences over your investment by choosing where to buy, but dealing with other aspects of government intervention requires the skill of St. George. You may never slay the dragon, but you can at least keep it at bay.

Ownership and investing

Real estate is subject to a variety of government controls and influences, ranging from legislation and planning guidelines to taxes. Taxes are unavoidable, but policies are open to challenges.

Before getting caught in scenarios you don't like, however, research the place where you're planning to buy. Some of the questions to ask yourself include

- ✔ Is it open to investment?
- ✔ Have property taxes increased on a regular basis?
- ✔ What are planning guidelines and development approval processes like?
- ✔ What are other investors and developers saying about the area, and what are demand projections like for local properties if current government policies continue?

The answers to these questions give you a sense of whether government influences are likely to have a significant impact on your investment.

Property taxes

Tax rates vary from town to town, and typically run higher for non-residential properties than houses. You can't avoid taxes completely, but you can choose to avoid communities where they are higher than average. Current rates are often posted on municipal Web sites, and the annual reports for a given city may also indicate trends.

Yet even in a jurisdiction with higher property taxes than others, remember that the lower the assessed value of a property, the less tax you pay the municipality. That means that a lower-priced asset with significant potential for appreciation in a community with a relatively high tax rate may be a better investment than a high-priced asset with little room for appreciation in a community with favourable tax rates. Remember to take all factors into account when deciding where to invest.

Tax policies concerning live-work units vary across the country. Some municipalities treat artist live-work studios differently from commercial live-work premises. Often, commercial live-work units are subject to business rates on the business portion and residential rates on the living portion, but not in all cases. Check with the municipality where you're looking to buy to ensure you're not hit with taxes you didn't expect.

Fortunately, tax assessments are open to challenge. You usually have a limited time frame to file an appeal, but if you believe you have been charged too much tax (and who hasn't, at some point?), challenge the ruling! Challenging an assessment that doesn't reflect market circumstances is common. Professional appraisers, not to mention lawyers, can assemble the appropriate documentation and handle the challenge for you.

Beware of bylaws

What you can and can't do with and on a property will affect its value, and your ability to sell it. Common bylaws include legislation regarding secondary suites and rental accommodation, business use of residential properties, land use and sanitation.

We mention limitations on secondary suites and rental units in your home in Chapter 2. Business use of residential properties may also be limited; although this doesn't usually affect home offices, it might be a factor if you plan to convert the property into a bed-and-breakfast or similar operation (like a couch-and-lunch). Some municipalities without civic sewage systems have legislated requirements concerning septic fields.

Zoning and density

Planning a renovation or a redevelopment of the property you've just bought? Be sure your plans comply with local zoning requirements. This is especially important if the property has what city planners call an existing non-conforming use — something that was allowed years ago, but isn't now. You may be required to secure a variance from the city allowing you to proceed with your planned renovation. You might even be forced to scrap your plans altogether, costing you not only the value you hoped to add to the property but some of the pleasure in your investment.

You might face similar restrictions if your renovation increases the floor area of your home. Some homes were cleverly built to the maximum allowable density on a site, meaning that you can't do anything more to the home. Clever, indeed.

You may immediately imagine battling it out with a grim-faced pencil-pusher when you think about approaching city staff, but try to keep a positive outlook and be willing to resolve issues concerning any renovations or redevelopment plans you have. Find out what the city is trying to achieve in your neighbourhood, and think of ways to meet them halfway. Creative solutions not only give you what you want, but also add value to your property!

Permitting and redevelopment

The time it takes to secure development and building permits for a site, and eventually realize a redevelopment plan, can have a significant impact on property values. A city that's open to development projects is typically a better place to invest in property than one that isn't, because the approval times are often shorter than in communities that are more resistant to new development. Typical approval times vary from city to city and project to project, but usually range from a few months to a year or more. The faster the approval time, the easier your job of developing or redeveloping a site. A lack of restrictions also attracts other developers to a community, leading to increased local property values all round.

Some properties come with development permits already in place, but for some reason the previous owner was unable to follow through with their plans. Depending on the circumstances, you may be able to secure the property for a good price. Pursuing a partnership that allows the planned development to proceed could net you a greater return than if you went through a new approvals process with your own plans.

Dealing with the Unexpected

You may be an optimist, but don't forget that bad things occasionally happen to good investors. Brace yourself for the worst, and consider in advance what you would do if you ran into some common pitfalls of owning an investment property. By addressing the factors within your control that could lead to a bad situation, you stand a better chance of not only limiting the chance of problems occurring but also the toll those that do occur take on your investment.

Coping with losses

Taking a loss when you sell a property may not feel like a successful move, but some benefits are possible. And yes, these go beyond any lessons you might have learned from the experience.

The most practical benefit, if the property was strictly an investment rather than your residence, is that you can claim the loss against capital gains on other properties. Check with the Canada Revenue Agency and consult your accountant for the current rules in such situations. (We explain why an accountant is a crucial member of your advisory team in Chapter 4.)

You can also take some comfort in knowing that the loss you take now may save you from seeing a further decline in the value of your investment in future. Several reasons may account for the problems you're facing:

- ✔ **Declining neighbourhood:** A loss sometimes indicates a declining interest in the property or area where it's located. This is sufficient reason to seek a buyer for the property before conditions get any worse. The sale also gives you a chance to renew your portfolio.

- ✔ **Weak economy:** Depending on the type of property you have, broader economic trends may have made the area unfavourable for tenants. You can't control the economy, but you can choose to wait for the economic clouds to pass and good times to return, or to investigate alternative uses for the property.

- ✔ **Failed hopes:** Whatever your hopes for the property, and despite your best efforts at research before making the purchase, perhaps it simply hasn't lived up to your expectations. Unless you have alternative plans for the property, it could be time to cut your losses and move on.

A loss in any one of these situations isn't good, but a sale could free up your cash for reinvestment in a property with the potential to deliver a better return.

Negative cash flow

One of the tricks of successfully managing a rental property is gauging the cost of variables such as heating and utilities, maintenance, and replacing tenants. Sometimes these can conspire to produce negative cash flow. Maximizing rents while you've got tenants is one strategy to ensure you're not losing cash. But what do you do when the losses begin to mount?

Preparation is key in managing utility costs. Because they're charged according to usage, make sure your systems are operating efficiently with minimum wastage. Standards from your power provider as well as rating systems such as EnergyStar exist to help you gauge energy usage and loss — so find out what you can do to save a few dollars. The federal Office for Energy Efficiency (oee.nrcan.gc.ca) also has guidelines worth checking. We discuss improvements to achieve energy efficiency in Chapter 18.

Maintenance is another issue. Regular monitoring of the building can help prevent regular wear and tear and random damage from contributing to the overall deterioration of a property and the resulting expensive repair bills. If you improve the appearance of the damaged suite (and others, as tenants leave), you can justify raising rents to a level that allows you to recoup losses and get the property back on track as an investment.

Routine upkeep doesn't mean you'll never shell out more than you expected for repairs. Obtaining a damage deposit from tenants will cover some costs, but you could be unlucky enough to end up with an unsavoury tenant who damages a suite severely enough to cost you a month or two in income in addition to repair costs.

Maintenance and upgrades can also lower the cost of finding new tenants. A tenants' market can put pressure on even the best of landlords. Onc landlord we know is proactive when it comes to securing tenants: He leases suites on a year-to-year basis, and touches base with tenants two months before the end of each term. This approach gives him the option of retaining a tenant or finding a new one. By initiating the discussion about the lease, he also benefits from having two months to find new tenants rather than being forced to respond to dissatisfied tenants and possibly having units sit empty when tenants decide to leave.

Expropriation

Canada has had its share of land *expropriation* — in short, government taking over private property. Many Quebec residents know the intense controversy in the 1970s surrounding the development of Quebec's Mirabel International Airport, when landowners had property expropriated for an airport that was eventually mothballed. The Mirabel saga remains a prime example of why expropriation leaves a bad taste in so many people's mouths.

You probably won't get caught up in a deal similar to the Mirabel fiasco, but sometimes something as simple as municipal infrastructure projects will result in land expropriation that could affect your investment portfolio.

The takeover of land by the government doesn't quite jibe with our notions of personal freedom, but take heart: you will get compensation. Unfortunately, it may not be what you hoped to get when you invested in your property, and little room exists for negotiating a higher sum from government. Typically, the only recourse you have is through court action.

In a best-case scenario, the expropriation leaves you with the majority of your property, which you can either redevelop or sell for a sum closer to market value than what you received from the government. Don't be sour — make lemonade with those lemons the government gave you.

Chapter 4

Establishing Your Investment Strategy

*P*eople can talk as much as they like about making money in real estate, but the proof is in the doing. And to do it right, you need a strategy. In this chapter, we discuss the importance of setting investment goals, and the properties that can get you there. We also cover the need for a group of trusted advisors to guide and direct you as you make the choices that will achieve (we hope) your investment goals.

Take time to research and develop your investment strategy, independently and in consultation with your advisors. The topics we cover in this chapter may be fundamental to developing a strategy, but the final development is something that will reflect your own unique circumstances and goals.

Knowing the Market, Knowing Yourself

Real estate investing probably isn't an exercise in self-discovery for you. But even if you think you know yourself, the experience of buying and selling property may shed light on skills and traits you didn't know you had. Those revelations may be empowering, or they could be chilling — particularly if they're pushing you into negative-return territory. That's why knowing what you bring to the table is as important as knowing the kind of market you're operating in, and having a sound strategy that helps you reach your goals.

Don't forget to include details about your financial standing and potential needs when you take stock of your own attributes. Although you're hoping real estate makes you money, you need at least some to start with, so it makes sense to consider all your assets — real and personal — when planning your investment strategy.

Taking stock of your real assets is easier than figuring out your personal skills and attributes. For real assets, you can review your most recent income tax return, tally personal net worth (assets less liabilities) and draw up a brief budget reflecting projected income and expenses for yourself. Together, these give you an idea of where you stand and of the kinds of investments you can consider. For a more detailed treatment of this topic, consult *Personal Finance For Canadians For Dummies* by Eric Tyson and Tony Martin (Wiley).

This chapter talks about selecting an advisory team, so we start with discussing the person without whom that team wouldn't exist — you! You need to focus on two areas as you consider your approach to real estate investing: your skills, and how your personal financial goals meshes with the long-term economic outlook.

Taking stock of skills

Being a successful investor depends in large measure on the skills, personal experiences, and research you've accumulated. Research and education can train you in ways of thinking about real estate, but it can't entirely make up for ineptitude or disinclination toward certain types of properties or a total lack of interest in real estate. Fortunately, because we all need a place to live, you have likely had some dealings with real estate and have a basic gauge of the skills you bring to buying, selling, and renting property.

First, however, some sobering news: No simple way exists to assess your skills. You won't find a special Myers-Briggs or Rorschach blot for determining your aptitude for investing in real estate. Taking an inventory of acquired skills and stacking them up against those needed to acquire and manage property is probably a better way to lay the groundwork for your investing career.

Some advocate an assessment of **s**trengths, **w**eaknesses, **o**pportunities, and **t**hreats (SWOT) assessment. As cliché as it sounds, it's good advice. A SWOT assessment requires you to take a close look at your abilities and shortcomings, and to consider the advantages and challenges facing the particular business in which you're involved. It gives you an idea of opportunities you're well-suited to pursue and threats to which you're particularly vulnerable.

We won't guess at your skills and vulnerabilities. But we offer the following list of skills we believe are important to real estate investors. It's not exhaustive or exclusive, but we hope it provides food for thought:

- ✔ **Initiative:** The ability to take initiative is an important skill for a real estate investor. After all, your first deal isn't likely to come to you: you have to find it.

- ✔ **Self-confidence:** A strong sense of self-confidence complementing your ability to take control will bolster your chances of success. And remember, self-confidence means being able to admit when you've made a mistake, and adjusting your plans accordingly.

- ✔ **People skills:** This skill set helps you relate to others and even win them over to your cause, whether they be partners, brokers, bank managers, or bureaucrats. Being a shy introvert won't necessarily work against you (especially if you exude confidence) but you may not make as many connections in the course of your investments. Then again, that could allow you to possess a mystique that awes — and inspires — those around you. (At least that's what we introverted writer types keep telling ourselves.)

- ✔ **Sales and communications skills:** These skills help you make your pitch to those with property to sell, buyers and tenants; they can also help you convince planners that a development you would like to undertake on a property will benefit all concerned. Being able to sell your project, whether for money or goodwill, is becoming more and more important as the demands and issues facing landowners and developers increase.

- ✔ **Research and analysis skills:** These are important for gathering and understanding the various threads of information that relate to your market, and knowing which information to ignore. The more efficiently you can absorb market information and the faster you can respond, the more dynamic an investor you are.

You can also ask yourself a few key questions that give you some insight into your personal investing style:

- ✔ **Do I like risk, or do I prefer stability?** Real estate has a reputation as a stable investment choice, with a proven record of returns over the long-term, but some assets are more stable than others.

- ✔ **Do I have the time needed to realize a return on my investment?** If personal circumstances limit your investment time frame, consider investments with a greater degree of liquidity.

- ✔ **Do I have a sense of place that will evoke gut feelings about a particular market?** Although a personal connection can get in the way of sound investing, familiarity with the community, local history and people with whom you're dealing can enhance your ability as an investor.

Gauging the market's future — and yours

Market cycles — a topic we discuss in Chapter 3 — is be a key factor in determining your investment strategy. You can't predict the future, but knowing general trends helps you plot out a strategy you can able to refer to as you go along.

For example, with real estate cycles running 5 to 12 years on average, you can bet that a 30-year investment career will take you through about three major cycles. The frequency may be greater in local markets, based on economic factors, but the big picture is what we want to keep in mind at the moment. It means that if the market is declining right now, odds are good that in a year or two you might be able to pick up some bargains, and in another 5 to 10 years, sell them for a profit.

Cycles are never exact, so timing your deals requires keeping an eye on circumstances as they evolve and create opportunities. In the meantime, you can estimate the time you have to hold, develop, and enjoy properties. Regularly review the time frames you establish for each property to develop a portfolio positioned to take advantage of cyclical trends, regardless of what the future brings.

Determining your own, personal investment future based on who you are now and what you want to do in the future requires some introspection and, of course, planning. Ask yourself a few basic questions:

- ✔ What are my long-term investment goals?
- ✔ Do I have plans to start a business?
- ✔ Do I plan on having children?
- ✔ When do I want to retire?

Though your goals may change from year to year, at least one stable element remains: You're not getting any younger! Knowing when you want to have kids, when your kids are likely to leave home, when you want to retire, and other key transitions in your life will help you develop an investment schedule.

For example, you may be 30 and single, with a career just kicking into gear. You've got a bit of money and can afford a down payment on a simple condo that gets you into the market. Perhaps in six years you'll marry and be able to trade on the value of that condo for a larger place, and then use the condo to generate income. Or perhaps you'll decide to sell and trade up.

On the other hand, you may be 45 years old with kids bound for college in eight years and plans to retire in 15 years. Your investment strategy reflects those plans. Once you check your strategy against the current market cycle, you may consider an income-producing property for a medium-term hold, and something with potential for longer-term appreciation that you can trade in when retirement approaches. Of course, if the market seems set to peak in 12 or 16 years rather than 15, you'll want to choose a property that gives you the flexibility needed to ensure the market serves your personal circumstances.

No one can read the future, so don't invest what you can't afford to lose. Although we want to help you understand and make judgment calls as you watch what the market is doing, and what your own needs demand, a measure of risk exists.

Selecting an Investment Type

Finding your kind of property isn't quite as easy as taking out a personals ad ("Single real estate investor seeks hot property for fun and profit"). Locating a property that advances your investment goals comes down to a lot of homework, an educated guess, and a gut feeling about what kind of property is going to serve you best (so maybe finding your kind of property is more like *answering* a personals ad).

Stacking up the options

Whether you invest in residential, commercial, or industrial properties, or any of the myriad types of real estate investments in Chapter 2, your success depends on matching them with your need to use them for personal use as well as investment purposes; the desire for relatively liquid assets or long-term investments; and the overall resilience of the assets to market cycles.

Investing with intent

Do you want a property you can use for your own purposes, or one strictly for investment? Knowing what you want from a property will help you determine the type of properties you'll consider buying:

- **Personal use:** Some forms of real estate are better suited to personal use than others. Investing in a property that will double as your home or place of business will have practical benefits for you as well as delivering a return. A house may deliver an equal return to a unit, or bay, in an industrial property, but you'll probably be able to do a lot more with the house than the industrial property.

- **Alternative uses:** Savvy property investment requires that you balance your personal needs against the qualities of the properties you're considering as investments. When you don't need the property for your purposes, who will? Will there be a market for it, or are your needs unique?

Special uses may fit some neighbourhoods better than others, meaning you may need to adjust your plans to include a broader geographic area. Are you comfortable with those changes?

✔ **Straight investment:** A property bought strictly for investment purposes may be just what you're looking for, because you have no interest in using it. For example, you may buy an apartment building with the sole purpose of being a landlord. Although the neighbourhood the building is in and the maintenance of the building appeals to you (not to mention the regular cash flow), you are quite happy not to live there.

Lapping up liquidity

Some properties have greater liquidity than others (we talk about liquidity in Chapter 2). Depending on the amount of time you have to hold an investment, you may want to buy a property to sell after a few years of generating income, or one to hold for years in anticipation of long-term appreciation in value. Gauging the liquidity of a property and making it work in your favour is a good aim. Here are the possibilities:

✔ **High liquidity:** Residential properties are generally the most liquid real estate investment. If you're unable to hold on to a property for an extended period of time, these are your best bet.

✔ **Medium liquidity:** Suites in resorts and other forms of operating properties are subject to trends in the sectors they serve, potentially reducing their liquidity. This makes them a good medium-term hold in a diversified portfolio.

✔ **Low liquidity:** Properties with a low level of liquidity come from a range of sectors and asset classes. No one type of property has a monopoly on low liquidity. The least liquid properties in a given market are those for which there's the least demand. Buying a property of this sort is typically a decision made with long-term hopes.

Balance a property's liquidity with your needs, which we discuss elsewhere in this chapter. Between the two you have the information you need to gauge a time frame for your investment.

Staying strong in soft times

Whether you're looking for a stable cash flow or are just plain conservative, a stable property is a good thing to have. The two mains gauges of stability when it comes to investing are stability in cash flow and stability in value.

Stability in value is self-explanatory. You want a property that's not going to lose its value, one that will — preferably — appreciate over time. A good means of ensuring this happens is to buy a property in a growing neighbourhood where land values are likely to increase. An established community is generally a good place to buy, whereas a home in a single-employer town carries more risk. But don't forget to look ahead and to buy in the path of development; a property can increase significantly in value if it finds itself engulfed by an expanding city (as landowners around Calgary have discovered in recent years).

Cash flow also depends on neighbourhood fundamentals. Because income-producing properties are often subject to cyclical factors, you may want to consider them for short- to medium-term investment. But less volatility means greater stability, so if you have an apartment block in an established residential area, chances are you're going to see both long-term cash flow and an appreciation in land values.

Doing your research

No matter what investment type you're leaning toward, you need to do your homework. If you're going to find properties with the potential to meet your needs and expectations, you need to not only know where to look, but also understand the specific trends affecting the *asset classes* (groupings of specific categories of assets, such as office properties, according to relative value) and properties that interest you.

Media outlets like your newspaper's real estate section are helpful in highlighting some of the trends affecting real estate, but don't overlook industry reports from real estate brokerages and their brokers, as well as most major financial institutions. The reports, usually available online or from the companies themselves, typically highlight sales and leasing trends and the factors affecting real estate activity. Associations for building owners, developers, and landlords are also useful sources of information, whether through newsletters or regular meetings.

We discuss reliable sources of information at greater length in Chapter 17.

Selecting Advisors

Even if you're relatively certain you don't want any partners in your real estate venture, you shouldn't go it completely alone. You need a team of advisors who will offer support — and challenge your assumptions — to make sure you stay on the right track as you pursue your investment goals.

You'll want several people with different sets of expertise on board, each with a particular contribution to make. At various times during your real estate investing career you might consult a real estate agent, a lawyer, an appraiser, an accountant, and a financial planner. In this section, we explain why you're only as good as the people who surround you, and offer some tips on selecting them — including some leads on organizations that can help you find the professional who's right for you.

The criteria

Knowing what to look for when you're sizing up potential members of your advisory team is important — and we're not just talking about qualifications and experience. Just because a real estate agent is good for one person doesn't mean the same person is going to be a match for you. Although references from family and friends can help, criteria for choosing your team of trusted advisors go beyond qualifications and experience to include personality, professional competence and fees.

You're going to have to depend on your interviewing skills, because, let's face it, you won't get along with everybody and some good questions may help you figure out who's right — and who's wrong — for you. Draft some questions that will provide a basis for interviewing your potential advisors. Don't be afraid to ask tough questions — the answers you get might prompt you to think twice about the candidate and steer you away from trouble before it finds you. We don't recommend something as formal (or as harsh) as the Spanish Inquisition, just a thorough but relaxed interview that makes candidates feel comfortable. You want them to open up and tell you how they can help you.

References and word-of-mouth referrals are particularly important when selecting any advisor who will be taking an overall approach to your financial affairs. Ask for professional references and then contact those professionals and ask about the advisor's strong attributes and any professional weak points. Also, ask how long the individuals have been dealing with each other. Don't ask for or expect an advisor to provide you with a list of clients, as this would breach confidentiality.

A short-list of three candidates will help you compare the relative merits of each, as well as provide alternatives in case your top choice falls through.

Qualifications and experience
Some of the advisors you are scouting have professional qualifications; others have specialized training. Be sure to ask if the people you're interviewing have the appropriate training and certification, and request the documentation to back up their claims. It's also important to find out how much experience they've had since receiving their training. Has the lawyer or appraiser cultivated

any special experience that can help you? An accounting firm that has a sizable clientele of small to medium-sized businesses will have in-depth expertise regarding small businesses, but if the firm also has several clients engaged in real estate, you'll be better served.

Personal compatibility

You may have a business relationship with your advisors, but don't discount the fact you'll have to deal with them on a personal level, too. The best candidate for the job should also be someone who doesn't tick you off. Attitude, approach, candour, and communication skills are all factors to take into account.

For example, you can reasonably expect your phone calls to be returned promptly. If your advisor is too busy for you, or is slack in returning your calls, you'll be grumbling about the situation. That doesn't make for a good relationship! Take charge, and make sure your needs are a priority.

Ask yourself these questions when selecting an advisor:

- ✔ Do you feel good chemistry (that is, do you like them and sense they like you)?
- ✔ Do you feel they understand your wants and needs clearly?
- ✔ Do they communicate clearly orally and in writing?
- ✔ Do you trust their motivation and judgment?
- ✔ Do you have confidence in their objectivity and expertise?
- ✔ Do they respond to your questions quickly and effectively?
- ✔ Do you feel they respect you and your opinion?
- ✔ Do you feel they will meet your needs in a timely way?

A solid rapport with your advisors makes you more confident in their ability to assist you. Not being comfortable with them could compromise your own decision-making.

Fees

Fees should be affordable, but also on a par with what others in the advisor's field are charging and — above all — a reflection of the advisor's training and experience. Accountants' fees, for example, typically reflect the work being done, so you may have to pay a bit more to receive the advice you need. But make sure you're comfortable with the rate, and that it's within your budget; otherwise, in an attempt to reduce expenses, you may not use the advisor as effectively as you might. Remember, not seeking professional advice when you need it is poor management! Table 4-1 provides a look at the cost of a range of advisors.

Table 4-1	Advisor Costs
Advisor	*Cost*
Buyer real estate agent	No cost as agent obtains the commission or part of the commission from the vendor.
Mortgage broker	Usually no cost to arrange financing, unless you are having difficulty financing, as there is more time and skill involved, in which case it could be a percentage of the amount obtained. Survey and appraisal cost is frequently waived by lender.
Home inspector	Depends on nature, age and size of property. Could range from $300 to $1,000+
Real estate lawyer	Depends on cost of the property being purchased, and amount of the mortgage, plus related disbursements such as search fees and filing costs; can range from $250 to thousands of dollars depending on various factors.
Accountant	Can vary based on time, skill, qualifications, and complexity and nature of advice and services. Could range from $200 to $1,000+.

The real estate agent

Real estate agents are important because they're the ones licensed to act on your behalf when buying or selling a property. For the purchaser, the agent can identify properties that may interest you and represent your interests to the listing broker. This arm's-length position can have its advantages when the time comes to negotiate a deal. As vendor, you benefit from the agent's listing services and ability to represent your interests in the marketplace. Agents may also have tips that expedite the sale of your property, ensuring that you see a return faster than if you handled the sale yourself. (We discuss the pros and cons of handling a sale yourself in Chapter 12.)

Though each real estate agent will have a different level of skill, and sometimes a unique area of expertise, matching your own needs with the talents of an agent isn't that difficult. Family, friends, and colleagues can often recommend particular agents. Real estate firms that handle the kind of property that interests you may also have recommendations. You can do some preliminary research by talking to people at open houses or checking out the agent's Web site.

The provincial real estate association for your province can provide further information on Realtors who may be helpful to you.

Coined in the United States in 1916, the word *Realtor* legally applies in Canada only to members of the Canadian Real Estate Association. The code of conduct to which Realtors adhere is available on the CREA Web site at www.crea.ca.

Interested in acting as your own agent? We discuss this option in Chapter 16, in the context of selling your own property.

The lawyer

The number of risks accompanying real estate transactions make legal advice indispensable when you're buying or selling a property, and especially so when it's intended as an investment.

References for lawyers are available from family, friends, or colleagues, or via a referral service operated by provincial law societies across Canada. You can easily locate law firms with expertise in particular areas of real estate law using the Yellow Pages or your favourite Internet search engine.

You may be able to save a bit of cash by having the lawyer handling your mortgage documents also handle the documents related to your property transaction. You must be careful that there is no conflict of interest, but this may not be easy if you live in a smaller community with a limited number of lawyers.

The bar association for your province should be able to provide further information on lawyers who may be of service to you.

A word about notaries

Though lawyers are almost always notaries public, not all notaries public are lawyers. This is important for you to remember, because only a lawyer is trained and qualified to provide a legal opinion, whereas notaries public may not be. But in Quebec, notaries (not advocates) are the people you want handling your property deal — they're what the rest of Canada knows as lawyers.

The appraiser

Traditionally, appraisers were trained in the valuation of real property. That makes them an important resource if you're trying to determine the value of your portfolio or what kind of financing you might be able to secure. They aren't always integral to a transaction but their knowledge may assist you in securing a better deal on a mortgage or taking a more strategic view of your investment.

Recently, many appraisal firms have been branching into consulting work. This can assist you when you're scouting properties to purchase, by helping you understand not just the financial worth of the property, but opportunities for increasing its value. Some appraisers will also provide assistance if you opt to appeal your property tax assessment.

The local chapter of the Appraisal Institute of Canada (www.aicanada.ca) maintains a list of appraisers for your area.

The accountant

In addition to always being the life of the party, accountants are integral to the financial health of your investments. Even if you keep close tabs on the day-to-day operating costs of your properties, an accountant can ensure you claim the appropriate deductions on your income tax and make prudent decisions toward achieving your long-term financial goals.

Unfortunately, anyone in Canada can call themselves an accountant. Though professional designations such as Chartered Accountant (CA) and Certified General Accountant (CGA) exist, be sure that the person you want to employ as an accountant has credible and recognized professional training and credentials.

That didn't happen for Doug's friend Don, unfortunately. Don wanted some money-saving tax strategies. Don decided that the staff at the tax preparation shop in his local mall were up-to-date on the latest tax rules. But the advice Don received was inappropriate for the type of investment Don was considering. The Canada Revenue Agency audited Don on receipt of his first tax return because of the strategy he employed on the basis of the tax shop's advice. The outcome of the audit cost him a pretty penny. If Don had used the services of a professionally qualified tax advisor, the outcome would have been very different. Your lawyer may be able to recommend a suitable choice. Some provincial chapters of the Canadian Institute of Chartered Accountants (www.cica.ca) also have searchable databases of their members. A call to any one of the provincial chapters can help narrow your search for an accountant specializing in real estate issues.

Rounding up advisors

You can consult several types of advisors regarding your real estate investments. Remember that prices for their services vary considerably depending on your requirements. Remember too to comparison-shop a minimum of three people in each area before you make your decision. You need that background as a benchmark, and also to make sure that the advice, recommendations, and price quotes you are given are consistent. And if they aren't, find out why! Put your questions in writing in advance of any meeting or telephone discussion so that you don't forget. Prioritize your questions in case you run out of time — a possibility, especially when you're paying by the hour. Make notes of all discussions with your advisors.

The financial planner

A financial planner complements the services your accountant offers by helping you set long-term goals for your investments. A planner can help determine if a specific property serves your long-term investment goals, and perhaps suggest alternative means of achieving those.

Because financial planners are not required to undergo any specific professional training, and only Quebec places legal requirements upon those who offer financial planning services, be cautious about the person you engage as your planner. References are essential, as are background checks. Family, friends, and accountants may be able to supply references, and a number of industry associations can also provide recommendations for your area. An interview can test whether you have the rapport necessary to work effectively together. This is especially important because your relationship will include frank discussions about your attitude toward life, death, family, and business.

Organizations able to assist you in your search for a financial planner include the Financial Planners Standards Council of Canada (www.cfp-ca.org) and the Financial Advisors Association of Canada (www.advocis.ca).

Other professional advice

A number of professionals may not have a high profile in your efforts to buy and sell property, but they can make important contributions during the due diligence period and other phases. These include building inspectors, structural engineers, and architects.

The building inspector

Building inspectors are responsible for ensuring newly built buildings conform to local building codes. Making sure any building you buy conforms to local standards and best practices for its particular kind of construction is in your interest.

Home inspectors are similar to building inspectors insofar as they examine a property to ensure it is structurally sound prior to your purchase. The regulations governing their activities vary from province to province; in some cases, no formal set of regulations governs their activities. For more information on the organization operating in your area, contact the Canadian Association of Home and Property Inspectors (www.cahi.ca).

The structural engineer

Planning a renovation? Check with a structural engineer to see if your plans impact the basic structure of the building. This includes walls, beams, and other elements that if removed or otherwise altered during renovations could destabilize the building. You may change your mind regarding your purchase if your plans do not meet with the approval of a structural engineer.

Structural engineers, like civil, electrical, and mechanical engineers, are registered professionals. Be sure to check their qualifications with the provincial registering body.

The architect

Architects are known as the coordinating consultants on building projects and play a key role in managing the major renovation of a property. They are also important in providing design services that can make the renovation you plan even better.

Though only registered architects are allowed to call themselves architects, intern architects and foreign architects living in Canada can provide basic design services for home renovation projects. You can obtain references to architects and designers willing to assist in your project from the local registering office and through local home builders' associations.

Part II

Preparing to Buy: Financing Real Estate Investments

The 5th Wave   By Rich Tennant

RICHTENNANT

I'm not sure this entirely justifies the "water view" increase in your selling price.

POOL WORLD

CHECK OUT OUR INVENTORY OUT BACK!

FOR SALE

In this part . . .

Getting your cash together may not be the easiest trick when you're just starting to invest in property, but this part aims to make your task a little simpler. We unravel the mysteries of mortgages, help figure out financing, and examine the potential of partnerships. We may not show you the money — but we help you identify places to look for it!

Chapter 5

Pulling Together the Cash: Assessing Your Resources

*R*emember when you were a kid and saw something you really liked? If you didn't have enough money, your parents probably told you to save up, or maybe shovel the neighbour's driveway for the extra cash.

Being a real estate investor is kind of like that. But because most of the things you want to buy are a whole lot more expensive than you can afford with a single cheque, less labour-intensive ways than shovelling driveways can get you the cash (lucky you). In this chapter, we discuss some of the ways you can optimize your saving strategies, as well as scrape together your own cash before approaching banks, private lenders, and other sources of capital.

We also cover finding, and cultivating, workable partnerships. Because many of the sources we discuss are friends and family, we also offer some tips on making sure you stay on good terms with them. Just because they're family doesn't mean you should be any less professional with them. Nor should they expect anything other than professional behaviour from you.

Building Up Your Resources

Let's go back to that item you wanted when you were a kid. Chances are that if you ever asked a sibling or friend for some money to help you buy it, you didn't go to the local bully. If your local bully was financially savvy, you might have been get charged as much as you were loaned in interest — but chances are better that you were just beaten up. More likely, you asked someone who wouldn't mind giving you the cash for nothing — someone who wouldn't even complain if you "forgot" about it (your grandma, maybe)! Those early lessons apply to buying a property — only, more potential bullies lurk on the block to worry about than when you were a kid.

Knowing your resources and who to ask for the extra capital you need to do a deal are key elements of successful real estate investing. Resources include not only you — your own finances, present and future — but the people with whom you partner, or who can put you in touch with prospective partners. These partners ideally include people who can match your investment with their own deep pockets to buy a property that can make you both rich (and maybe even famous).

Before you turn to others for help, look at your own financial situation. Take stock of your *assets,* the funds you have at your disposal, and *liabilities,* such as outstanding debts and other claims that reduce the amount you have to invest. You won't be able to secure a great rate on a mortgage if you're carrying hefty debts.

Financial resources to tally may include the following:

- ✔ Cash and savings, including Registered Retirement Savings Plans and Registered Education Savings Plans
- ✔ Investments, such as term deposits, mutual funds, equities and properties

Once you've tallied up your financial resources, subtract the amount of debt you're carrying. Calculating your net personal worth based on the difference between your assets and liabilities helps you determine how much money you have to invest.

Running a credit check on yourself could reveal important information about your eligibility for a loan. Even when all else indicates you could be a good risk, a bad credit rating will weigh against your ability to secure the best possible financing deal. The major agency providing credit reports in Canada is Equifax (www.equifax.ca), which will provide you with information about your own credit rating free of charge.

Personal Finance For Canadians For Dummies by Eric Tyson and Tony Martin (Wiley) can provide you with further tips on laying a firm financial foundation for your first foray into the world of real estate investing.

Social capital is just as important as financial capital. Some cultures avoid financial institutions in favour of cooperating among themselves, and some of them have enjoyed huge success in the real estate market. Don't underestimate the value of your social connections when assessing your own investment abilities. We go into further detail on this topic in the section of this chapter that deals with tapping friends and acquaintances for financing. You may even wish to establish a formal partnership with your supporters, an option we discuss elsewhere in this chapter.

Identifying Resources

So, how much cash do you have to play with, anyway? And how are you going to use it to fund your real estate purchase? Tapping a mix of resources is just as important as investing in a diverse range of assets. Reducing your reliance on a single source of investment funds limits the chance you will be caught short if that source of financing dries up. Cultivating other sources may also create opportunities for funding future investments as you grow your portfolio.

Resources fall into three categories:

- *Liquid,* such as savings in your piggy bank or bank account, which you can access and pour into alternative investments relatively easily;

- *Illiquid,* which aren't easily converted to cash you can use to fund other types of investment and typically include bonds and other long-term, locked-in investments or investments whose risk inhibits conversion;

- *Vaporous* (okay, *vaporous* isn't a legitimate financial term but it fits!), which are difficult to pin down until they take the form of liquid resources; they usually come from other sources on request.

Typically, you want to supplement any liquid resources you're ready to invest with illiquid resources converted for the purposes of the investment you're about to make. Shortfalls in your own resources can be made up with funds from others who are game to support your investment: friends, family, or even strangers.

Liquid: Savings

Savings and other liquid resources typically account for no more than one-third of a balanced investment portfolio. Whether you're working with an old-fashioned bank account or a low-risk, income-oriented mutual fund, you've got cash on hand.

The advantage of liquid resources is that they're available in the event of unexpected circumstances such as job loss, emergency travel, or medical expenses. But compared to other investments (something we discuss in Chapter 1), they're probably not advancing your personal wealth to any extent. Fortunately, they're available when an investment opportunity comes around.

Depending on your investment strategy, however, you may not have a lot of liquid resources sitting around waiting for an investment opportunity. Perhaps you haven't had a lot of cash to play with and have kept most of your available resources in relatively liquid forms. More aggressive investors tend to have less in liquid resources.

Savings and other low-risk investments don't offer high returns and tend to grow slowly. Some low-risk investments lose value over the long-term in exchange for a greater degree of liquidity.

Limit the amount of cash you keep in liquid investments to make the most of these vehicles. Restricting yourself to three months' worth of expenses frees up more cash for investment in higher-yielding options that may offer better returns, building the amount you're able to invest in less time.

Savings don't include just the money you set aside, however. Although putting aside a set amount each month is a good plan, don't forget to review your spending habits and look for savings in your day-to-day expenses. Most of us have heard (and maybe even taken) the advice to cut down on expenses such as that daily hit of java, but don't forget that unused gym membership, public transit rather than a car (if possible), and even reading material from the public library rather than the bookstore. (One old codger we know of made a fortune in real estate but never bought his own copy of the newspaper!)

Illiquid: Long-term investments

Planning is critical if you hope to use long-term investments to finance a real estate purchase. Whether you're waiting for market conditions to improve before you cash out, or simply waiting for a bond or GIC to mature, planning can help ensure your illiquid investments melt together to provide you with the cash you need when you need it for other purposes.

The challenge you face highlights the need for a diverse investment portfolio. We're not talking just diversity of investment types but diversity of liquidity. Although the latest darling of the stock market may have spectacular growth potential, you want to be sure you can cash out at an appropriate time. A stable stock may offer a lower return but ensure you get to see the gains it has made since you bought it. With the advice of a financial planner or broker, consider a mix of stock types and set goals for the ongoing sale of shares that will allow you to secure the greatest gains possible for your ultimate goal of real estate investment.

Similarly, if you favour bonds and other fixed-term investments, make sure they mature on a regular basis rather than all at once. Known as *laddering,* spacing maturity dates limits your exposure to changes in interest rates. You also have an opportunity to top up your investments or shift them into either higher-yielding vehicles or more liquid forms for investing in property.

Something you want to minimize — and if at all possible completely avoid — are penalties and fees for early redemption or transfers. Good planning should limit the risk of paying too much for sound management of your investments. Tax implications may also accompany the redemption of shares, so consult your accountant for advice on how to minimize taxes as you line up your resources to invest in real estate.

A financial planner can advise you on balancing your short-term and long-term needs, and identifying the resources you should keep in liquid, short-term investments and less liquid, higher-yielding long-term investments. Financial planners are important people to have on your advisory team (something we discuss in Chapter 4), and this is just one of the reasons why!

Tallying cash

Determining the amount of cash you have available at any given time for real estate investment depends largely on your having a clear financial plan in place and sticking to it. No formula exists, as the amount you have depends wholly on your risk or debt comfort-level, your goals and priorities, your borrowing leverage from a lender or mortgage broker, your family connections and borrowing abilities through them, and your creativity and initiative. However, here are some tips on elements of your spending and saving habits you may want to monitor, assess, and update on an ongoing basis:

✔ The amount of cash you need and want for a down payment

✔ Your disposable income, net after tax

✔ The maximum personal line of credit that you can get from your lender

✔ Additional sources of income that might be available to you, such as working a second job, or working overtime, or starting a part-time home-based business on the side

✔ Money your family or relatives may be prepared to lend you, or possibly invest with you in real estate, and the amount, their expectations for the investment, and any restrictions

✔ How much RRSP borrowing room there is for a first-time home buyer, if that is applicable, for you and your partner

✔ Your credit rating (set out a plan to improve it if required)

✔ A pre-approved mortgage for the maximum amount possible and to be held for the maximum length of time possible (say, 90–120 days)

✔ The amount of rental revenue you could obtain from a property through a basement suite as well as the rest of the house to maximum revenue for mortgage eligibility purposes, if that is the investment scenario of interest

✔ The members of your investment group and why they would be assets (if you are thinking of group investing); also look at developing such a group of people with a clear investment plan in writing so that you can exploit purchase opportunities

Vaporous: Friends and acquaintances

Other people's money may be as important to the success of your investment as your own. We discuss institutional financing and mortgages in Chapter 6, but don't forget the people you see every day. You may not have told people you're thinking about investing in real estate, but they may not have told you *they're* thinking about it, either!

A shortfall in your own resources and a desire to not involve an institutional lender, for whatever reason, may make a friend or other acquaintance a good source of funding. That's especially true if they're also looking for investment opportunities. A casual conversation may be an effective way of broaching your need for capital and gauging a friend's interest, but having a plan ready to discuss won't hurt. To reflect a professional approach be able to tell potential investors:

- ✔ What you need, and for how long;
- ✔ Why you need it, and
- ✔ The way you hope their participation will benefit them

A realistic and confident attitude about the amount you need, and willingness to offer a competitive return (either through interest payments, a share of the cash flow if it's an income-producing property or a stake in the property itself that will deliver a return when you decide to sell the property (see also the section on partnership in this chapter) bolsters your ability to secure the support you need. Setting a realistic time frame for the investment will also give your potential financier the information required to decide whether to buy in.

Because you're approaching someone you know, be sure to limit the potential for personal conflict by having a legal agreement in place that safeguards interests on all sides. Don't let the convenience of tapping a friend for the cash you need become a source of bad feeling. You want the deal to be a winning prospect for all concerned. By the same token, don't promise something you can't deliver.

Even more vaporous: Family

Some people make a habit of treating their family differently than they treat their friends. Ironically, that sometimes means worse rather than better. However, we feel strongly that you should treat everyone with whom you do business in a professional manner. That's especially true of family, because the close relationship and trust you have with them is more at jeopardy where money's involved.

Although family members can help boost your own resources, and even provide expertise when it comes to real estate investing, make sure you manage the relationship properly. This includes everything from the moment you raise the possibility, through any challenges or difficulties you face, right up until to the time you cash out and distribute the proceeds of the investment.

Approaching family to invest in your next real estate venture doesn't always have to be an option of last resort. In several situations it's more than just a convenient idea, it's good business sense, too:

- ✔ If a family member has the cash you need to close a deal
- ✔ If a family member has not only cash but also expertise that can help you develop your investment portfolio as well as your investing skills
- ✔ If a family member is willing to become a full partner and meets the criteria you would set for any other business partner

Don't let the ties that bind blind you to professional practice. Make sure you have a formal contract outlining the terms of loans and any other support that family members provide, and the benefit to them of the arrangement. Don't take the support of family for granted, unless you wish to invite resentment. Honour your agreement as you would that with any other lender.

Family matters

Jordan recently moved to Halifax and was enthusiastic about buying a property in a part of the city that was beginning to see a lot of redevelopment. The upside was good, and he wanted to get in early. He found a property with a two-bedroom suite in the basement and planned to renovate and find tenants for the upstairs. He would live in the basement with Kim, his partner. Jordan's parents agreed to provide a $50,000 loan towards the purchase and renovation of the house, but didn't insist on a written agreement outlining the terms. After all, Jordan had always been a responsible person and this was a way of helping him out.

But, after a year of renovations and a few months of being landlords, renting the property,

Kim and Jordan broke up. She went to a lawyer and brought a claim forward arguing that because she had helped make monthly payments and contributed to renovations and maintenance of the property, she was entitled to half the equity in the house.

Because there was nothing in writing proving that the money from Jordan's parents was a loan, and there was no mortgage securing the funds, the cash was accounted as a gift. After much legal haggling, Jordan and Kim reached an out-of-court settlement for $25,000 (not to mention legal fees). Proper documentation could have avoided the mess that resulted, and ensured that all parties benefitted, at least financially, from the break-up.

Providing cash

Many tycoons got their start with a bit of seed money from a parent, an uncle, or some other family member. Whether as start-up capital or last-minute financing needed to close a deal, family money can play an important role in your career as a real estate investor.

Having financial support from family is an advantage insofar as your family knows your needs and you know the source of the cash. The ties that bind also promise to ensure you respect each other's interests. You may even enjoy easier terms than any institutional lender would offer. In some ways, family can play the role of so-called "angel investors," financiers we discuss at greater length in Chapter 6.

To reassure any family members from whom you secure financing, provide some form of security, either through a mortgage agreement or a security agreement. This will ensure they are ranked as secured creditors should you be unable to meet your obligations and declare bankruptcy. This guarantees they have a chance of seeing something when your assets undergo liquidation, whereas unsecured creditors enjoy no such guarantee. We discuss these ideas at further length in Chapters 6 and 7.

If you buy a home with a brother or sister (say, during university), make sure you have an agreement outlining your respective rights and responsibilities associated with the property and the particulars of your ownership stakes. (We discuss joint ownership in Chapter 8, including several points worth keeping in mind when buying residential real estate with siblings.)

Passing on skills

Family members are sometimes logical sources of financing because you can also learn more about investment from them. Giving them a stake in the success of your investment may encourage them to share advice based on their own experiences as investors.

Having an older, wiser, better-heeled family member serve as both an investor and mentor has its advantages if you're a younger investor. The experience can teach you how to handle a purchase through negotiation to close, and how to manage the property. In exchange, on top of simple repayment of the loan, you could offer an equity stake in the property.

Clearly define the involvement of the relative with whom you're working. This ensures your relative knows the limits of her participation in the venture and also limits her exposure to potential legal claims in the event the investment goes sour.

Defining roles and responsibilities is particularly important where family is involved because emotional sensitivities may heighten the tension or any feelings of betrayal when things don't work out as expected. Safeguards in the shape of formal agreements help ensure you don't act solely on emotions.

Partnering up

Finding out that a family member wants to go into business with you may be the last thing you expect when you approach them for financing. But it's not necessarily a bad idea. You have a right to consider your options, however, and subject your potential partner to the standard gamut of trials you would put any other business partner through. We discuss some of these factors in Chapter 4.

Family members deserve both greater and less scrutiny. Less, because you have a long-standing connection with them that gives you special insights into their character and some expectation of how they'll behave. Greater scrutiny of their role in your venture is necessary, however, because even if you've known each other since birth your objectives won't necessarily be the same. Make sure you're on the same page, and have a common understanding of your respective motivations, long-term goals, and the skills you will each be bringing to the investment.

Family includes spouses! Although a business relationship with a blood relative can be sensitive enough, you probably don't have to go home with them at the end of the day. Not so with a spouse! We're not marriage counsellors, but we respectfully advise that before you enter an investment or business relationship with your spouse, you make sure you're prepared for the venture going sour. Discuss what would happen, for instance, if other creditors called their loans or the bank started to foreclose on your primary residence.

Working with Professional Financial Partners

Given all the cautions we've issued about working with family, maybe you would prefer to turn to professional or institutional financiers, the folks for whom real estate financing is as natural as breathing. Even if you've enlisted the help of family and friends, you may need a little extra cash to round out your financial backing. The options are many, from financial institutions such as a bank or credit union to independent-minded career investors looking for opportunities to invest their loose cash.

Regardless of whether you seek institutional or independent financiers, shop around. Services and rates will vary among financial institutions, and even among branches of the same institution. You want to be sure you're getting not just the best deal, but also the best service for your purposes.

Private lenders, who may be friends of friends or contacts you'll discover in the process of networking, require particular caution to ensure that the deal is fair and equitable for all concerned. Even if they're hoping the purposes to which you're putting their cash brings them a return, you want to make sure interest is reasonable for the purposes and that you're being treated fairly.

Keeping the peace

Peace of mind is difficult enough to maintain in your business when family aren't involved. Their involvement can open up whole new possibilities for frustration and anxiety. Many disagreements are avoidable if you follow a few simple principles:

✔ **Don't request personal guarantees from family members.** Asking a spouse, family member, or friend to guarantee or co-sign a loan may sound innocuous enough, but it invites bad feelings if the lender requests immediate payment (a step colloquially known as *calling the loan*). The relationship may not survive the financial loss, depending on the amount and the related circumstances. It's always best, where possible, to bear the responsibility yourself.

✔ **Avoid collateral mortgages on your primary residence.** No sense risking your home just to get into the real estate market. Although you and your spouse may think the idea is a good one, and that you won't fail as an investor, don't even put yourself in a position where creditors could place a claim against your home. You need a roof over your head,

and losing your home would rob you not only of that but possibly of your marriage as well.

✔ **Don't assign life insurance proceeds.** Among the assets you shouldn't calculate among your available financial resources when you're gearing up to do a deal is your life insurance policy. If you assign the proceeds of the policy to your creditors and you die unexpectedly, your creditor could receive the money without your family ever seeing a cent. A far better option is securing mortgage insurance (we discuss this in Chapter 7), which assures concerned creditors that any loans you've taken will be satisfied on your death.

✔ **Don't ask family or friends to serve as directors of your investment company.** Directorships carry a lot of responsibility, not to mention liability for claims made against the company. This can leave directors open to personal lawsuits from creditors, threatening their own assets rather than just those of the investment company. We present some strategies for handling directors' liability in Chapter 8.

Squaring accounts

Getting the best deal from a financial partner, and ensuring the best treatment possible, demands attention to the three *R*'s: rates, results, and references.

Rates

Of course, if you need additional cash to close a deal, you want to receive it for the lowest possible price. The benchmark interest rate is known as the prime rate, which banks give to their best customers. You can find both current and historical rates on the federal Bank of Canada Web site (www.bankofcanada.ca). Comparing interest rates, and the terms of mortgages, is vital. Some bargaining room exists if you're looking for a better rate or terms, so muster whatever persuasive skills and goodwill you can in an effort to reach an arrangement that work for you.

Other lenders typically charge a higher interest rate than the major financial institutions, but the persuasion can also help you secure a better deal from them.

Results

Once you've identified lenders offering the best rates on the financing you need, have a look at the results they've been able to secure for others. You can tell a lender by the company it keeps, and institutional lenders are generally happy to tell you who they've done business with and the deals they've made happen. It's to their credit if they've played a role in a landmark transaction, and it works in your favour if they know the kind of deal you want to do, whether it's a simple house purchase or a land transaction.

References

References are invaluable whenever you're investigating a partnership. That's especially so when it comes to lenders, as their integrity is vital to the success of your venture.

Check with others who've done business with the lender you're considering. What was their experience, especially in terms of service? Was the lender responsive, and easy to work with? Knowing the experience of others may bring to light issues that didn't appear in either your preliminary investigation or in the documentation they provided.

Run a credit check of your potential financial partner. You probably don't have to worry about a major financial institution or credit union, but if you're considering receiving financing from an individual or small business, you should check their credentials. A search of provincial court records, for example, may turn up information that steers you to safer partners. Most provincial courts have searchable databases of judgments (or decisions) available online.

Recognizing danger

It usually happens in only the most desperate of cases, but lenders may want to charge interest at levels approaching the maximum rate allowed by law (that's 60 percent in many jurisdictions). That's hardly competitive with prime! Though 60 percent and under isn't legally considered *usury,* the practice of charging an exorbitant rate of interest in these days of cheap capital is close, and brings to mind Dante's reservation of a special place in Hell for usurers.

More common dangers include inflexible agreements and the lack of adequate leeway for yourself, especially if you run into cash flow difficulties or other circumstances that temporarily prevent you from meeting obligations. References from other investors who have worked with the lender should clear up any concerns in this area.

Real estate fraud, a topic we discuss in Chapter 11, is something else to watch for. It's a growing problem that could cost you your investment, your property, and, if identity theft is involved, your ability to invest in the future.

Optimizing Saving Strategies and Leverage

Regardless of whom you decide to team up with, building your resources to a point where you can actually do something with them is one of the greatest challenges you face as an investor. Once you have a stake in the market, however, things gradually become easier, as you are able to use your existing assets to back future deals and grow your portfolio.

This section looks at how you can gather together the resources you need to invest, and also takes a look at *leveraging,* which at the most basic level simply means borrowing money to make a purchase. Borrowing money requires security, however, and once you've closed a deal or two you may have the option of using an existing property to leverage your next buy.

Assembling a war chest

Your real estate empire may be about as tiny and aggressive as Lichtenstein next to some of the bigger dealers in the business, but you still need a war chest, or funds to finance your real estate conquests. Regardless of the kind of assets you include, you've got to make the numbers work before you head out on the acquisitions trail. To get started, you need to stock your chest with enough capital to finance the assets you want.

Developing a comprehensive strategy is key, and there are four steps:

1. Set investment goals.

2. Develop a budget that help you achieve your goals.

3. Establish an investment strategy that makes the most of your investments, through laddering and other techniques.

4. Plan an exit strategy, or a timeline for when you want to begin pouring your non-real estate investments into property.

Setting investment goals

Knowing how much you want or need to raise to begin investing is important. In some parts of Canada you may need just a few thousand dollars to buy a property; in others, the cost of entry will be a lot more. Setting an investment range will help determine your purchase strategy as well as give you a sense of the investment timeline you're looking at.

For example, if you need just $10,000 to make a down payment on a cottage or piece of land, you may have that in the bank. But if you need $50,000, you will likely have to save up and cash in some investments to become a buyer. Achieving those goals could take one to three years, or more, and requires you to meet ongoing expenses while saving up.

Developing a budget

A budget keeps you on track as you put together the cash to fund your real estate purchase. The budgeting process forces you to assess your income sources and your expenses, perhaps encouraging you to become a more responsible manager of your cash. You may even find yourself inspired to seek higher paying employment!

TIP

A disciplined approach to saving for a major investment will also get you in the habit of setting aside funds for ongoing investment in the management and operation of the asset you acquire.

Having set a budget for yourself, calculate the resources you will likely be able to invest in the future. This requires drafting a simple budget, and perhaps setting some realistic goals for savings. Budgets may not be your thing, but they play an integral role in maintaining the discipline you need to invest in real estate. Your budget should identify how much you can afford to devote to real estate investments. This amount is important for two reasons:

- ✔ If you are preparing to invest in real estate, it focuses your saving efforts towards a specific goal, such as a down payment, and signal when you are able to make your move into the market.

- ✔ If you already own a home or investment property, this amount tells you how much you have to pay down existing properties and channel toward new investments.

Finally, because you've likely made some initial contact with lenders (see the section in this chapter on approaching financial partners), try to identify how much cash you can expect to secure through mortgages, personal loans, and other means. The answer could help determine your investment choices.

Establishing an investment strategy

Money in the bank is great, of course, but it's not going to do a whole lot if it's just sitting there. That's where a solid investment strategy comes into play, helping you reach your goals more effectively — and, we hope, quickly. A financial adviser can assist you in structuring your portfolio to help you retain the gains you make. Though fluctuations in market value will occur, you need to avoid losses and translate gains into further gains in order to meet your goals faster.

Many financial planners provide assistance only after your portfolio reaches a certain size, but it doesn't hurt to make contact early. Cultivating a relationship with an adviser familiar with your long-range plan ensures someone has an established understanding of your goals and objectives as your portfolio expands. You reap the reward in advice tailored to your specific needs. See the discussion of financial planners in Chapter 4.

Planning an exit

What do you do when you've reached your investment goals? An exit strategy gives the answer, defining the process by which you can convert part or all of your investments into more liquid (that is, accessible) forms for financing a real estate purchase. It should include a start date, timeline, and what you'll do with the funds (in your war chest) in preparation for acquiring a property.

Depending on the deal you strike to acquire a property, and the kinds of assets you have, full liquidation may not be necessary. You may be able to close a deal by committing to paying your investments to the vendor as they become available, effectively resulting in a graduated purchase. This could shorten the timeline required for your exit strategy. Offering investments in lieu of cash may have tax implications, however. Again, talk to your accountant and financial planner regarding the best way to structure such an arrangement.

Weighing the opportunities and risks of leveraging

Leveraging is the practice of using a small amount of your own resources and borrowing the rest to buy a property. Your resources may be the down payment that allows you to secure a mortgage (something we discuss in Chapters 6 and 7). Sometimes another property will secure financing for a property or project that will boost the value of your portfolio. The Greek philosopher Archimedes famously boasted, "Give me a place to stand and I will move the earth," a poetic expression of the fact that a fixed point can support a bar capable of shifting great weights. Similarly, real estate investors can use a single property to leverage subsequent purchases several times the value of the original property.

The opportunities leverage offers real estate investors is an advantage of this form of investment, something we discuss in Chapter 1. But a deal that's *over-leveraged* can also create trouble, and sometimes even cost you a property.

Gaining ground

When successful, leveraging allows you to build a portfolio more rapidly than if you were just paying cash. If property values are increasing and you can trade up, leveraging is a low-risk endeavour that can rapidly build your wealth. The risk to the lender is low or nonexistent because the expensive property into which you've leveraged yourself can be sold should you not meet your obligations; the proceeds will cover your outstanding debt.

Risking losses

History is full of investors who purchased properties they couldn't afford to buy, then found themselves forced to sell because the payments were more than they could bear. But a wise investor won't let leveraging opportunities outrun an investment's potential. Building a portfolio by leveraging deals should still respect fundamental principles of good financial management.

Higher than desired leveraging can happen if you buy at the top of the market and conditions begin to weaken. A decline in the value of the property puts the lender at risk. The conditions could also jeopardize your ability to see steady cash flow from the property, putting you at risk of defaulting on those hefty payments.

Staying within your means isn't always easy to do, but guidelines exist. One considers it unwise to leverage a property unless it has seen sufficient appreciation to purchase a property twice the size of the original property. You may not acquire a property worth twice as much as your current holding, but you can at least buy one that's of equal value relatively worry-free.

Another rule recommends making down payments of no less than 25 percent of an asset's value, regardless of how cheap financing is. However cautious that sounds, it prevents you from ever approaching a point where you are too highly leveraged.

Chapter 6

Getting Help: Mortgages and Other Financing

....

....

*I*n this chapter, we discuss mortgages, their sources, and some alternatives in case you find yourself unable to strike a deal with a bank, credit union, or some other financial institution. We also take a look at a few options that aren't mortgages at all but may be just what you need. We wrap up the chapter with a section on how to limit the risk you face when financing your real estate investment.

Getting to Know Mortgages

Mortgages aren't the sort of thing one laughs about. When people talk about adult responsibilities, the omnipresent mortgage is one of the items on the list, alongside kids and credit cards. When you take out a mortgage to buy a house or property, the mortgage is in effect until you pay it off. If you fail to make your payments, you're in *default* (a topic we cover in Chapter 7), and responsible for a debt typically satisfied through *foreclosure*. Foreclosure proceedings terminate your legal right to the property, which is typically sold through a court-ordered sale with the proceeds going toward satisfying the outstanding debt.

Dead pledge

A glance at the origins of the word has a grim touch, too: *Mortgage* literally means "dead pledge." The term reflects the original, thirteenth-century French understanding of a mortgage as a deal that dies when payments cease — either through fulfillment of the terms of the deal, or failure to meet its obligations.

How mortgages work

So, how do mortgages come to be? How do they work? The borrower, also called the *mortgagor,* mortgages property — in the say, a building, land, and the like — in exchange for the cash needed to purchase the property and gain title. A mortgage document filed against the title of the property in the appropriate provincial land registry provides security to the lender against other creditors the borrower may have. In the event the borrower defaults on the mortgage, the lender (or *mortgagee*) is first in line to receive any proceeds from the sale of the mortgaged property.

Discharge, or satisfaction of the terms of the mortgage, must occur before a new owner can claim title to the mortgaged property. Typically, the seller's lawyer is responsible for making sure this happens.

Mortgages typically run for a fixed period of time during which the property owner makes regular payments of a fixed sum. Because a mortgage represents debt, regular payments ensure that the value of a mortgage decreases over time, building *equity,* which is the difference between mortgage and other claims against a property and the sale value of the property.

The regular payments include the *principal* of the mortgage, the amount actually loaned to you for the purchase, as well as *interest,* the amount you're charged for the use of the money. The time during which you make payments to repay the loan is the *amortization* period. We explore these concepts in greater detail in Chapter 7.

Renegotiation of the terms of a mortgage is possible. We discuss this in Chapter 7, which deals with managing mortgages.

Mortgages are subject to both federal and provincial regulations, but they're registered in the land registry office of the province in which the borrower has mortgaged property. Although the laws governing mortgages may differ from province to province and in the territories, the mortgages themselves function in pretty much the same way.

Useful resources for mortgage information

Most major real estate firms and the main sources of mortgage financing in Canada offer plenty of information on mortgages, and in some cases mortgage calculators available on their Web sites that will give you a better sense of how mortgages can serve you.

Web sites you may find of particular interest or use include the following:

✔ **Canadian Institute of Mortgage Brokers and Lenders** (www.cimbl.ca), which represents the majority of mortgage providers across Canada.

✔ **Canadian Mortgage and Housing Corporation** (www.cmhc.ca), the federal Crown corporation that provides various forms of mortgage financing and whose Web site is a mine of housing market research.

✔ **Genworth Financial Canada** (www.genworth.ca), the main private-sector provider of mortgage insurance in Canada, includes information on its products and the rationale for mortgage insurance on its Web site.

✔ **Google** (www.google.ca) is a great way to dredge up huge amounts of information on mortgages in Canada, but you may also want to consult.

✔ **Moneysense** (www.moneysense.ca), which provides a variety of personal finance information including a section on mortgages.

✔ **National Real Estate Institute Inc.** (www.homebuyer.ca), a site with which Doug has an affiliation that can fill you in on mortgages and other aspects of home buying.

The major real estate firms in Canada offer their own share of information. Have a gander at these sites:

✔ **Royal LePage** www.royallepage.ca

✔ **Re/Max Canada** www.remax.ca

✔ **Century 21 Canada** www.century21.ca

✔ **Coldwell Banker Canada** www.coldwellbanker.ca

Many of the above sites also feature mortgage calculators that will help you get a handle on how much mortgage you can handle.

The major voice for real estate professionals in Canada is the **Canadian Real Estate Association** (www.crea.ca), which provides a wealth of information for buyers and sellers of properties, including the financing aspects.

For specific information regarding the mortgage registration and enforcement laws in your province or territory, consult your local land registry office or the lawyer you've chosen to handle your purchase.

Types of mortgages

Far from being homogeneous creatures, mortgages come in many forms to meet the diverse needs of property purchasers. A conventional mortgage satisfies the needs of most residential property purchasers, but knowing the alternatives may suggest means for you to structure a deal that suits your particular situation.

A glance at the various types of mortgages reveals straightforward, conventional mortgages for single or multiple properties, arrangements that reflect the circumstances of a particular property, and options for those who would rather avoid institutional lenders or who have special needs. Approximately 95 percent of all mortgages are of the conventional or high-ratio forms; the others we discuss are available for the specific purposes described.

Though the conventional route may be familiar to you, some forms of mortgage may be better suited to certain properties than others. Examine the pros and cons of each type of mortgage and become familiar with the benefits and risks they present.

Conventional mortgage

Conventional mortgages involve loans representing no more than 75 percent of a property's appraised value or purchase price, whichever is less. The federal National Housing Act requires insurance for mortgages for a sum greater than 75 percent, a measure that protects lenders in the case of default. Purchasers who seek a conventional mortgage must provide the remaining 25 percent of a property's purchase price through a *down payment* or other means, such as a vendor-back mortgage. The major financial institutions generally offer conventional mortgages.

The benefits of a conventional mortgage are that they allow you to secure a property in exchange for regular payments, with the major risk being that you may not be able to make the payments. Should the property, or your own circumstances, not fit with the lender's policies, you may either have to get mortgage insurance or seek an alternative source of funding (we discuss some of the options in the "Securing a Mortgage" section later in this chapter).

High-ratio mortgage

A high-ratio mortgage provides financing for between 75 and 95 percent of a property's value. Because they carry a greater risk, federal law requires that they be insured. The insurance is designed to protect the lender, encouraging lenders to provide financing when they might otherwise consider the risk of the loan may too great. The two major providers of mortgage insurance in Canada are the Canada Mortgage and Housing Corporation (www.cmhc.ca), a federal Crown corporation, and Genworth Financial Canada (www.genworth.ca), the largest private mortgage insurer in the country.

The benefits of having two different options available for high-ratio mortgage insurance is to provide the public with a competitive marketplace, rather than having the federal government monopolize the business. The private insurer provides some additional competitive options that CMHC does not, and vice versa. For example, CMHC recently agreed to permit mortgages to have a 30-year amortization period if the borrower wants, rather than the traditional 25-year amortization period for calculating mortgage payout. Genworth also has a 30-year amortization period option, but recently added a 35-year amortization period option as well. CMHC may or may not decide to provide the additional option.

You typically require a high-ratio or insured mortgage if you're unable to provide 25 percent of a property's purchase price. A high-ratio mortgage and insurance is good if you need a hand getting into the market, but it also lays a greater burden on you — your monthly payments are generally higher and you will consequently pay more interest to service the loan. These two factors make such a mortgage a more costly proposition.

High-ratio mortgages are available from most major financial institutions, but your specific circumstances determine the exact amount of financing a lender provides. Check with your Realtor and banker regarding any conditions that may affect whether a high-ratio mortgage is the only — or best — option for you.

Condominium mortgage

Condos are eligible for conventional mortgages but because purchasers also enjoy an interest in the common elements of the development, special conditions apply. This interest is considered *undivided,* that is, the condo owner shares an equal right to the common elements of the property (such as the grounds, rec centre, swimming pool, and other amenities) with every other unit owner in the condo development.

The lender requires the borrower to comply with all the terms of the bylaws, rules, and regulations of the condominium corporation. Any default on the borrower's part will constitute default under the mortgage. Also, if the borrower doesn't pay the appropriate portion of maintenance costs of the common elements, the lender is entitled to pay the costs on behalf of the borrower and add these onto the principal amount outstanding on the mortgage, with interest charged to this amount.

In the case of default, the lender is has a right to use the unit owner's vote or consent in the condo corporation. This protects the lender's interest in the property subject to the mortgage. Though the lender doesn't usually vote on any and all decisions in normal circumstances, the lender can require the borrower to provide notice of all condominium corporation meetings and is entitled to receive copies of all minutes and information the council gives to owners.

In short, condo purchasers face greater pressure to comply with the terms of their purchases than home buyers who purchase single-family homes.

Leasehold mortgage

Leasehold mortgages allow the person who holds an interest in land to use it for a fixed period of time. An agreement between the landlord, who owns the property, and the owner of the leasehold interest, or tenant, sets out the terms and conditions of the relationship. The leaseholder can sell only the right to use the land for the time remaining on the lease, subject, of course, to the conditions of the lease. See Chapter 8 for more on leasehold ownership.

Mortgages for property on leased land are always for a term less than that of the lease, and are therefore in a class of their own. Normally, a lender won't grant mortgages for such properties unless the lease runs significantly longer than that of the mortgage, because the lender may have to sell the property if the borrower defaults. The longer the time on the lease, the better the chance of selling the property.

For example, if a condo is on leasehold land with a 99-year lease and 85 years remain on the lease from the end of the mortgage, the lender has a good chance of selling the property. On the other hand, if the lease runs 30 years and 5 years remain after the scheduled end of the mortgage, the lender will likely consider the risk too high.

Buyers typically want an assurance of the terms of leased property when they buy. The last thing most property owners want is to see the terms of a lease change, possibly increasing the cost of the land on which their buildings sit. Five or ten years is rarely long enough to reassure potential purchasers that a property will have the value they saw in it when the time comes to sell.

Blanket mortgage

Blanket mortgages, in which several properties come under a single mortgage, are cozy arrangements — at least for the lender. A blanket mortgage provides the lender with additional property as security, enabling a borrower to access more money than the lender would typically provide on the basis of a single property. In the event of default, the lender could proceed against one or several of the properties in order to get sufficient funds to satisfy the outstanding debt.

When one of the properties covered under a blanket mortgage sells, all or a portion (for example, half or three-quarters) of the purchase price of the property has to be paid to the lender to reduce the blanket mortgage. The payment is a condition for the lender's releasing the encumbrance on the individual property. After that, the lender releases the portion of the blanket mortgage that was filed on that property in order for the purchaser of the property to place his own mortgage.

Blanket mortgages are an efficient means of mortgaging several lower-value properties within your portfolio with a view to consolidating their value through the purchase of a more valuable asset. This is an attractive means of trading up if you've gotten a foothold in the market with several low-value properties. For example, an investor with three apartment properties valued at $1 million apiece may secure a blanket mortgage that facilitates the purchase of a $4 million apartment block with a greater number of units in an up-and-coming neighborhood. The new purchase promises not only greater cash flow in the short term, but if the property values in the neighbourhood rise, you could be sitting on a property worth more than those initial three apartment buildings ever were.

Collateral mortgage

Collateral mortgages, in practical terms, provide lenders with a form of backup protection for loans filed against property. Rather than the mortgage agreement itself serving as the main security for the loan, the security is typically a *promissory note* (a legal agreement regarding the loan signed by both the lender and borrower), personal guarantee, or the assignment of some other form of security. Discharge of the collateral mortgage occurs when the borrower fulfils the terms of the promissory note.

A collateral mortgage resembles a conventional mortgage, with the difference that a subsequent buyer can't assume it when a property sells. This makes the collateral mortgage a common option for raising funds for purposes other than purchasing property, such as home improvements or other investments.

Builder's promotional mortgage

To encourage buyers of new homes, a builder may offer mortgage packages arranged through the lender that's financing the project. For example, the builder's lender could offer buyers a mortgage at half a percentage point less than the posted rate for a mortgage and include all legal costs for transferring title and doing the mortgage work. The arrangement provides more business for the builder's lender, which could result in a better deal on project financing for the builder. The builder may even receive a commission for sending business the lender's way.

When it comes to a builder's mortgage, beware! Ask a mortgage broker if you can get a better deal. If a builder has arranged with its lender to offer a half-point discount on a mortgage complete with legal costs, you're probably going to be able to find an institutional lender that can offer to cover your legal costs as well as reduce your interest rate by a full point. When a builder offers a special mortgage, it has made arrangements with the lender to subsidize the discounted or incentive cost of the mortgage by paying the lender for its calculated loss. Conversely, the lender may have a deal with the builder, that if the lender gets more than 50 percent of the mortgage business — say, a minimum of 200 out of 400 condos for sale — it will absorb the discounted mortgage. Another reality is that it might just be a one- or two-year mortgage with a discount. If you want a longer mortgage than that, you would pay extra for the additional years.

Make sure you obtain legal advice to ensure the terms of the mortgage meet your requirements. You may want to investigate the option of renegotiating the mortgage from the builder's lender at a future date should your needs change (we discuss the question of renegotiating mortgages in Chapter 7).

Construction mortgage

A *construction mortgage* is actually a line of credit secured by a mortgage on a property under development. You must provide documentation for the construction, including the contractor's detailed costing estimate, house plans, and other information. After the mortgage is approved, the lender provides a document for you to sign that sets out the terms of the mortgage, including a schedule of advances up to an approved amount that will cover each stage of construction. The lender will want confirmation from the builder or contractor when each stage completes before release of the next payment.

The close scrutiny to which a lender subjects a construction mortgage aims to ensure that you manage construction smoothly and don't invite claims against the project. The property should remain free of *liens,* claims that could prevent the lender from retrieving the full value of its loan. The lender registers the mortgage on the property where the construction is taking place and may even register it against your current residence to ensure sufficient security in case of default. When construction completes, the lender converts the construction mortgage to a conventional mortgage.

Vendor mortgage

A *vendor mortgage* is one in which the party selling a property (the vendor) offers to lend part of the purchase price to the prospective buyer. This is useful if you require assistance securing institutional financing, because the vendor can supplement the cash you need for a down payment. For example, if you don't have enough funds to provide a 25-percent down payment, the vendor may provide 15 percent of the purchase price in an arrangement that would effectively serve as a second mortgage on the property. You would only need a down payment of 10 percent.

The vendor may also offer a mortgage with a lower interest rate than what institutional lenders are offering. The arrangement may help you buy the property, but beware of drawbacks. In some cases, the vendor may boost the price of the property to make up for the discounted rate of interest; in others, the discount may last for a short period of time, after which you need to secure a regular mortgage. The arrangement has advantages if you need some help buying a property before other financing becomes available, but it may be false economy.

Assumed mortgage

An *assumed* mortgage is one that already exists — for which you *assume* responsibility to repay. (Not one that you just *think* is there.) This can save you legal fees and disbursements for registering the mortgage, among other expenses. Whenever you assume an existing mortgage, make sure your lawyer obtains a statement that shows the principal balance outstanding, the method of paying taxes, the remaining term on the mortgage, and a copy of the mortgage that shows other features such as prepayment privileges and the like.

If you're the vendor in a vendor mortgage

Because vendor mortgages often work in tandem with institutional financing, vendors frequently won't run credit checks on purchasers requiring such mortgages. If you're the vendor, however, we think it's a prudent move to check the credit-worthiness of your purchaser. Requesting a clause to this effect in the offer to purchase is a simple step that can forestall major headaches. To request a credit report on a potential purchaser, tenant, or even yourself, contact Equifax (www.equifax.ca) or Transunion Canada (www.tuc.ca).

A credit check is a standard requirement if the vendor intends to sell the mortgage to a mortgage broker when the transaction completes. The arrangement allows the vendor to recover the loan, leaving the risk in the broker's hands.

Although the purchaser avoids the fee payable to the mortgage broker, the vendor may refuse to sell the property unless a mortgage broker is willing to purchase the mortgage.

A bad credit rating isn't the only danger vendors face when offering a mortgage to a purchaser: A purchaser may refuse to repay the vendor's mortgage if problems exist, or appear to exist, with the property after sale. This is where legal advice in the wording of the loan agreement is important. The vendor or mortgage-broker may, of course, attempt to commence foreclosure proceedings, but the purchaser may put up a fight that could create headaches. As with any business partners, know who you're dealing with when you grant a loan, and have appropriate advisers on your side to defend your interests!

When someone else assumes your mortgage, obtain a written statement from the lender that granted you the mortgage that clearly states your freedom from liability. Without such a statement, the lender is able to go after both yourself and the person who assumed the mortgage to recover the outstanding debt or any mortgage shortfall after any future sale of the property. Make sure you obtain legal advice before allowing someone to assume your mortgage.

Government-assisted mortgage

In Canada, the Canada Mortgage and Housing Corporation (www.cmhc.ca) is typically the source of government-assisted mortgages, but some provinces also offer second mortgage funding or funding guarantees to assist in the purchase of a principal residence. You can find more information on the various financing opportunities available in your province at your chartered bank, trust company, or credit union.

Second and subsequent mortgages

Second and subsequent loans rank lower in priority when it comes to payment than those registered before them, so they typically bear a greater rate of interest that reflects their riskier nature. The risk stems from the hierarchy of repayment for the various mortgages. For example, a $200,000 property may have, say, three mortgages: one of $125,000 at 5 percent; $75,000 at 7 percent and $20,000 at 10 percent. But the largest mortgage doesn't carry the most risk to the lender; the smallest one does. When the property sells, the proceeds pay the first mortgage first, then the second mortgage, and so on. Repayment of the third mortgage happens only after the others are satisfied. Should the sale price cover only the first two mortgages, the third lender could be out of luck.

Second and subsequent mortgages sometimes supplement the financing obtained through the first mortgage, and typically represent up to 75 percent of the value or purchase price of the property that secures them, whichever is lower. Some mortgage brokers, among other lenders, offer second mortgages for 90 percent and even higher of the purchase price or appraised value (again, whichever is lower).

If a borrower can obtain sufficient financing to buy a property with only a first mortgage, that is the best option, because the rate is the lowest. However, maybe the lender will only lend up to 75 percent of the financing, and the borrower needs to find the other 15 percent in order to borrow a total of 90 percent of the purchase price, because he has a 10-percent down payment.

Or you may want a second mortgage because you're buying from someone whose mortgage you can assume and that mortgage is 3 percent lower than the prevailing rate. To make up the shortfall on the purchase price, you would need to get more financing, which, after the mortgage is registered, would constitute a second mortgage. If you required more money still, you might have yet another mortgage registered, which would constitute a third mortgage in the security lineup ranking.

When your second mortgage has a term longer than your first mortgage, make sure you have a postponement clause in the agreement governing the second mortgage. A postponement clause enables you to automatically renew or replace the first mortgage when it becomes due, if you wish to do so, without having to obtain permission from the second mortgage lender to do so. The clause ensures that the mortgage you renew or replace continues to rank ahead of the existing second mortgage in order of priority.

Keep an eye on the value of the property you're mortgaging and the size of the debt you're carrying. All that cash may look good right now, but if you need to sell a mortgaged property, make sure you can discharge in full the mortgages registered against it. Talk to your accountant or financial planner to ensure you're not loading yourself down with more debt than you can handle.

Mortgage limits

Regardless of how you finance your real estate purchase, you need to know how large a mortgage you can take on. Why over- or underestimate your abilities when you can get some hard facts? First, calculate the size of mortgage for which you're eligible; next, consider strategies for stretching your limits.

Calculating your limits

Different lenders have different criteria for approving the amount of mortgage they're willing to grant, but you can ballpark what you're eligible to receive by calculating your *gross debt-service ratio* and the *total debt-service ratio.*

The gross debt-service ratio is the total of your monthly mortgage principal, interest, and taxes divided by your monthly income. Typically, you want to use 30 percent of your gross income to pay the mortgage principal, interest, and taxes. The total debt-service ratio is higher, usually 35 to 40 percent of your gross monthly income, though this varies among lenders. The calculation is the same as for the gross debt-service ratio but it includes not just your mortgage payments, interest, and taxes, but all other debts you're carrying.

Online mortgage calculators

Checking out the mortgage calculators on bank or other Web sites is easy and convenient. Some sites have a range of different types of mortgage calculators. Plug in your numbers at one of these sites:

✔ Google (type in key words, such as "Canadianmortgage calculators" www.google.ca

✔ Canada Mortgage and Housing Corporation www.cmhc.ca

✔ Genworth Financial Canada www.genworth.ca

✔ Moneysense magazine www.moneysense.ca

✔ Royal LePage www.royallepage.ca

Stretching your limits

If you want to boost the amount of mortgage you're eligible to carry, a couple of options exist:

✔ **Purchase a home with a rental suite.** Tenants provide an ongoing cash flow that most lenders will factor into your debt-service ratio, allowing you to carry a larger mortgage. (We discuss this strategy in Chapter 2.)

✔ **Use a mortgage broker to source a mortgage with the best interest rate and mortgage terms possible.** The lower the rate, the lower the risk of carrying costs. If you have a variable-rate mortgage to pay less interest, make sure you monitor the market so you can quickly convert your mortgage into a fixed-term mortgage for budget purposes if rates begin to increase.

Securing a Mortgage

Our goal in this section is to outline the financing options available to you. We cover the various types of institutional and non-institutional lenders available, as well as the standard criteria they look for. We also discuss mortgage brokers, what they can offer and how to select one.

Banks, credit unions, and brokers

Two main sources of financing are available for property purchases, *institutional* and *non-institutional*. The major institutional lenders include banks, trust companies, and credit unions, all of which are established by and subject to government regulations. Non-institutional lenders are a wider-ranging lot, including everyone from mortgage brokers to partners, friends, and family (we discuss some of these non-institutional sources of financing in Chapter 5). Mortgage brokers are also subject to government legislation, setting them apart from most other non-institutional lenders, but like other non-institutional lenders they're often willing to take on greater levels of risk.

As with any other business relationship, your time shopping around to find a match that's right for you is well spent. You may already have a relationship with a particular financial institution but the branch you deal with may not have the expertise you need. A competitor may offer a better interest rate, or offer to advance an amount that broadens the range of properties you can consider. You can afford to put your interests first when selecting a lender; the research you do can only help improve your ability to negotiate a deal that serves your needs.

Tough negotiation pays off, and sometimes isn't that tough to pull off. Ask what incentives are available to attract your business, and whether the lender can offer a discount from the rate posted at the door. Try to achieve a one-point reduction in the posted rate. Cite your history with the lender if you do most of your financial business there, or mention that you're comparing rates; the mortgage business is competitive, so a lender will strive to keep you as a customer.

Consider obtaining a credit report on yourself. This is usually free, and lets you see whether any elements in your credit history are likely to make a lender nervous. It also assures you that lenders are receiving accurate information about your credit. (For more on credit reports, see Chapter 5.)

What lenders require

Knowing what lenders require, and being prepared to deliver it, can go a long way toward securing you the best possible mortgage in the shortest possible time. Of course, you won't have control over all parts of the process, but you can do your best to make the best impression and negotiate the rest to secure a workable deal.

During the one to five days it takes to approve a mortgage for the winning investment you're about to make, a lender investigates two key areas: your potential purchase, and you, the borrower. This information is supplied in the mortgage application, which typically has three parts:

- ✔ Description of the property
- ✔ Details of the property's purchase
- ✔ Borrower's financial background

Getting to know the property

The most important aspect of the property to the lender is its ability to serve as collateral. If you get the loan needed to buy the property and the lender eventually has to sell the property to recover the loan, the lender wants to make sure the property is valuable enough to cover the outstanding debt.

When you apply for a mortgage, provide a copy of the agreement of purchase and sale, the basic document that will become the sales contract when the deal closes. An appraisal, usually at your expense, provides the information the lender needs to both verify the description in the sales agreement and determine the property's future market potential.

Thanks to the vast stores of information available about property transactions, appraisals are a much simpler process today than they once were. However, the basic criteria factoring into the valuation remain the same:

✔ Location

✔ Previous selling price

✔ Current condition of the property and the surrounding neighbourhood

✔ Available services, infrastructure, and amenities

✔ Comparative sales in the area

Because lenders typically prefer a more conservative valuation, the bank settles for a lower valuation than necessary. This may decrease the size of the mortgage the lender is willing to give, but it also invites you to make a case for yourself.

A lender could refuse to provide a mortgage following an appraisal, but if so, you'd probably be wise to get out of the deal. For example, the appraisal may say the property you want to buy is only worth about 80 percent of what you've agreed to pay for it, or that significant problems exist with the property, all of which could put the lender's security at unacceptable risk.

Getting to know yourself

Character and capacity for debt are the two criteria lenders take into account when deciding whether to grant you a mortgage. The two factors are unique yet in many ways interdependent. Your capacity for debt will indicate how much debt you can realistically handle, while your character will give the lender an idea of how you're likely to handle that debt under different circumstances.

The main verification of your character the lender seeks is a credit check. The lender also wants to know your employment history, and the stability of the sector in which you work. A letter from your employer (if you have one)

that confirms your position, length of time with the employer, and salary is important. If you're self-employed, be ready to provide copies of your financial statements and/or tax returns for the past three years. Historically, self-employed individuals have been considered higher risks than those with conventional employment, but this attitude is steadily changing.

The greater stability you can demonstrate in both your credit and employment history, the better you appear to a potential lender. Be ready to make a forceful case for yourself, and negotiate the best possible mortgage!

Calculating your total debt-service ratio will give you an idea of how much debt you can handle, and the size of mortgage a lender may be willing to grant. To secure a mortgage that allows you to consider the broadest range of properties, back up your case with an accurate statement of your assets and liabilities and detail the exact financing (and sources) you intend to supply. Identify strategies, such as renting a suite, that may convince the lender you can support a larger mortgage than usual for that particular property.

Presenting a sound financial plan developed with the help of your accountant or financial planner could help make your case stronger and sway the lender in your favour. Don't forget to seek the help of these advisers!

Coming clean

So, you've requested your credit report and found out why the lenders have been denying you that mortgage you desperately need. What to do?

First off, review it to make sure the information is correct. This is especially important if your credit rating has been ruined by identity theft. If anything is inaccurate or not updated, you can write to the credit reporting agency and set out your side of the story. This is added to your report history, so that potential lenders can see your version of events.

You should also contact your creditors to request that they immediately update their records and remove any inaccurate or incorrect information that may be hurting your credit rating. The credit rating agency will only remove the offending information at your creditors' request.

After you update your credit bureau history, review your credit history to see whether any black marks can be improved. For example, pay your monthly credit charges on time to establish a reliable pattern.

If your credit history is poor, consider speaking to a credit counsellor about consolidating your loans or establishing a system for the orderly payment of your recurring debts whereby you just make one payment to the credit counsellor company who then pays the other creditors. Every province has this type of service available to assist people in improving their credit history. Contact information on credit counsellors is readily available in the phone book.

A relatively simple way to determine the amount of mortgage available to you is to go to Google (www.google.ca) and type in "Canadian mortgage tables," "Canadian mortgage eligibility calculators," or "Canadian mortgage calculators" and see the range of Web sites that show up. (Keying in "Canadian" before the search words will help ensure the sites are indeed Canadian, but be sure to double-check.) The calculators will be able to provide customized calculations for your personal situation. Still having trouble? Contact the mortgages rep at your bank or credit union, or a mortgage broker, and request the information you're looking for. You usually receive it at no cost or obligation.

Selecting a mortgage broker

Traditionally, when people couldn't secure mortgages through institutional lenders, they turned to mortgage brokers who, for a slightly higher interest rate, would match them with the funds they needed.

Today, a mortgage broker remains an intermediary between those who want money and those who have money to provide. This could include traditional mortgage lenders, as well as private lenders, pension funds, and insurance companies, who lend money for residential mortgages. If a mortgage brokerage is large enough, it may also lend money, but generally brokers, well, broker other people's money.

Mortgage brokers enjoy a booming business thanks to their ability to tap into a broad range of financing sources from the conventional to the unconventional. Mortgage brokers frequently get the best discounted rates from lenders due to the volume of business they command. Here are some common sources of funds:

- Banks, trust companies, and credit unions
- Canada Mortgage and Housing Corp. (CMHC)
- Private and union-sponsored pension funds
- Real estate syndication funds
- Insurance companies and private lenders

The process of selecting a mortgage broker is pretty much the same as for selecting any other type of lender. References from friends and associates may help make the decision easier and, as always, it pays to compare. Mortgage brokers generally charge a fee of between 1 and 5 percent for their services, based on the standard lending criteria as well as the difficulty and urgency of your particular situation.

We recommend the use of mortgage brokers in all cases for many different reasons. It will save you time and money: Time running around doing your own comparison shopping, and money because mortgage brokers can submit your request to multiple lenders who will give their best rate within the competitive marketplace. Mortgage brokers are in the mortgage money business. That is all they do. They know which lenders are anxious to lend money at any give time, and the incentives that will be offered to make a deal. Also, mortgage brokers get a referral fee from the lender, so you don't pay for the service. The lender is glad to pay a referral fee to the mortgage broker as a cost of marketing in a highly competitive money-lending environment.

The mortgage broker you choose should be a member of the Canadian Institute of Mortgage Brokers and Lenders (www.cimbl.ca), whose membership handles 90 percent of mortgages in Canada. The new professional designation of Accredited Mortgage Professional (AMP) promises to further establish mortgage brokers as trusted players in the financial service sector.

Considering Other Sources of Cash

Sometimes circumstances require creative financing as the only way to make a deal work. A conventional mortgage is the height of workable but distinctly unimaginative financing. This section provides some alternatives with a creative flair that are all legal — but not necessarily your grandpa's mortgage.

Don't pay now: Interest deferral

Interest deferral is actually meant to hold your interest in a property. It allows you to defer interest payments on a mortgage in favour of paying down the principal. Deferral typically occurs for a set period of time prior to payments returning to normal. Although interest accrues according to the agreed-upon interest rate, you don't have to pay it until the agreed date. For this reason the arrangement is sometimes billed a *balloon payment* mortgage.

Interest deferral can help tide you over if you don't have cash now but expect a windfall in the future. Be prepared to demonstrate that you've got the cash coming, however; this is one case where your credit- and trustworthy character will stand you in good stead!

Share the wealth: Equity participation

Sometimes the best way to get money from a lender is to give her a stake in the property you're buying. And we're not just talking about giving the lender the option to foreclose on the property. An equity position allows the lender to enjoy any appreciation in the property's value and interest on the loan you require to buy it. This could benefit both of you, so long as you keep paying and the property appreciates at a relatively rapid rate that more than makes up for the loan required to secure it.

Conventional lenders are not typically in the equity participation game. Instead, that's a role left to private lenders and individuals. Family members or relatives often play this role, as they know and trust the person to whom they are lending money and have a mortgage on the property to secure the loan. The downside of this type of loan is the ties that bind — what expectations, investment criteria, or reporting requirements are involved, and who has the ultimate say or control in decision-making such as when the property is sold.

Float your boat: Variable-rate mortgages

Fixed-rate mortgages offer a stable interest rate for the term of the mortgage. But if you're caught in a cycle of declining interest rates, you're not likely to want to lock in at a high rate that's bound to be much lower within weeks of your locking in. Enter the variable or floating rate mortgage.

The interest on a variable rate mortgage is adjusted according to an index, such as the Bank of Canada prime rate, but at certain intervals and with a limit on the amount of interest. Many lenders allow you to set the terms such that you can quickly convert your variable-rate mortgage into a fixed-term mortgage if you think interest rates are about to rise.

Some variable-rate mortgages may compound interest monthly. This could boost the total interest you pay compared to a mortgage with a higher but fixed rate of interest.

Divine intervention: "Angel" investors

Some consider them the lenders of last resort, others the drivers of the real estate market, but one thing's for certain: angel investors are willing to provide financing when no one else will. The greater the risk and appeal, the better the prospect for these lenders.

Locating angels is best done not through prayer — though we don't discourage that — but through networking. Angels keep a low profile, but those in the know can direct you to them.

Angels' taste for risk means you'll often wind up paying a heftier interest rate. Even when conventional financing is cheap, they'll often require payments that are ten percentage points above the going bank rate. Alternatively, you'll find yourself offering up an equity stake or devising some other form of the creative financing methods we've discussed in this section. Keep your wits about you!

Walk the line: Lines of credit

Using a line of credit is another form of getting cash. If you have a home, you can get a home equity loan. Depending on the amount of the loan, if you provide the lender with an additional mortgage to provide security for the loan you will receive the very best rate — maybe even the prime rate, or less than prime. That is all negotiable. Remember, if you don't ask, you won't receive! Depending on how many mortgages you already have on your home, the home equity loan would rank last in priority — for example, it may be the third mortgage registered, which would make it a third mortgage, and it would rank in security as third in line after the previous two mortgages.

Limiting Risk

Risk takes many forms for a real estate investor. We discuss some of the general factors that make real estate a risky investment in Chapter 1, but financing a real estate investment brings its own risks.

Understanding the pitfalls of financing a real estate investment can help you limit the risks you face. Some of the common ones include

- ✔ High interest rates
- ✔ High debt to service ratio
- ✔ Inflexible terms

These three risks aren't always in play at the same time, nor will they always demand the same amount of attention. Fortunately, certain strategies can limit the dangers they present.

High interest rates

High interest rates haven't been a problem for most of this decade. Instead, rock-bottom rates have fuelled a lot of the investment in real estate that's been going on. But back in the early 1980s, when parachute pants were cool and double-digit interest rates were the norm, financing real estate was a lot more expensive. Any increase in interest rates increases the cost of financing a real estate purchase, potentially making it less of a deal than you originally thought.

To limit the risk you face from high interest rates, try locking in the rate of interest on any loans required to finance your investment for as long as possible. It may pay to hold off on making an investment in some cases for six months or a year if research suggests interest rates are poised to fall. However, as property values could go up considerably during this time, appreciation in property values could negate any benefit of waiting for lower interest rates.

A better strategy may be to go for a short-term fixed-rate mortgage of, say, 6 to 12 months, which could be paid off at any time (open), or to obtain a variable-rate mortgage, which tends to be about one to two percentage points less than a fixed-rate mortgage. Then, when rates drop to a level you consider attractive, you can lock in a fixed-rate mortgage for 5, 7, or 10 years.

Usury begins at 60. Sixty percent interest, that is. By definition, it's a rate beyond what the law allows. We trust you'll never see a 60-percent interest rate in any loan agreement you're asked to sign. If you are, run far, far away.

High debt-to-service ratio

Believing you can take on more debt than you can comfortably service is a major risk for investors. Spurred by ambition and betrayed by reality, more than one investor has woken up to find themselves carrying more debt than they can handle.

Don't be sucked in by irrational exuberance, or hype in the marketplace, or greed, or the experience or enthusiasm of others. Calculating the amount of debt you can manage and staying within your limits can help you avoid over-extending yourself. Here are some guidelines:

- ✔ Don't borrow any more than you can afford to lose if the market goes soft and your property decreases in value. It's one thing to lose the equity you have — it's another to go further into the hole to pay off your mortgage. Some simple long-term planning can help you ride out cyclical fluctuations, but this requires knowing when to lock in your mortgage at an interest rate that will suit you for an extended term!

✔ Have a contingency buffer plan in case you have vacancies, a net short-fall in revenue, or unexpected repair costs. This could take the form of personal savings or a line of credit.

Inflexible terms

Real estate financing is subject to contracts, terms, and conditions like any other business agreement. But an agreement that expects more than you're comfortable with — or just plain can't deliver — isn't in your interests.

Avoid agreements that dictate payments beyond your means or an acceler-ated repayment schedule that could jeopardize your financial stability. Have your financial and legal advisers, people we discuss in Chapter 4, review the terms of your agreement. If they voice concern about the deal, renegotiate. If you're still not comfortable with the terms of the agreement, walk away.

You can also take some concrete actions to limit risk:

✔ **Finance yourself.** Though only a lucky few people can finance a real estate portfolio themselves, it's one way to limit the risk you face in having creditors. And, hey, if you've got a lifetime ahead of you and are content to wait until that five acres of backwoods you bought for a song turns into a property worth selling to developers for a huge profit, go right ahead.

✔ **Work with reputable lenders.** A bank, credit union, or other well-established lender exposes you to less risk than working with a lender whose own stability may hurt yours. The stability of a major bank may allow you to secure more favourable terms than those available from a smaller lender. Favourable terms have an impact on everything from the interest rates to the repayment schedule under which you operate.

✔ **Work with your advisers.** We've said it before, but we'll say it again: Nothing beats the value a good team of advisers can provide, especially when you're negotiating a loan. Regardless of the financial resources you bring to a deal, you'll usually require some level of financing. A lawyer, accountant, and financial planner can each provide observations and insights that can make sure a lending arrangement carries as little risk as possible for your budding real estate empire. For tips on choosing advisers, see the appropriate section in Chapter 4.

Chapter 7

Cutting Costs: Making Financing Go Farther

. . . .

In This Chapter

▶ Managing mortgages like a pro

▶ Keeping on top of payments

▶ Renegotiating or refinancing strategically

. . . .

*N*o matter how you finance your property purchase, you will undoubtedly end up paying interest on some portion of it. Although financing comes in many forms (we discuss these in Chapter 6), the most common form is a mortgage. So, favouring the numerical majority, this chapter discusses managing a mortgage. Keep in mind, though, that the principles often apply to other types of financing as well. The main topics we cover in this chapter are the basic concepts you encounter as you gear up to manage a mortgage. We also take a look at some of the methods of managing payments, and also the one thing you don't want to do — default on your obligations. And we look at refinancing, an important tool that can help both manage your mortgage and your cash flow.

Managing a Mortgage

Preparing to handle a mortgage requires familiarity with a handful of key concepts and their lingo. Knowing how each works in the context of a mortgage — even if the terms are familiar from other parts of your life — will prepare you to manage everything, from payments to discharge, more effectively in partnership with your team of trusted advisers. You'll also have a grasp of what they're talking about when they mention open and closed mortgages (something we discuss in the next section).

Interest

By definition, mortgages bear *interest* — the price a lender charges for you to use the money. The lender may charge interest at a rate that remains fixed for the term of the mortgage (for six months to ten years), or a variable rate, in which the rate fluctuates in tandem with a base rate the lender sets. Though the actual monthly payments are usually constant, the proportion of the payments that pay down the principal of the loan will vary.

Mortgages, like bonds and other fixed-term investments, may bear *compound interest* — that is, interest charged on interest owing. When interest compounds, the amount of money you pay in interest charges increases. Mortgage agreements must contain a statement explaining how the lender calculates interest. Mortgage interest traditionally compounds every six months.

The initial rate quoted for a mortgage is called a *nominal rate,* while the *effective rate* is the actual rate of interest you're paying. For example, a mortgage that quotes a nominal rate of 10 percent has an effective rate of interest of 10 percent when compounded yearly, 10.25 percent when compounded half-yearly, and 10.47 percent when compounded monthly.

Variable-rate mortgages often compound interest monthly, reflecting monthly fluctuations in interest rates. Taking this into account when you're scouting mortgages is important in deciding the term of the mortgage, and whether you want a variable-term mortgage at all.

Are you considering assuming an existing first mortgage because the rate and term are attractive, but concerned that a higher rate of interest on a second mortgage might make the deal not so hot? Calculate the average interest of the two to see how much interest you'll end up paying overall. You may find the average interest rate varies significantly from the prevailing first mortgage rate.

For example, if the first mortgage is for $60,000 at 5 percent and the second is for $30,000 at 8 percent, you'll pay $5,400 each year in interest. But that works out to a 6-percent interest rate on the total debt of $90,000 (see Table 7-1). How does that compare to the best offer a lender is making you for a single mortgage on the whole property?

Table 7-1		Averaging interest	
Mortgage	**Amount**	**Interest rate**	**Interest owing**
1	$60,000	5%	$3,000
2	$30,000	8%	$2,400
3	$90,000	6%	$5,400

When the term of a mortgage ends, the principal and unpaid interest of the mortgage become due and payable. Unless you are able to repay the entire mortgage, you typically either renew the mortgage with your lender on the same terms, or renegotiate or refinance the mortgage (two strategies we discuss at the end of this chapter). Renewing a mortgage usually costs between $100 and $250.

Renewing the mortgage with a new lender may involve paying administrative charges. Because considerable competition exists among lenders, many will waive the administration fee or absorb it when you transfer. You can use this as a negotiating point with the new lender, if you wish to transfer your mortgage.

Interest payments

The amount of interest you pay on a given mortgage depends in part on the frequency of your mortgage payments. Shown in the following Table 7-2 is the difference in interest payments per thousand dollars of mortgage when interest compounds semi-annually during the payment period.

Table 7-2		Tallying interest payments		
Interest rate %	**Weekly $**	**Every two weeks $**	**Twice a month $**	**Monthly $**
3.50	$0.67	$1.33	$1.44	$2.90
4.00	$0.76	$1.52	$1.65	$3.31
4.50	$0.85	$1.71	$1.86	$3.72
5.00	$0.95	$1.90	$2.06	$4.12
5.50	$1.04	$2.08	$2.26	$4.53
6.00	$1.13	$2.27	$2.47	$4.94
6.50	$1.23	$2.46	$2.67	$5.34
7.00	$1.32	$2.64	$2.87	$5.75
7.50	$1.41	$2.83	$3.07	$6.15
8.00	$1.51	$3.01	$3.27	$6.56

Amortization

Amortization is the length of time over which the regular (usually monthly) payments are calculated. The calculation assumes that you will pay off the mortgage by the end of the period. The standard amortization period is 25 years, although you may have the option of a 5-, 7-, 10-, 15-, or 20-year amortization period.

The advantage of a shorter amortization period is the savings on interest, while a longer amortization period may allow payments that suit your monthly budget but require you to spend more servicing the debt. The drawback, of course, is a lower net return on your investment.

Assuming a $50,000 mortgage and an interest rate of 6 percent (interest being compounded semi-annually), the following Table 7-3 indicates the standard monthly mortgage payments for various amortization periods.

Table 7-3	Amortization and Payments			
	Amortization period in years			
Payment	*10*	*15*	*20*	*25*
Monthly payment of principal and interest	$553.26	$419.95	$356.10	$319.91
Total of mortgage payments over the amortization period	$66,390.31	$75,558.58	$85,461.45	$95,968.63

Insurance

Three types of insurance are critical elements of mortgages. The first two offer you protection; the other protects your property. And all three protect your lender from potential loss. We go over all three in detail in the following sections.

Insuring your mortgage

Mortgage insurance protects you from circumstances that may lead to your defaulting on your mortgage obligations, and also ensures that whoever has loaned you money for your property purchase gets paid. Mortgage insurance is a requirement whenever the down payment provided for the mortgage is less than 25 percent of the purchase price. The insurance fee typically runs between 1 and 2 percent of the amount of the mortgage. You may pay it in a single payment, or pay it alongside your mortgage.

Mortgage life insurance serves a similar purpose to mortgage insurance but kicks in only when you die. Mortgage life insurance guarantees that the lender will receive full payment of the mortgage in the event of your death.

Think mortgage life insurance is for you? Consider term insurance from a general insurer, which can often do the trick for cheaper. Your own term insurance is another option. Payable to your estate on your death, it guarantees your estate sufficient funds to pay off your mortgage.. Talk to your financial planner and insurance broker about the kind of policy that best serves you and your real estate investment strategy.

Insuring a good deal

Trying to get the best possible deal on your insurance policies? Insurance premiums vary from policy to policy and situation to situation. The rate you pay will reflect the insurance company's assessment of the risks you face, such as the age of the property, location, crime statistics for the area, and other factors. You should always compare and get written quotes from at least three insurance brokers for any type of insurance you are considering. Also, ask about obtaining discounts, each of which could range from 5- to 10-percent off the original premium. You could use several of them, but most insurance companies don't allow the aggregate amount of discounts to exceed 50 percent of the original premium. Common types of discounts given for property insurance coverage may be available if you have

- ✔ No claims in the previous 5 years, or at all
- ✔ A mortgage-free discount
- ✔ Three or more years' standing as a client
- ✔ A Block Watch or similar volunteer monitoring program in your community
- ✔ Eligibility for an age-related discount for property owners over the age of 65, and sometimes as young as 50
- ✔ A new home ten years old or less (this may result in a depreciated premium discount for based on the home's age)
- ✔ A monitored fire and burglary alarm in place
- ✔ Local alarm systems (not monitored)
- ✔ Different types of insurance products with the same insurance company or broker (may result in a multi-line discount

Insuring the property

Because the property that secures a mortgage is the lender's basis for advancing cash in the first place, the last thing you — or the lender — want to see is that building damaged or destroyed. Most mortgages therefore require that you insure your property against fire. The insurance policy must show that the mortgagee is first in line in case of a claim.

Because the lender's interest in protecting your property isn't insignificant, the insurance policy typically includes a clause allowing the lender to pay the premium in the event you don't. The lender also typically has the right to augment the amount of coverage on the property.

Should the lender act in your stead, you may find the extra premiums part of the principal of your mortgage. You'll also pay interest on the payments, something you wouldn't have done had you made the payments or taken the coverage yourself.

Tax considerations

Mortgages and taxes are a mix of good news and bad news, but sharp management can ensure that the two work in your favour.

First, the bad news: The lender's interest in your property extends to property taxes. To ensure the property has the best possible value in the event it has to go to market, your lender will most likely require you to pay property taxes on a monthly basis into an account that holds the funds in trust for you until the July 1 deadline for paying the annual tax bill. The lender may also require that you pay your property taxes by rolling payments into your monthly mortgage payments. Watch out: This may boost your interest payments.

Now, for the good news: Mortgage interest is a deductible expense for investment properties, because it's cash spent as part of your business activities. So, even if the amount of interest you're paying looks like a significant amount (and it is), take heart in knowing you can write it off, lowering the overall tax you have to pay! Talk to your accountant or financial planner.

Scheduling Payments

Strategies for managing your mortgage, and especially its ultimate cost to you, focus on the *amortization schedule* — that is, the schedule determining how quickly you pay off the mortgage.

You may plan to sell a property before paying the mortgage on it in full. Because you're likely to have a mortgage on one property or another as long as you're a real estate investor, however, you should focus on building equity in your properties. The greater the equity you build in a property, the greater the wealth you'll be able to recoup when you sell the property. Scheduling payments that let you build equity quickly and efficiently will play a key role in your success.

Make a date: Payment schedules

Mortgage payments occur within two types of arrangements, open and closed systems. Most mortgages take the form of a *closed mortgage,* which defines payments for the term of the mortgage and levies a penalty on advance payments. A standard closed mortgage usually requests three months' interest in the event you sell the property before paying off the mortgage. The lender may waive the penalty if the purchaser takes out a new mortgage with the same lender.

An *open mortgage* allows you to boost payments of the principal at any time. It allows you to pay the mortgage in full at any time with no penalty or extra charge. In exchange for this flexibility, which can limit the amount a lender sees in interest, open mortgages often charge a higher interest rate.

The actual mortgage payments occur at regular intervals regardless of whether the mortgage is open or closed. These range from weekly to monthly and annually. The more frequent your payments, the lower the amount of interest you pay.

Mortgage payments themselves include both principal and interest. The payments are traditionally a set amount calculated assuming monthly payments. However, variations in payments may occur. We mention the idea of balloon payments in Chapter 6, a strategy that allows you to defer interest payments, and variable-rate mortgages, in which the mix of principal and interest in your set payment fluctuates on a monthly basis.

You may choose to negotiate with your lender a graduated payment schedule. *Graduated payments* are lower at the beginning of the term of the mortgage and increase over time, so that payments at the end of the mortgage's term are considerably higher. This is a useful arrangement for revenue-generating properties, or if you expect your ability to pay down the mortgage will increase over time.

The risk of graduated payment strategy is that you could find yourself paying more interest than you had expected if interest rates rise and you have the greatest amount of payments yet to make. You also build equity in the property at a slower rate than if you make set payments throughout or larger payments at the beginning of the term.

Opening doors: Prepayment privileges

Most closed mortgages have a prepayment feature that allows you to pay off the mortgage faster than you initially thought possible.

Prepayment privileges create a mortgage that's a cross between an open and a closed mortgage, permitting prepayment at specific stages and in a certain manner (but not at other times). For example, a prepayment feature may allow you to prepay between 10 percent and 20 percent on the principal amount of the mortgage each year. This would allow you to prepay up to a certain amount, giving you a useful measure of flexibility while assuring the lender you're going to be paying down the mortgage for some time to come. You may also have the option of increasing the amount of your monthly payment once a year.

Based on a $50,000 mortgage at a 6-percent interest rate, with interest compounded semi-annually, the following Table 7-4 shows the savings you can achieve.

Table 7-4	Prepayment or increased payment savings		
Standard mortgage 25-year amortization		**10% annual increase in mortgage payment**	**10% annual prepayment of principal**
Mortgage repaid in months	300	164	97
Total interest charged	$45,968.63	$29,504.54	$14,060.22
Interest savings vs. standard 25-year mortgage	N/A	$16,464.09	$31,908.41

Exercising your prepayment privileges can save you an incredible amount of interest while reducing the amortization period and building the equity in your investment. Make sure that you completely understand your prepayment options, as they could save you a lot of money.

Passing the torch: assumability

Assumability allows a buyer of your property to take over the obligations and payments of the vendor's mortgage. Most mortgage contracts deal with the issue of assumability very clearly. The lender can agree to full assumability without qualifications, assumability with qualifications, or no assumability.

Assumability is an important issue to consider. If you go this route, you may have a wider range of potential purchasers interested in buying your property when it comes time to sell. This is because purchasers who may not otherwise qualify for a mortgage are able to assume your mortgage without qualifications (we discuss this angle briefly in Chapter 6).

 We believe you should place some qualifications on the assumability of any mortgage you seek, if you agree to its assumability. If you're the vendor, qualifications allow you to check out the creditworthiness and debt-servicing ability of the owner assuming your mortgage so that you can be sure the new owner is a good risk.

 Should the person assuming your mortgage default, you might find yourself on the hook for their unfortunate circumstances if your name is on the mortgage document. You can avoid this scenario by obtaining a statement from the lender that the lender will not hold you liable under the mortgage agreement after the new property owner assumes the mortgage. Make sure your lawyer has reviewed the document to ensure that your interests are properly protected.

Mortgage to go: Portability

Portability is a feature some lenders offer that allows you to take a mortgage from one property and apply it to another. In practical terms, you could save money if interest rates have increased since you bought your previous property. Higher interest rates would mean higher interest payments and a lower available mortgage. (Remember, the higher the interest rate, the lower the mortgage amount available to you.) Conversely, if mortgage rates have gone down since you bought the first house, you would probably not be at all interested in continuing your existing mortgage.

 Portable mortgages can be beneficial when you're seeking to trade up, especially in an environment of escalating rates. You may even find that averaging the interest rate between the first, portable mortgage and a second mortgage in such circumstances works in your favour if the property you aren't able to purchase the property you want with a first mortgage alone. Talk to your mortgage broker and, if you wish, your accountant and financial planner to see if a portable mortgage can take you places.

Default: Don't go there

Sometimes the best-planned schedules fall apart. When that happens to the payment schedule of your mortgage, and you fail to make the payments you've agreed to make under the mortgage agreement, you may find yourself in a state of *default.* Technically, default occurs if your payment isn't received within 30 days of the due date. Defaulting on a mortgage has potentially serious consequences. If you're consistently late, you could jeopardize your credit rating, your ability to renew your mortgage, and even your ability to obtain mortgages in the future.

Lenders are typically generous about grace periods before they consider legal action, sometimes allowing grace periods of three to six months before commencing any legal action. How quickly a lender acts will depend on the circumstances and how effectively you have communicated the reasons for the lack of payment (for example, reduced income, sickness or injury, or a family breakup). A lender usually only commences foreclosure or sale legal proceedings if the property is at risk and you have failed to communicate the reasons. A lender generally aims to work things out with you first.

We hope you never default on your mortgage (we want you to be a successful investor, after all), but you should know how default occurs and its consequences.

Understanding default

Because the mortgage agreement sets out in considerable detail your obligations as a borrower, you should have a pretty good idea of what you can and cannot do. But defaulting on a mortgage may involve more than simply not making payments on time; it also includes the following:

- ✔ Failure to pay your taxes
- ✔ Failure to have insurance, or sufficient insurance
- ✔ Failure to obey municipal, provincial, or federal law as it relates to the premises that you have mortgaged
- ✔ Failure to maintain the premises in a habitable condition
- ✔ Failure to keep the premises in proper repair
- ✔ Deliberately damaging the property that secures the mortgage

Many of the factors that place you in default of your mortgage require a fair amount of intention. Because your investment fortunes run parallel to those of your lender, chances are that lender won't forget to make sure you're taking care of business.

Avoiding default

A state of default is something you can probably see coming and take steps to avoid. Your team of advisers can also help with this, but don't rely on them. Some common strategies include the following:

- ✔ **Arrange with the lender for a waiver of payments for a set period of time or arrange for partial payments to be made:** This is a wise choice if you find yourself temporarily unable to make payments but know you are able to resume payments after a certain date (say, after a medical leave of absence from work or when a new job starts, or if you're expecting an inheritance). Having substantial equity in the property helps your case.

- ✔ **Reschedule the debt and make new payment arrangements that accommodate whatever difficulties you're having:** Be sure to do this in consultation with your accountant or financial planner.

- ✔ **Refinance the mortgage with another lender:** The terms may be more flexible and appropriate to your current circumstances.

- ✔ **Negotiate with the lender to provide either additional security or to secure concessions under the existing mortgage:** You may also invite the lender to acquire an equity stake in either part or all of the property.

- ✔ **Pre-empt the lender by selling the property yourself:** Selling the property yourself may avoid default, the shame of foreclosure, and — best of all — may even garner you a small return on the property if the value has increased sufficiently.

- ✔ **Exercise your *right of redemption:*** Mortgages that lack an *acceleration clause* (a clause that allows you to speed up, or accelerate, payments) give you an opportunity to exercise your legal right to pay the arrears outstanding under the mortgage through a right of redemption. The right generally prevents the mortgagee from commencing or from continuing foreclosure proceedings. However, if an acceleration clause exists, the lender may deem the full amount of the mortgage immediately due and payable in the event you default; this requires you to pay the full amount of the mortgage in order to stop foreclosure proceedings.

Some provinces have legislation restricting the application of acceleration clauses. Many provinces allow you to exercise your right of redemption anytime from one and six months into a state of default; otherwise, the lender is legally entitled to move on the property and begin foreclosure proceedings. If you know that you will not be able to pay off the lender within the right-of-redemption period, you are entitled to ask the court for an extension. Whether the court grants an extension depends on the circumstances.

The circumstances of your default determines what you do to resolve the situation. Contacting the lender and attempting to negotiate a resolution is clearly the first step. Your lawyers' advice is particularly useful in situations such as this, as you require full awareness of your rights and options. Your lawyer may also be able to negotiate with the bank on your behalf.

Dealing with default

When your best efforts to stave off default fail, you'll find yourself facing not only legal wrangles but also the potential court-ordered sale of your property. Should the matter end up in court, however, you will have a chance to plead your case through your lawyer.

More often, a lender will pursue one of the following courses of action when a borrower defaults before seeking a court-ordered sale:

- ✔ **Pay taxes, maintenance fees, or insurance premiums on the borrower's behalf:** The lender will add these payments onto your total mortgage debt and charge interest on the amount.

- ✔ **Obtain a court injunction preventing you from engaging in activity the lender considers improper or plain illegal:** The order may require you to perform some specific obligation under the mortgage to protect the property from damage. You would have to pay the lender's costs of obtaining the injunction.

- ✔ **Obtain a court order appointing a receiver of rents from the property:** A receiver of rents effectively takes the place of the borrower, receiving the rents you would otherwise have received and using them to cover your outstanding mortgage payments. Most lenders will only take this step in serious situations involving a rental property, however. In reality, if you borrowed money for revenue property, the lender probably asked you at the outset to sign an *assignment of rents.* Under the assignment, the lender may notify your tenants to direct rent payments to the lender if you default on the payment terms of the mortgage.

- ✔ **Obtain a court order placing the property in receivership:** In this case an independent party, called a *receiver-manager* or *receiver,* takes possession of the property on behalf of the lender and maintains it. This procedure is usually implemented if the property is held by a corporate entity that has given the lender a security document known as a *debenture,* which takes the place of collateral. Receivership is often a more efficient means for the lender to secure its interests in such cases.

- ✔ **Accelerate the mortgage:** The lender can either request the arrears under the mortgage or deem the full amount of the balance outstanding on the mortgage as immediately due and payable. The lender cannot request this latter course unless there is an acceleration clause in the mortgage. Some provincial legislation restricts the use of acceleration clauses.

✔ **Sell the property:** Defaulting on your mortgage may prompt the lender to put your property up for sale and sell it. Each province sets a specific period of time after which this can happen. In many cases a lender will seek a court order for the sale. This enables the court to monitor the ultimate sale price, minimizing the risk that the borrower could claim the property was undersold if there is outstanding debt remaining after the sale. In other cases the lender does not have to go to court to list the property for sale.

✔ **Sue the borrower personally for the debt outstanding:** The lender may take advantage of the borrower's liability under the mortgage agreement whether or not the property sells. If the lender sells the property, the borrower remains responsible for any debt not satisfied by sale proceeds. When a corporate entity holds the property, the lender usually requests a personal guarantee of the people behind the corporation. The lender is not required to commence other actions such as foreclosure or sale of the property.

✔ **Foreclose:** The lender may request that the court extinguish your rights in a property and transfer all legal interest that you have, including the right of possession and legal title, to the lender. In this situation the lender secures rights to the equity accumulated in the property. The courts are generally involved in this procedure, guaranteeing your rights and the fairness of the sale, but you have little chance of seeing a return from the property (farewell, investment).

Fortunately, courts usually advise an order for sale of the property rather than a formal foreclosure. That means more than 99 percent of court-ordered sales are exactly that — orders by the court, rather than foreclosures proper.

Renegotiating and refinancing

When the term of your mortgage ends, usually six months to ten years after negotiation, you have the option of renegotiating or refinancing it.

When to renegotiate

Renegotiation can help you achieve a better deal, or tailor your existing agreement to more closely meet your needs. Renegotiation is an attractive option if significant changes appear in the lending environment between the beginning and end of your mortgage term:

✔ **Changing lending environments:** Renegotiating makes sense if interest rates have fallen over the course of the previous term and you want to reduce the cost of servicing your debt, freeing up more cash to put toward paying down the principal of your mortgage. Conversely, if interest rates have increased, and your income allows it, you may wish to boost the amount of your monthly payments to shorten the amortization period.

✔ **Changing personal circumstances:** Changes in your personal circumstances may also prompt you to renegotiate your mortgage. Regardless of what interest rates have done, changes in household income may allow you to boost the amount you pay to your mortgage each month. Or perhaps you find yourself worse off, financially, than you were when you first negotiated the mortgage. Renegotiating can extend the amortization period to accommodate your straitened circumstances.

Adjusting the length of the term of your mortgage may also accommodate current or pending changes in either the lending environment or your own circumstances. A falling interest rate may prompt you to renegotiate for shorter periods, whereas a short-term mortgage may tide you over temporary changes in your personal finances or help you prepare for a possible sale of the property.

Why refinancing can make sense

Refinancing, the strategy of paying off an existing loan with the proceeds from a new loan (in this case, a new mortgage), can help you manage your mortgage payments as well as access equity that has accumulated in the property since you acquired it. Whereas renegotiation adjusts the terms of the mortgage, refinancing allows you to reapply for a mortgage on the same property.

Refinancing is a good move if interest rates have decreased, as you will be able to service a greater debt, potentially secure a larger mortgage and pay less interest per month than you would otherwise. It also makes sense if you've experienced a significant improvement in your gross debt-to-service ratio, for similar reasons. Changes that allow you to access, and service, a greater amount of financing will potentially benefit your ability to invest in better-quality properties.

On the other hand, refinancing may not be such a wise move if changes in the value of your property and your personal financial situation conspire to limit your ability to borrow. You may find yourself able to access a greater volume of debt but facing a longer amortization period that costs you in terms of interest payments. Speak with your mortgage broker and, if you wish, your accountant and financial planner before you refinance, to ensure you are doing what's best for your long-term investment success.

Refinancing in action

For Michel, a property owner in Montreal, refinancing made sense. The five-year term on his current mortgage was due for renewal in two months' time. When he spoke with his lender about renewing for a further five-year term, he was told the interest rate would be 7.5 percent. Michel decided to approach a mortgage broker and comparison shop.

The broker was able to provide the same five-year fixed-rate term at a rate of 6 percent from a competitive lender, who would also pay all legal fees and costs to discharge the old mortgage and register the new one. The competitive lender would guarantee this rate for two months, regardless of whether interest rates went up. If interest rates had decreased by the time Michel's mortgage was due, the new lender would reduce the new mortgage's rate accordingly. In addition, the new lender would permit a mortgage lump sum pay-down of 20 percent annually, anytime in the year, without a pre-payment penalty — Michel's current lender would permit an annual pre-payment of just 10 percent without penalty on the mortgage's anniversary date.

The new lender's policy was far more flexible for Michel, who frequently earned large commissions from his work throughout the year. Michel committed to the new lender. He saved a lot of money on interest payments over the next five years of the mortgage, and paid down the mortgage faster than he could have under the original lender.

Chapter 8

Look Before You Leap: Ownership and Legal Considerations

In This Chapter

▶ Finding an ownership arrangement that works

▶ Strategizing for gain

▶ Limiting risks

▶ Minimizing litigation and legal wrangling

*R*eal estate deals have legal implications, and that means you need a lawyer (see Chapter 4 for more on finding and choosing a lawyer). A lawyer is especially helpful if you're buying for investment purposes, because of the expectations you have for the property and also the number of other people the transaction potentially affects. Your investment doesn't serve just your interests: the loan you need to do the deal is someone else's investment in your success, and you probably plan to lease your property to yet more people.

We discuss some of your legal obligations to lenders in Chapter 7 and explore tenant relations in Chapter 13. In this chapter, we look at the legal implications of ownership. We discuss the kind of ownership structure you want to have for the property, and explain some of the strategic benefits of the various types. We also cover the forms of liability you assume when you invest in a property. Finally, we speak candidly about litigation, its dangers, and strategies for making peace when disagreements between partners and associates threaten to become lawsuits.

Determining an Ownership Structure

One of the first decisions to make when buying investment real estate is the legal structure by which you hold the property you purchase. We discuss various forms of ownership in Chapter 2; this chapter looks at some of the legal ramifications and strategic benefits of the various forms.

Types of ownership

The real estate investments you make determine the kind of ownership structure you choose for your portfolio. The potential risk and liability, amount of money needed to start, what you expect to earn, and whether you have partners (not to mention the tax implications) all factor into your decision. Your main alternatives for ownership include

- Sole proprietorship
- Joint ownership
- Partnership
- Corporation

After we briefly explain the ins and outs of each type of ownership, we take a more detailed look at some things you need to consider when forming partnerships and corporations.

Whether you choose joint ownership, form a partnership, or incorporate, be sure to have a written agreement among the partners or shareholders that outlines their interests and responsibilities in the business. This helps avoid legal disputes and may defuse arguments arising from misunderstandings of each person's role or entitlements. An accountant and lawyer will advise you regarding the specific structuring of the agreement.

Sole proprietorship

A *sole proprietorship* has nothing to do with the bottoms of your feet, though it may mean you foot more bills than you would under other ownership structures. You have sole responsibility for the income and debts of your properties, and enjoy control of what happens — but you also assume full liability.

Sole proprietorships exist when you own and operate property under your own name rather than through a partnership or corporation. The government considers your personal income and income from your real estate investments (if they're revenue properties) the same ball of wax for tax purposes.

Separate personal and business bank accounts help distinguish between your personal funds and those related to your business. This helps the Canada Revenue Agency if it decides to audit you, and also reduces your liability in the case of a court case. You don't want your personal income caught up in a nasty legal dispute; instead, pay yourself a salary from your business account for personal expenses such as food, clothing, lodging, and savings.

Joint ownership

You may own the joint you just purchased, but with whom? Two types of joint ownership exist if you partner with one or more people in a real estate purchase and plan also to occupy the property yourselves. Neither provides a *divided right,* or right to sole use of a specific part of the property. Here are the two forms of joint ownership:

- ✔ **Joint tenancy,** which gives each owner an equal share with all other owners, who are listed on the title of the property equally. The main feature of a joint tenancy is the right of survivorship. This means that if one of the joint tenants (that is, owners) dies, the surviving owners each receive an equal portion of the deceased person's share. Joint tenancies are common arrangements between couples.

- ✔ **Tenancy in common,** which allows tenants — those who own (rather than lease) the property — to hold equal or unequal shares in the property. A tenant in common is allowed to sell, mortgage or will his interest in the property. Tenancy in common is a good option when the partners want joint ownership but aren't investing equal amounts of cash, or want to preserve their specific interest (say, in the case of partners who aren't family members).

Partnership

A partnership is a proprietorship with two or more owners. Unlike joint ownership, the partnership — rather than the partners — holds the property.

The partners' interest in the partnership reflects their investment stake. The partnership has to file a tax return but it doesn't pay any tax. Instead, the partners pay tax on the basis of their portion of the partnership's net profit or loss. As in a sole proprietorship, each partner is personally liable for the full amount of the business's debts and liabilities. Unlike sole proprietorships, however, partnerships operate under relevant provincial legislation.

Corporation (limited company)

A corporation is a business that operates as a legal entity separate from its owner or owners. Corporations are registered in a provincial or federal registry and must file annual reports, submit tax returns, and pay taxes.

The shareholders who own the company aren't personally liable for the company's debts unless they have signed a personal guarantee. Corporations may have one or more shareholders, who typically enter a shareholders' agreement setting forth the conditions of their involvement. They also elect directors who manage the corporation on a day-to-day basis.

Choosing a partnership type

Partnerships take various forms in Canada. Select the one that suits you based on your goals as an investor, as well as those of your partners.

The broadest form of partnership is a joint venture, which allows both individuals and corporations to combine their skills as well as capital, land, and other assets in investments or development projects. Typically focused on one project, it can take any of the following forms. Consult both a lawyer and accountant to determine which one is right for you and your partners.

General partnership

General partnerships typically involve only a few people, but many risks. The major concern is that this arrangement leaves you open to bearing all claims against the partnership, regardless of how many partners there are. A typical example of this type of partnership risk is a law firm partnership. If one lawyer gives bad advice and is sued by the aggrieved client, all the other partners in the law firm are sued at the same time. Each partner is liable for the financial claim for losses, as if each personally provided the bad advice.

Limited partnership

Limited partnerships grant you a share in the partnership's business in proportion to your investment, and limit your liability for claims against the partnership. Your interest in the firm is in proportion to your investment, and is represented by units that can be sold to other investors. To minimize your risk, secure a written commitment from the general partner, who handles the day-to-day management of the partnership, to purchase your units by a set date.

This type of business structure is suited to large property investments requiring a substantial amount of money. For example, the overall cost may be $5 million to $10 million, with each partner holding investment units worth $25,000.

Corporation

Corporations are a convenient means for investments by groups of two or more people. Partners hold shares in the company that can be bought, sold, or transferred. This provides a possible exit if you need or want to leave the partnership.

Corporations are subject to strict reporting requirements, but the advantage for you, as a shareholder, is that the company accepts full responsibility for all claims made against it. Unless you sign a personal guarantee for claims against the corporation, claims are limited to the corporation's assets.

You also want to have a buy-sell clause and a shareholder's agreement signed in advance of going into any deal or providing any money. These documents set out formulas for dealing with issues and possible scenarios. Your lawyer can help you with this type of protection.

Co-tenancies and equity sharing

Co-tenancies and their cousins, equity-sharing arrangements, are common means of becoming an owner-occupier of a property if you can't quite make the down payment.

In the case of a co-tenancy, each co-tenant will have her interest noted in the property's title deed. That ownership stake becomes part of the co-tenant's estate if she dies rather than being distributed among the other owners as it would in a joint-tenancy arrangement. Though the rights, duties, and responsibilities of the various partners should be stated in the co-tenancy agreement, the agreement is easier to withdraw from than other joint-ownership arrangements.

Equity-sharing agreements allow a prospective owner to pay a rent slightly above the going market rate in exchange for having a house to live in and maintain. The agreement typically requires the buyer to stay for a minimum period, after which the option exists to purchase the home for the appraised value less the standard commission and an agreed-upon percentage of the increase in the equity value of the home. If the buyer isn't able to buy the home, then the option to purchase lapses.

Equity sharing benefits the existing owner as an investor by ensuring positive cash flow while potentially securing a buyer for the property. The main disadvantage is having to share the equity with the owner-to-be, who has paid a higher rent and invested time in maintaining the property in return for that privilege.

Understanding the obligations

A workable partnership should have some guiding principles setting forth the rights and obligations of the partners. Because not everyone is looking out for your interests, we'd like to outline a few issues you should raise when drafting a partnership agreement.

Getting to know one another

Business partners don't have to know everything about each other, and that's probably a good thing. Why have a decent business relationship tainted with knowledge of your partner's least-savoury quirks? But you should find out some basic information before you get involved with the wrong — or right — group of people. Of prime importance is making sure you get along, and that you're getting involved for similar reasons. No sense in one of you looking for a quick return while everyone else hopes the property will deliver a stable cash flow over the long term. And just imagine what it would be like if half the partners want to sell in three years, while the others have a gut feeling that it's better to wait five.

A good mix of expertise can help your group gauge the market and research properties. Be sure, however, that everyone is comfortable with the skills and expertise each member brings to the group; strategies that are second-nature to some may be unfamiliar and even threatening to others. Assess the experience and abilities each person brings to the partnership, the contribution they'll make, and decide how they'll be rewarded.

Ultimately, the success of your partnership depend on your willingness to work out concerns and issues that arise. You deal with relationships, some of which may be intense, so the more compatible the partners are, the better. Take into account not just the business and investing experience of the people you work with, but the perspectives that come from age, life experience, and long-term goals.

Taking control

Don't be afraid to control your interests in a partnership — this is as important to reaching your investment goals as controlling the steering wheel is to reaching the destination on a road trip. Certain partnerships allow more control to the individual investor than others, especially in the decision-making process.

Remember, too, that the amount of control you have in the partnership's operation could affect your exposure to risk and liability.

Control doesn't relate just to management. You may be asked to invest time and money that you can't easily afford into making the partnership work. Knowing the demands that will be placed on you will limit any feelings of resentment that could sour the deal. Also make sure the demands being placed on you are in line with the cash investment you've made in the partnership.

Getting out

Managing your exit from the partnership is important. This could be an advantage if you believe the partnership is shifting from the goals it had when you became involved, or if you want to secure the return on your investment. Assess the liquidity of your investment (discussed in this chapter), and if possible, make sure to include a clause that allows you to sell your interest to your partners should you wish to leave.

Putting it in writing

A written agreement, drafted by a lawyer, will help establish the ground rules for your partnership. Here are a few of the points it should cover:

- Type of legal structure
- Name and location of the partnership
- Goals, objectives, and duration of the partnership
- Names of investors, their interest and responsibilities
- Financial investment by the investors, and means (if needed) for securing additional capital
- Management responsibilities, and the role any of the partners will play
- How the partnership will handle financial matters, from operating expenses and accounting to signing cheques
- How investors enter and leave the partnership
- Settlement of disputes, and non-competition clause should a partner leave
- If a co-tenancy agreement, the relation between the co-tenants and their respective responsibilities and fiduciary duties

Being creative with ownership

Creative ownership arrangements aren't as dubious as creative accounting!

Take the case of Duane and Madelyn, for example, a professional couple in Red Deer whose three children were on track to start university in Edmonton within two years of each other. Because the kids would have to leave home, Duane and Madelyn decided to buy a property a 15-minute walk from the university and renovate a portion for rental purposes. They planned to rent out the basement while their children and their friends (who would pay a nominal rent) would enjoy the run of the main floor. The total amount of rental revenue from the property paid the operating expenses of the house, such as the mortgage and related interest, property taxes, utilities, maintenance, and insurance. And $1,500 was left over for Duane and Madelyn to put towards their retirement.

To make the deal work, Duane and Madelyn sought expert legal advice. They decided to put the house in the names of their three children, and received three key documents from their kids in return. One was a declaration of trust stating that the children were holding the property in trust for their parents and would, upon their parents' request, transfer title back to the parents. The document also stated that any rental income in excess of operating expenses belonged to the parents. The parents also obtained a transfer of title document signed by the children, which the parents kept unfiled. The third document was a letter from the children assuring Duane and Madelyn that the property would remain free of all financial encumbrances, such as another mortgage, line of credit, or judgment filed against it for a debt.

The agreement gave Duane and Madelyn full control over the property, but also ensured that their kids had a place to live. When their children graduated, they could arrange to sell the property and allow the children to retain the net proceeds without any capital gains tax as the property was the children's principal residence. This could pay off most, if not all, their student loans. However, if the parents needed the money, or the children turned out to be prodigal, Duane and Madelyn could exercise the trust declaration and file the transfer document giving them full ownership. They could sell it, and pay any capital gains tax as an investment property, after getting tax advice on the best tax strategies.

The price of liquidity may be a penalty. Make sure you have the terms of any penalties for leaving the partnership in writing. In exchange, you are able to secure the liquidity of your investment on commonly agreed terms.

Working out the terms

Never go into a partnership without considering the legal implications of a dispute. Remember, 80 percent of business partnerships fail, and yours may be one. Knowing what to do when things go bad could save you the time and anxiety of a protracted and fractious legal dispute. Your backup plan could be as simple as a withdrawal strategy for disgruntled partners, or a buy-out clause that allows you to make an offer to a partner who no longer fits with the others. Or it may be an agreement to seek the mediation of a third-party should conflict arise (we discuss mediation and arbitration in more detail at the end of this chapter).

Having a limitation on liability can also be helpful, especially if one partner leaves and decides to sue the partnership for whatever reason. Even if the allegations are proven untrue, you could face spending several thousand dollars to defend yourself unless you've vested responsibility for all claims in the partnership.

By addressing the potential for disputes before they happen, you increase the chances of the partnership surviving — and working for the remaining partners — if good terms go sour.

Types of interest in land

The ground on which properties stand is subject to its own unique forms of ownership — freehold or leasehold:

- ✔ **Freehold,** also called *fee simple,* is an ownership form that entitles the owner to use of a property for an indefinite period. The owner deals directly with government and is responsible for compliance with laws and contractual obligations regarding the land as well as any charges that encumber the title of the property, including mortgages, liens and judgments, et cetera).

- ✔ **Leasehold** allows the person who holds an interest in land to use it for a fixed period of time. An agreement between the landlord, who owns the property, and the owner of the leasehold interest, or tenant, sets out the terms and conditions of the relationship. The leaseholder can sell the right to use the land only for the time remaining in the lease, subject, of course, to the conditions of the lease.

Both freehold ownership and leasehold ownership can be left in your will as an asset of your estate, or specifically bequeathed in your will.

Tax implications

Taxes are a significant consideration as you choose an ownership structure for your real estate investments. From a tax point of view, you experience either direct or indirect benefits from the ownership form you select.

Partnerships: The bad and the good

Doug's work as a real estate lawyer has treated him to all sorts of scenarios when it comes to partnerships. He offers the following from his broad experience.

Greg and Sudhir decided to enter a real estate investment partnership, having been pumped up on the partnership's prospects during a seminar the partnership's promoters hosted. The seminar speaker was a slick presenter and his sales team followed up afterwards to make sure attendees didn't miss out on "the investment opportunity of a lifetime. "We had to act quickly," Sudhir said afterwards.

Greg and Sudhir invested $100,000 in the partnership, which the partnership used to purchase properties on their behalf. The properties would remain in the name of the partnership, which would manage the assets for a half-share of revenues from the properties plus a 50-percent incentive fee in the form of an equity stake in the property for finding the properties in the first place. The partnership's investors agreed to split net revenues from the property and any net equity as well as equity build-up proportional to the amount of their investment.

The dream opportunity turned out to be a financial nightmare.

Because the investment properties were located in another province, Greg and Sudhir were unable to check out the assets themselves. They relied on a few selected photos to make their investment decision. Nor had Greg and Sudhir completely read or understood the documents making them partners in the partnership. They hadn't obtained independent legal advice from an experienced real estate lawyer, nor had they consulted a professional accountant.

Because vacancies and turnover in the properties were high, and the buildings required extensive repairs, investors enjoyed relatively little rental revenue and were on the hook for significant repair bills. To make matters worse, investors had to keep their money in the partnership for a minimum of five years or face a 25 percent penalty if they sold out early. Those who sold also had to pay a portion of the rental losses and repair expenses.

For Greg and Sudhir, the investment left a bitter taste. They lost their entire investment, and have steered clear of partnerships ever since.

Sandra, Rachel, Simone, and Jerome were luckier. Combining their skills as a lawyer, accountant, contractor, and real estate agent, the four merged their collective talents to form Quartet Estates. Quartet focused on buying old houses in Winnipeg, upgrading them, and turning them into boarding houses accommodating about ten tenants each. The four partners each had a quarter-interest in the company, and provided $25,000 each in seed capital. They each signed personal guarantees to a maximum of $100,000 with Quartet's bank for a company line of credit to a maximum of $400,000. A detailed business plan was written for the venture, and a detailed shareholder agreement signed.

Over a period of two years, six houses were purchased, renovated, and filled with tenants who allowed Quartet to see a monthly cash flow of $10,000 after all fixed and variable costs were taken into account. The equity in the houses rose by about 25 percent over the same period, thanks to the improvements and market forces, so the company enjoyed about $1 million in additional equity than when it started.

Unfortunately, Jerome was diagnosed with a long-term illness and wanted to withdraw from the partnership and recover his equity. Fortunately, the shareholder's agreement had foreseen the possibility and allowed him to withdraw with just a small penalty.

The clause in question allowed Jerome to withdraw by paying 15-percent of the net equity in his portion of the partnership for withdrawing before the partners unanimously voted to wind up the company, dissolve its assets, and split the proceeds. The clause, intended to discourage partners from withdrawing, allowed Jerome to exit under extenuating circumstances. The clause preserved the integrity of the company and allowed it to pursue its business plan, while avoiding hassle and discord among the partners.

Paying up front

Sole proprietorships, joint ownership, and legal partnerships all allow you to claim income directly from your investment property just as you would claim the income from a term deposit or similar investment. Although partnerships must file a tax return, they don't pay taxes; that's your job, as a partner.

Because the government treats your personal income and income from your real estate investments (if they're revenue properties) the same way when you hold property through sole proprietorships, joint ownership, and partnerships, you're able to lower your taxable income by claiming business expenses such as utilities and book-keeping fees related to management of the property (a detailed discussion of deductions and business expenses appears in Chapter 15).

Letting others pay

Ownership of properties through a corporation may open up various tax advantages not available if you hold the properties directly.

Among the benefits corporations enjoy is a rate of taxation that's often lower than that a proprietorship faces, up to a certain level of income. Because the corporation operating your properties files its own taxes, you can claim only the income flowing to you as a shareholder in the business. The business-related expenses of the corporation are unavailable for the shareholders to claim.

Tallying Strategic Benefits

With a variety of ownership structures available, you need to examine your situation and weigh the merits of each possible option. A partnership isn't a possibility if it's just you making an investment. But why not opt for incorporation? And why choose joint ownership over a partnership?

Looking into the whys and wherefores can help you make your decision. In this section we walk you through some possible scenarios that we hope will help you reach the right decision.

What to consider

Drafting a strategic plan is an important part of preparing to invest in real estate. You want to know where you're going and how you'll get there. The strategic plan probably assumes a particular type of ownership — perhaps you expect to own most properties yourself, and maintain tight control over the suites. Or perhaps you want to partner with someone and leave management to a management company. Which ownership structure do you choose?

Here are a few of the key factors you should take into account in tallying the benefits (and drawbacks) of each structure:

- ✔ **Cash available for investing** determines whether you go it alone in the market or involve others in your investments. A sole proprietorship probably isn't the best form of ownership if you require a significant range of investors to buy a property; joint ownership or a partnership might be better. At the same time, if you see the opportunity to secure a large amount of cash on a regular basis from yourself and a handful of friends, it may make sense to incorporate. (We talk more about sources of financing in Chapter 5.)

- ✔ **The number of investors** influences the ownership structure not just because of the amount of cash they bring to the business, but because of their specific interests and priorities. Partners who wish to use part of their interest to fund other ventures may prefer a tenants-in-common structure that allows them to sell or mortgage their share in a property; husbands and wives may opt for a joint tenancy arrangement that allows for one of them to automatically inherit the property in the event the other dies. Still others may want to render the properties relatively independent, allowing individual investors to come and go with greater ease.

- ✔ **The type of real estate** plays a role in determining the ownership structure because a large property may require several investors whose needs are best met through a more complex form of ownership than a partnership. Residential properties or a retail unit may be no trouble for a sole proprietor, but commercial and industrial properties carry a degree of liability that makes corporate ownership a more attractive option.

- ✔ **Portfolio size** determines the ownership structure because of the opportunities for various tax advantages. A large portfolio is probably best handled through a corporate entity, but a few straightforward rental suites won't complicate your standard tax form.

You probably won't exercise just one form of ownership in your investing career; you may have two or three. A lawyer and tax accountant can assist you in determining which structure will best serve your investment strategy.

Personal advantages

An appropriate ownership structure may help forward your investment goals beyond the mere ownership of property. You may want to consider the following points as you weigh the various ownership structures:

- ✔ **Direct control:** Tenancy in common allows direct ownership of your stake in a property, whereas ownership under a partnership structure is vested in the partnership. Direct control over their individual interests allows participants in a tenancy-in-common arrangement to trade their stakes in the property, which are commonly larger than any one party in the arrangement could afford alone. You may be able to leverage a mortgage you couldn't otherwise access in order to finance a venture outside the investment property.

- ✔ **Limited involvement:** A corporation structure lets you invest as much cash as you would through a partnership, but the directors of the corporation handle matters such as property maintenance, management, and sale. The advantage for you is a return that may be as significant as if you had invested through a partnership — but with less hassle.

- ✔ **Better value:** The form of ownership you adopt may allow you to build a more valuable portfolio than if you made investments by yourself. This is an important consideration if you're investing in multi-family or commercial properties, or investing in blocks of raw land that have greater value together than as individual units. The value of the portfolio could very well be greater than the sum of the individual parts, and thereby deliver a better return.

Strength in numbers

Although real estate investors often enjoy having direct control over their investments, you may be a social type who enjoys being with others. On the other hand, you may want to work with a more experienced investor. Whatever the reason, investing with others can be source of strength.

Some of the strength is financial, to be sure: More investors means a greater pool of cash and a greater range of investment properties open to the group. And it never hurts to have multiple perspectives, and more sources of advice.

Here are some of the strengths you enjoy when investing with others:

- ✔ **Joint responsibility,** which prevents full responsibility from resting on your shoulders, is an asset if you are managing a large or complex property

- ✔ **Capital gains and losses** from the investment accrue to the partners rather than become the responsibility of a single investor

- ✔ **Stability,** a primary benefit of incorporation, is also a feature of partnerships and joint tenancies that limits the disruption in ownership when a partner dies or wants to sell his interest

Despite the strengths partnerships can offer, weaknesses also exist. For example, joint ownership is a more difficult structure from which to extricate yourself than, say, a corporation where you can trade your shares. A partnership arrangement exposes you to the risk that a partner may do something with which you don't agree, raising the possibility for conflict. One of the best defences against such weaknesses is to lay out, from the outset, the rights and obligations the various owners enjoy, and the decision-making and exit procedures partners should follow. A lawyer's help can ensure the agreement is fair and equitable.

Managing Risks and Liabilities

Ownership brings with it responsibilities, and responsibilities mean liabilities. You may not get sued the moment you become a property owner, or at all, but the chance exists. An ownership structure that limits the risk to you and your estate helps protect you if any portion of your portfolio takes a hit.

Getting personal: Protecting yourself

Personal liability, plainly stated, is the potential for someone to make a claim against you rather than your business. Written agreements can help protect you from claims, but your choice of ownership structure is also important. A handful of strategies can further reduce your personal exposure to claims that could easily consume your savings.

Going corporate

Corporations may be vilified by many for their cold, impersonal style, but they can help protect you from the slings and arrows tossed about in an increasingly litigious environment. Most other ownership structures expose partners to some form of personal liability. A corporation, as a separate legal entity controlled by but independent of its individual shareholders, acts on its own legal behalf and bears responsibility for its actions.

Taking advantage of the protection from personal liability corporations offer is easy. For example, always sign business documents as an authorized signatory of the corporation of which you're a part. A clear statement that you are acting as a representative of the corporation rather than in your own personal capacity will help ensure the corporation — and not you — bears the brunt of any claims.

Similarly, if you make loans to your corporation, become a secured creditor. The corporation is independent from you, unlike in a sole proprietorship, so you can lend money to it like any creditor and receive security. This protects your interests should claims come forward that push the company into bankruptcy.

A corporation's directors typically bear some liability. Be aware that if you serve as a director of your corporation, you may take on the liability you're trying to avoid. Provincial and federal legislation lay out areas where directors are liable, including the following:

- Corporate tax
- Sales taxes
- Provincial employment standards legislation
- Builder's liens

To protect your interests as a director, consider not owning personal assets of consequence — such as a car or real estate. You may wish to transfer these assets to your spouse to limit what claimants can seek from you. (Hey, why not make your better half not only better but richer?) Worried about a marital split? The courts typically break down the family assets 50/50 — ensuring you receive part of the gold mine, not just the shaft. Of course, if you're in business with your spouse, he or she should avoid being a director if you want to limit the impact of otherwise devastating financial claims all 'round.

Living lightly

Two key strategies exist to reduce your personal and financial exposure from legal claims against your incorporated business. One strategy is to reduce your personal direct legal involvement in your business as a director by not being a director. Directors could be liable under provincial and federal legislation for monies owing by the business to government creditors, such as corporate taxes, employee deductions or to employees for employee holiday pay and arrears of salary, and to contractors, trades or suppliers for builder's liens.

Another strategy to minimize personal financial exposure in a business, is to reduce the number of possessions you hold in your personal name, such as property, by having them in the name of your partner, assuming they are not in business with you. All these strategies require advance customized legal and tax advice.

Whatever form of ownership you have, avoid signing a personal guarantee for the debts of the business. Try, instead, to limit the guarantee. For example, if the company is borrowing $45,000, and there are three partners, agree to limit liability to a maximum of one-third only, or a proportion that reflects your stake in the business. Similarly, don't pledge personal security such as your car, house, or life insurance policy. It doesn't make sense to lose your house for the sake of your business.

A competitive marketplace for lenders may enable you to use a demand for a personal guarantee as leverage when scouting loans. You may also be able to use a personal guarantee you've signed to prioritize payments.

Doug is well-versed in protecting the interests of small-scale entrepreneurs. To find out more, have a look in *The Canadian Small Business Legal Advisor* (McGraw-Hill) by Douglas Gray and *The Complete Canadian Small Business Guide* (McGraw-Hill) by Douglas Gray and Diana Gray. And don't forget the current edition of Margaret Kerr and JoAnn Kurtz's *Canadian Small Business Kit For Dummies* (Wiley).

Estate liability

"The evil that men do lives after them," Mark Antony intoned over the body of Julius Caesar. That may be so, but we hope that you'll protect your estate from any claims people bring against you after your death. Even if you keep your accounts up to date, you can't prevent your unexpected death from leaving some debts unpaid. Moreover, if you are liable under a personal guarantee or as a director, creditors could make claims against your estate.

Consider a few options to ensure your estate faces minimal risk from creditors and potential claimants. In all cases, you want to have your will drafted by a lawyer who specializes in will and estate law issues, for your peace of mind and legal protection.

✔ **Make a will.** We discuss the importance of wills in Chapter 1. Without a will, your major beneficiaries could in effect be the provincial and federal government tax departments. Also, other beneficiaries are determined by a provincial government formula for family members, and most likely would not reflect your wishes at all. In addition, you want to consider two other documents that would come into effect during your lifetime. One is an enduring power of attorney that gives the legal right to one or more designated persons to look after your financial and legal affairs if you lack the mental capacity to do so (due, for example, to a stroke or a head injury).

The other document is a living will or representation agreement or health care proxy. Different terms are used in different provinces for essentially the same intent; that is, to designate your wishes for your health care needs, and possibly to designate a proxy to act on your behalf, and to set out your wishes if you have a terminal illness or life-threatening condition. For example, maybe you don't wish to be kept alive by heroic means. You can obtain information on living wills in each province of Canada and free downloadable forms from the University of Toronto, Joint Centre for Bioethics (www.utoronto.ca/jcb). For further information, read the latest edition of Douglas Gray and John Budd, *The Canadian Guide to Will and Estate Planning* (McGraw-Hill).

✔ **Have a shareholder's agreement with a buy-sell clause.** This enables one owner to buy out the other's interest in certain situations, as set out in the terms of the agreement, while the individual is alive or from her estate, It is important to have this type of document if you own a business with other partners. If you don't have it, there are no formulas to resolve issues that might be anticipated. This may result in legal issues that would need to be resolved through litigation. At a minimum it would involve everyone concerned hiring their own lawyers, which costs money, delay, and frustration.

✔ **Designate beneficiaries.** Designating beneficiaries for insurance policies, registered savings including RRSPs and RRIFs, and some non-registered investments allows the proceeds to bypass your will, and hence your estate. Because creditors can claim only from assets in your estate, the funds are beyond their reach. Another reason you want to designate beneficiaries is to save on provincial probate tax. For example, any insurance proceeds are tax-free to the recipient. However, if the insurance funds go to your estate first, and then the will states where they should go, those funds would be included in the amount covered by probate fees.

✔ **Establish a trust.** Setting up a living trust while you are alive allows the contents of the trust to bypass your will, and in turn, your estate. A testamentary trust, set up through your will, takes effect on your death. Both types of trust can remove assets from your estate, and away from creditors. However, if you set up a trust before you die, it bypasses your will completely and therefore is not covered by probate tax. However, including a trust in your will may create uncertainty. If your will is challenged by some interested third party who wants the judge to vary the will in favour of the person contesting the will, the trust may be subject to review.

Because this book is about real estate investing, rather than wills, we suggest you speak with your lawyer or an estate planner about strategies to minimize the liability your estate could face. You can prime yourself with the insights offered in Douglas Gray and John Budd, *The Canadian Guide to Will and Estate Planning* (McGraw-Hill) and Margaret Kerr and JoAnn Kurtz, *Wills and Estates For Canadians For Dummies* (Wiley).

Avoiding Litigation

Sometimes you can't avoid a confrontation; it comes looking for you. Patience really is a virtue, if you want to avoid legal fees! Keeping your cool helps stave off anger and prevents disputes from ballooning into lawsuits. When cooler heads *don't* prevail, use the tips in this section to address the situation and defuse the crisis.

Controlling emotions

Remember the old school-yard rule of counting to ten before unleashing your anger on someone? The same tactic can help you as an investor when you feel that you've been wronged. No matter how upset you are, remain professional and have as clear-eyed a look at the situation as you possibly can. Give yourself some time, perhaps several months, to see if the dispute really requires legal action.

A dose of legal advice may give you a more reasonable, even philosophical, perspective on the situation getting under your skin. Although the lawyer you've selected for your advisory team may be skilled in litigation, you may need to look further to find a lawyer that has some expertise suited to your particular situation. After all, you wouldn't choose a lawyer who practises family law to handle a case of medical malpractice! The same holds true for real estate disputes.

Before deciding what course of action to take, ask at least three lawyers for objective feedback on your chances at trial, the possible length of the court proceedings, and the approximate costs. The process is essentially the same as for selecting a lawyer for your advisory team, something we discuss in Chapter 4. After you've received the opinions of various lawyers and before deciding whether to pursue legal action, take time to sleep on it.

Courting losses

Doug offers the following anecdotes about the legal snags litigious investors can run into when dealing in real estate:

John Doe, a home purchaser, decided he would sue Bob Smith, vendor of the house, for breach of contract. A beautiful chandelier was not hanging in the house when John took possession — but it *had been* there when he did the walk-through before making the offer and he assumed it came with the house. Indeed, the chandelier clinched the sale for him as another house he had considered buying boasted nothing quite as beautiful. John put a lot of money out for a lawyer but lost at court, for a number of reasons. The agreement of purchase and sale did not make any mention of the chandelier being included in the deal.

Oral representations made when dealing with a property are difficult or impossible to enforce or prove, which is why these details should always be in writing. In the absence of a written agreement, there can be honest misunderstandings. The chandelier was considered by the court to be a chattel that could be removed without damage to the ceiling, rather than a fixture that would automatically be considered part of the integrity of the building structure (that is, it would cause structural damage on removal).

As a result of losing at court, John had to pay not only his own lawyer, but a portion of the legal costs awarded by the court to the defendant Bob Smith. When all the financial dust settled, John could have bought a solid 14k-gold chandelier for the legal expense he incurred.

Peter, Paul and Mary decided to go into a group real estate investment together. Because they were old friends who had known each other for years, they felt it was unnecessary to incur the expense of seeing a lawyer about doing up an agreement, or even having a written agreement, as they "trusted each other." They planned to hold some raw land for five years until property values went up, and then subdivide it into small parcels of land, make a lot of money, and retire at the tender age of 55. However, Paul died a year after the property purchase. His partner Sue inherited his interest in the land. Sue and Peter never got along, and did not agree with the group's development plans — all of which had been discussed but never written down. So, Sue sued the group and asked the court to order a sale of the property, which was granted.

However, the timing with the market cycle was out. There was a financial shortfall on sale due to property values declining as a result of a real estate slump, low demand, and oversupply of raw land in that geographic area. The mortgage company sued on the outstanding debt. Peter and Mary had sold all their assets and left the country to be folk singers in Peru. Sue was the only one left in the country with assets. So, the lender went after Sue to collect on the full debt shortfall of $200,000, which resulted in Sue losing everything and declaring personal bankruptcy. The morals here: Be careful what you wish for, and have a lawyer draft your investment deal in detail.

Don't commence your action before you have all the facts! This may sound simple, but a lawyer may point out gaps in your case that you'll want to address before you take the matter to court. Without all the facts, your lawyer will have trouble arguing your case effectively.

We hope you can control your emotions just enough to not make any rash decisions. Most court actions have to take place within a specified time of the incident that you're targeting. Don't wait too long, or you may find yourself unable to sue. Time limits vary from province to province and according to the action, so make sure you don't miss your chance!

Assessing your chances

Many people assume that if they're right, they will win at the end of the day. However, court proceedings can take surprising turns; few issues in law are as black-and-white as the prosecution or the defendant try to argue! Moreover, even a victory can mean a financial loss as an award of costs typically garners just 15 to 35 percent of your legal fees. And the responsibility is yours to collect the judgment, which could mean another legal wrangle.

Before rushing into court, consider whether:

- ✔ **You have a chance of winning:** We advise in the previous section to consult three lawyers before launching your case. Your consultations should shed some light on whether you have legitimate grounds for a case, and its chances for success.

- ✔ **The defendant has enough cash to pay up if you win:** Winning the court battle doesn't mean winning the war. The defendant you're tackling may have no assets in his name or have all the assets tied up with debt. A corporate entity could be a hollow shell without any net worth.

  Objectively assess the real potential of collecting on a judgment. Your lawsuit may only deepen your losses, especially if the costs end up being more than the judgment you hope to collect. Though the learning experience may be rewarding, watching how other people conduct their court cases is a cheaper way to find out what goes on in court.

- ✔ **The exercise is worth the time, money, and cost to your reputation:** Launching a lawsuit, especially if you're trying to establish your portfolio, could paint you as a litigious hound. That's not a great reputation to have. Instead of going for the jugular of your opponent, assess the relative pros and cons of litigation. Take into account lost time and productivity. Keep in mind, too, that the defendant may decide to launch a countersuit, protracting the battle. An unsuccessful suit will bolster neither your reputation nor your bank account, and — to add insult to injury — may even leave you liable for your defendant's court costs.

Making peace

Settlements occur all the time; only about 5 percent of lawsuits ever actually reach trial. Settlements allow both parties to strike a deal and get on with life, saving a lot of court time and legal fees. Regardless of whether you're the claimant or the defendant, a settlement may make the most sense. But we'll leave that to your lawyer to decide!

Lawsuits aren't the only way to reach a satisfactory conclusion, however. Options open to skirmishing business associates include mediation, arbitration, and alternative dispute resolution (ADR).

Arbitration and mediation

The terms *arbitration* and *mediation* are most commonly heard when there's a labour dispute, but these strategies can help you too.

Mediation is an informal resolution-facilitation service, and arbitration is a formal procedure governed by provincial arbitration legislation. Many lawyers are also accredited mediators and arbitrators. When going to a mediation or arbitration hearing, you should select a lawyer who is an expert in the legal area of dispute, such as real estate or contract law. A skilled and experienced lawyer can present your case in a compelling, organized, and objective fashion. This enhances the chances of an outcome in your favour. However, the outcome depends on the issues in dispute and its financial and legal implications. For example, if you're involved in a landlord-tenant dispute where the value is, say, under $1,000, you may choose to represent yourself. In that context, it is common for mediators and arbitrators to deal with laypeople unfamiliar with the process, and who need to be coached and educated.

Alternative dispute resolution

The first step to resolving a dispute is obviously for both parties to sit down together and attempt to work out a mutually acceptable solution. If this approach fails, a method growing in popularity in business circles is alternative dispute resolution (ADR).

Parties that engage in ADR invite trained professionals to provide mediation and arbitration services, including mediating contract interpretations, disputes or negotiations. The professionals provide a written opinion proposing a pragmatic, equitable, and reasonable resolution of conflict.

Looking for alternatives?

Professionally trained arbitrators and mediators across Canada offer expertise in a wide range of areas. Many of these people are also lawyers. The best way to get the name of a mediator or arbitrator is through a trusted referral, from your lawyer, or through the Internet.

Various associations, groups, and private Web sites list Canadian mediators and arbitrators. Research several sites to familiarize yourself with the jargon, process, options, costs, and the names of qualified and experienced professionals. Initial consultations are commonly without charge. Here are some helpful Canadian Web sites that list both mediators and arbitrators:

- ✔ **Canadian Commercial Arbitration Centre** (www.cacniq.org): Established in 1986, the Canadian Commercial Arbitration Centre is a private, non-profit organization with offices in Quebec City and Montreal.

- ✔ **ADR Web** (www.adrweb.ca): Touts itself as "the complete online solution to the requirements of those wishing to research and book mediators or arbitrators across Canada."

- ✔ **ADR Chambers** (www.adrchambers.ca): Established in 1995, this Toronto-based organization numbers retired judges and senior counsel among its dispute resolution experts.

- ✔ **Google** (www.google.ca): Use key words such as "Canadian arbitrators and mediators" plus the name of your city, and you should find professionals with the skills you're seeking.

Part III
Selecting Properties: Where to Look, What to Watch For

The 5th Wave   By Rich Tennant

Looks good to me, but you're the inspector. What makes you think the foundation is sinking?

Well, for one thing, we're standing on the third floor balcony.

In this part . . .

Don't be caught out — bad market timing, real estate fraud, and not doing your due diligence are hazards you face as a real estate investor. We spend time in this part preparing you to face these and other challenges in the quest for your ideal investment property. That perfect property is out there! And we make sure you have the basic knowledge needed to work your way through a deal, close a sale, and embark on your role as a property owner — all without losing your shirt.

Chapter 9

Scouting Properties: Where to Look, and What to Look For

In This Chapter

▶ Identifying the best time to buy

▶ Finding the home or rental property for you

▶ Choosing a location to invest in

▶ Knowing when everything is "just right"

*F*inding the right property takes skill, luck, and a whole lot of intuition. But the hard work of scouting properties will give you the feelings in your gut you need to make the hard decisions that promise success as a real estate investor. This chapter is something of a scout's handbook, and we can't help but advise, "Be prepared!"

We discuss everything about finding properties, from the big picture down to the specific property. Some of the basic issues are tackled in Chapter 1, but in this chapter we get into the nitty-gritty of sizing up the conditions in specific markets, neighbourhoods, and even the property you're looking at investing in. We can't know the specifics of every situation you have to choose from, of course, but we hope we can provide some useful examples and guidelines.

Assessing Current Market Cycles

An overview of market cycles can be found in Chapter 3, along with concepts important to understanding the market. These basic elements help you to decide when to buy and sell properties. Putting the concepts to work requires research, keen observation, and a measure of intuition.

This section walks you through an analysis of market cycles as they apply to the process of purchasing a property. Three main steps go into assessing the current market cycle: conducting research, doing an analysis, and making a decision.

Research: Doing your homework

The first step is to figure out what type of market you're in (we describe the three market types in Chapter 3). Is it a *buyer's market,* with plenty of product to choose from? Or a *seller's market,* with rising prices and limited supply? Or are conditions stable, reflecting a relatively *balanced market*?

To help you figure out where the market stands, we look at the key factors we identify in Chapter 3 as affecting market conditions.

Knowing where to find basic information — and when to dig for more — is an important skill for researching market cycles. In this section, we give you the pointers you need to be an effective market analyst! More sources of information appear in Chapter 17 in the Part of Tens that rounds out this book.

Tracking interest rates

Though you may not appreciate higher interest rates, the lenders financing your investment certainly will! The lower the interest rate charged on a mortgage, the greater incentive there is for you to borrow to buy a property. The higher interest rates are, the more you'll end up paying to borrow the money and the lower the return you can expect on your investment.

The primary source of information on interest rates is the Bank of Canada (www.bankofcanada.ca), the Ottawa-based bank that the leading lending institutions across Canada pay attention to when setting their interest rates. The bank's Web site provides information on its own rate, including reasons why it is where it is, and offers charts with historical interest-rate data that allows you to see where rates have been and where they seem to be going.

Canada's major chartered banks and other lending institutions often issue newsletters discussing their own monetary policies and their outlook for interest rates. The updates and newsletters from their chief economists are important resources to consult when trying to figure out where rates are heading and how real estate markets will respond.

Though we don't recommend trying to second-guess interest rates, a close look at past rates, current trends, and the projections of the various banks should indicate whether rates are set to rise, plateau, or fall. Your assessment of rate trends assists you as you decide whether financing will be more or less expensive in future, and whether you should select a variable or fixed-rate mortgage. Interest-rate trends also indicate whether you should buy now, wait a few months, or sell while low rates are encouraging buyers to hop into the market.

Locking into rates

The Bank of Canada is cautious and conservative in determining when to raise or lower interest rates. Normally, any change — and the reasons for the change — is the focus of economists' speculation for days beforehand and much discussion in financial and other circles. The Bank of Canada looks at various factors when making a decision to change the prime rate of interest. For example, the rate might be increased to dampen inflationary trends by increasing the cost of borrowing, or decreased to encourage borrowing to stimulate the economy. Another reason for the Bank of Canada to change the interest rates is to make the Canadian dollar more attractive for international institutional investors. The bank takes into account a lot of factors prior to making its decision.

The relevance of interest-rate fluctuations to investors is the degree of financing risk. That is why a lot of investors will take out a long-term fixed-rate mortgage — say, for 5, 7 or even 10 years. This way, investors can budget with certainty regardless of what happens to interest rates.

On the other hand, some investors prefer a variable-rate mortgage that fluctuates based on the Bank of Canada rate. However, the interest rate difference can be 1 to 2 percent less than a fixed-rate mortgage. Money can be saved, but the risk is the uncertainty as to when interest rates might go up. It could be that over time the variable interest rate could be higher than if you had locked in your fixed-term mortgage six months earlier. Most investors prefer the stability of a long-term guaranteed rate mortgage.

We discuss mortgages and their management at greater length in Chapters 6 and 7.

Rising rates may make financing more expensive but they can sometimes create opportunities for buyers by putting pressure on buyers who have overleveraged their portfolio. Selling when buyers are active can provide financing you can use to purchase properties when debt-burdened buyers have to unload assets.

Determining property taxes

Property taxes may seem like a fixed cost but they are an important consideration for investors analyzing market cycles. A booming market with rising sale values pushes up assessors' valuations of properties. A slack market, by contrast, could see property values fall. This has a direct impact on the annual tax assessment, not only in the coming year, but often in the three years following the change in value. Taxes levied on a property will affect the return you see as an investor, and possibly your financing costs.

Different investors have different expectations and projections for their profit margins. Most investors want a *double return,* that is, a positive cash flow for a rental revenue stream, and a capital gain over the original purchase price. Traditionally, real estate has gone up an average of about 5 percent a year for the past 30 years. However, that figure can be higher or lower depending on the real estate cycle, location, type of property, and other factors. Most investors would like a gain of at least 5 percent a year in equity in the property, due to appreciation.

When determining your margin, you have to consider the capital gain aspect. If you average 10 percent a year in value over ten years, for example, that property would have doubled in value. If you buy it for $100,000, and sell it for $200,000, you have a $100,000 gain in your original capital investment. You are taxed by the Canada Revenue Agency on 50 percent of your gain. In this example, that means you could keep $50,000 tax-free, and pay tax on the remaining $50,000. At the top marginal tax rate of approximately 50 percent, you would pay approximately $25,000 tax. At the end of the day, that would mean that you could keep $75,000 of your original $100,000 gain, after tax.

If your original purchase price was $100,000, that would mean a 75-percent return over ten years, or an average of 7.5 percent a year non-compounded. But you also had positive cash flow from rental income to factor into the equation.

In addition, maybe you just put down 10 percent and borrowed the other 90 percent on a mortgage. Therefore, you actually received a 75-percent return on your original personal resource down payment of $10,000 over ten years. The reason is that your original $10,000 down "investment" resulted in a $75,000 net gain, or an average of $7,500 a year on your original $10,000, or 75 percent return a year. Better than obtaining, say, a 6-percent return on a term deposit that is taxed as investment income in your hands in that taxation year. Depending on your tax bracket, you could pay 30 percent or more on that interest income, meaning that net after tax, you only actually received about two-thirds of your interest, or 4 percent in the example given.

Property tax assessment records are available through municipal offices or provincial assessment authorities. You will also find explanations of trends in the annual reports of the municipality in which you hope to buy. Often, local media cover trends in property taxation, providing you with insights into overall municipal approaches to setting tax rates (in some provinces, the provincial government sets the rates).

Be sure to discuss the impact of property taxation policies on your investment with an appraiser, who is often able to coordinate appeals on any assessments you consider out of line with the reality of your holding. Given the range of factors that affect the value of a property, and its performance in any given market, you should understand how property taxes will influence your own cash flow as well as the property's appeal to future investors. Assessments that indicate opportunities for investment can easily rise after investors move in, improve the properties, and improve the tone of the surrounding neighbourhood.

(We discuss the role appraisers can play in helping you determine the current value and potential uses of a property in Chapter 10.)

Reviewing leasing conditions

Fully leased properties with long-term tenants make for great investments from a revenue perspective, but a close look at the tenant mix may reveal nothing more than a good tease. The last thing you want to do is enter a market on the basis of an apparently healthy lease market, only to find that leasing activity is actually heading south and taking property prices with it.

Fortunately, several sources can help you investigate the current and long-term history and prospects for local leasing markets. If you're looking at residential rental properties, have a gander at the annual rental housing market survey the Canada Mortgage and Housing Corp. (www.cmhc.ca) produces. Commercial brokerages such as Colliers International (www.colliers.com) prepare similar reports on a quarterly basis for commercial and industrial markets. Retail leasing reports are also available from the big brokerages, but high rates of turnover make these more difficult to produce.

Knowing where vacancies stand in your market, and the rents tenants are paying for their spaces, will indicate investment opportunities and reflect landlords' capital requirements. High vacancies may indicate buying opportunities as existing owners may want to sell out because of cash flow pressures; alternatively, low vacancies may make assets attractive to purchasers, resulting in a vendor's market as buyers compete for assets.

A good leasing market doesn't necessarily mean a good investment market. Conversely, high vacancies won't always prompt landlords to sell. Still, knowing rental conditions can help you build an argument for investing in particular locales and devising a negotiating strategy that will win over vendors.

Gauging consumer confidence

Buyers' confidence in markets is as changeable as the markets themselves. The two, after all, have an intimate relationship. Confident investors contribute to a strong market, while conservative investors limit the volume of activity taking place in the market.

But short of doing psychological assessments of a random sampling of active investors, how can you gauge the level of confidence in the market? Let others skilled in the art research it for you, of course!

The Conference Board of Canada (`www.conferenceboard.ca`) is just one of the organizations that issues business and consumer confidence surveys. For a fee, the board also provides detailed analyses for specific regions. Newspapers also record perceptions of where markets are heading. The information gleaned from these sources, like interest rate projections, can help you gauge whether markets are in for a boom or a downturn.

Rising consumer confidence may indicate an increased willingness to invest in real estate. As an investor, you may consider preparing your residential property for sale to the potential buyers, or perhaps you'll opt to buy before the market heats up. On the other hand, falling confidence in the market may signal purchase opportunities as people retrench in anticipation of harder times.

Consumer confidence is less definite than monetary policy and interest rates, and relies on a good grasp of the current economic climate. Unforeseen events can put the kibosh on existing predictions, so although we recommend consulting assessments of the market's mood, know that the mood is just that — a mood. It won't necessarily obey scientific laws.

Considering local planning activities

Urban planning activities have a peripheral influence on market cycles but may play a role in spurring demand in local areas. Including a glance at urban planning initiatives in the areas where you're considering investing is therefore a good plan!

Here's how planning has an influence: An area that has languished at the bottom of the local market cycle may find itself at the top of a council's priority list because of public concern over its status or the potential for improvement if it is rezoned for certain purposes. A community planning process may identify certain goals and uses for the area. Perhaps planners will propose development incentives. A combination of these factors may spark a rush into the area.

Knowing the pressures coming to bear on specific neighbourhoods, and where these areas rank in the city's planning priorities, will give you clues to where the market in these areas is likely to go in the future. This gives you an advantage over other investors, potentially allowing you to get in when the market is low and sell when the market is high. Conversely, if an area is set for rezoning, you want to be aware that the market for properties with uses allowed under the previous zoning is about to collapse.

Analyzing thoroughly: Tallying the variables

Making sense of the information you glean through your research into market conditions and perceptions of the market may seem like voodoo. And, to be fair, seeing the big picture takes a good deal of intuition. Of course, we face similar decisions. To make life easier for you, we offer a chart in the Sizing up the cycle sidebar that will help you determine where the market sits and what your course of action should be. Find the set of criteria that comes closest to what you've discovered about the market, and gauge how you'll respond!

	A	B	C	D	A
Values	Depressed	Increasing	Increasing	Declining	Depressed
Rents	Low	Increasing	Increasing	Declining	Low
Vacancy level	High	Beginning to decrease	Low	Increasing	High
Occupancy level	Low	Increasing	High	Decreasing	Low
New construction	Very little	Increasing	Booming	Slowing	Very little
Profit margins	Low	Improving	Widest	Decline	Low
Investor confidence	Low	Negative to neutral	Positive	Slightly negative	Low
Media coverage	Negative and pessimistic	Positive and encouraging	Positive and optimistic	Negative and pessimistic	Negative and pessimistic
Action	Buy	Second best time to buy	Sell	Be cautious	Buy

Sizing up the cycle

To make your job of determining market conditions a bit easier, Doug has put together a table that assembles various variables and suggests an appropriate action based on the variables most prevalent in your corner of the market. Of course, determining a market's character is hardly an exact science, but this table should help you put circumstances into perspective.

The decision: Trust your gut

Whether you're buying or selling, don't make your decision lightly. Consult your long-term investment plan and take stock of what your advisers are saying. Knowing when you're ready to sell is as important as knowing when you're ready to invest. (We discuss selling a property in Chapter 16.)Though you may consider selling a handful of properties in your portfolio, the range of properties you can buy is typically larger. Knowing whether the market is at the right point for a purchase, however, is just one aspect of your investment decision.

Few markets are uniform, after all. Even an unfavourable market can harbour good investments. Finding the good deals in difficult circumstances is part of the challenge — and joy — of investing in real estate.

X Marks the Spot: Identifying a Target Market

Well, you could try throwing a dart at a list or map showing the areas where market conditions are favourable, but we hope you'll put a bit more effort than that into your decision. A number of factors may sway you in favour of (or against) a particular locale.

We explore some of the considerations you'll want to take into account when you're narrowing down your list of potential neighbourhoods for investment. We want you to keep the fundamentals of the local market in mind, looking past the fads to the actual investment potential of the area. Of course, your perception and affinity for a particular neighbourhood may count more than the hard financial stats. To ensure your investment balances financial wisdom with personal feeling, find out what conditions on the ground are really like.

Separating the fads from the fundamentals

Successful real estate investment requires that you know what you're buying and trust that it's going to deliver a return. Remember the old joke about diplomacy being the skill of telling someone to go to Hell in a way that they actually look forward to the trip? Real estate marketing can be a lot like that; a marketer will sell you a piece of Hell and you'll enjoy the heat and other amenities!

Although the marketing of new developments tends to focus on lifestyle and neighbourhood options, you may look at other aspects of the property and be wondering if that development is really so great. The hottest new neighbourhood under development or redevelopment may not fit your investment strategy, no matter what advantages the marketers tout.

Points to consider when comparing a property in a hot neighbourhood to one in a locale generally considered less favourable include not only their price, but also their potential for appreciation, maintenance costs, and cash flow:

✔ **Price** is an important factor when stacking up properties, and especially when gauging the relative merits of two properties whose neighbourhoods differ in quality. Check whether the list price of each property is within area norms, and whether either of the two is undervalued. An undervalued asset in a better neighbourhood is probably a good bet, but steer clear of an overpriced home in an undervalued neighbourhood because you'll have less room for long-term appreciation.

✔ **Potential for appreciation** will indicate the return you can expect on your investment. The greater the potential for appreciation, the better the investment. Consult an appraiser for a prognosis on the kind of return you can expect on the various properties you're considering. (We talk more about working with appraisers in Chapter 10.)

✔ **Potential maintenance costs** could cut into your margins, especially in a less-favourable neighbourhood. We're not talking only about deferred maintenance that's contributed to the lower asking price of the property and greater potential for appreciation, we're talking about the ongoing maintenance associated with graffiti, litter, vandalism, and the like. You may be able to make something of the property, but will you be able to *keep* that something?

✔ **Potential for cash flow** could moderate your enthusiasm for that high-end asset if you find tenants hard to come by. Depending on your investment strategy, it may be better for you to invest in a more modest property with solid cash flow potential than a trophy few can afford to rent from you. On the other hand, if you have a chance to pick up two residential properties, and can swing the financing, you may opt to live in one and rent the other — effectively having *two* slices of cake and eating them too. (Just be sure you know which piece is sweeter.)

Getting to know markets and neighbourhoods

Bearing in mind the fundamentals of sound investing, part of your job as a diligent investor is to familiarize yourself with the neighbourhoods you're targeting for investment. There are several ways to do this, from research or walkabouts, and a number of factors to consider.

We recommend identifying three neighbourhoods, based on your research into market conditions, that could serve as investment opportunities. This will allow you to see how each compares with the others, tally up the relative advantages and disadvantages of each, and generally get a feel for which neighbourhood you're most comfortable with.

Basic factors to consider before you even visit a neighbourhood relate to its age, its character, and its unique mix of properties and infrastructure.

Sizing up age

Older neighbourhoods either are well-to-do and established, or show their age. The good news is that a neighbourhood with an aging stock of properties with rock-bottom values can offer great value. You may be able to renovate the property and make it into something people want, either as tenants or owners. On the other hand, an established neighbourhood with good-quality homes may offer few opportunities for you to enter the market.

A new neighbourhood may be the hottest place for some investors, but it also has the potential for surprises. Where an established neighbourhood has a reputation, a new neighbourhood has yet to prove itself. The quality of the homes may be good and the infrastructure may be there, but what will it become?

Sizing up character

The kind of neighbourhood character we're talking about isn't necessarily the vibe you'll pick up during a stroll down the street. Rather, it's the mix of people actually in the neighbourhood, the age and income levels, and education and employment indicators. These factors are worth considering because they contribute to the kind of tenant you attract, and also how the locale maintains itself.

For example, an upper income neighbourhood in a suburb with a growing working class population may have a prime piece of real estate to offer. Buying the upper-end property hoping to lease suites to workers or students may not be the best idea because the rents you'll have to charge to make ends meet on the property probably won't match what the workers and students are able to pay.. Chances are the better opportunity will lie in an asset that can provide affordable housing to the growing population of workers.

We don't recommend a snobby attitude in selecting properties, but as an investor you should consider what serves the market. Paying attention to the demographics and overall character of a neighbourhood helps you find an asset that's the right fit, not only with your own goals but also with those of the people to whom you hope to lease.

Sizing up the mix

The right mix of properties in a neighbourhood ensures a match made in heaven between the kind of property you want to own and the needs of any tenants you hope to secure.

Perhaps you've got a penchant for a small industrial building. The three mid-size bays inside are perfect for light industrial users. But a glance at the uses of surrounding properties indicates that it's nowhere near any amenities, and neighbouring properties don't really complement the kind of users you hope to secure. However good a deal it is, and whatever the future growth potential of the industrial area where it's situated, chances are the small industrial users you're looking for may not want to lease the premises. Therefore it won't suit their needs, and the investment won't live up to your expectations.

Amenities are key to supporting the needs of the users you hope to attract to a revenue-producing property. Several electronic resources allow you to gauge the potential of a neighbourhood before you even see it; some real estate listings offer 360-degree views of the surrounding neighbourhood, for example, while Google (not to mention many municipalities) provides satellite views of your potential neighbourhood that give a sense of the area's layout (a simple Web search will pull up others). Some even allow you to cross-reference business listings with satellite imagery so you know what amenities are available locally.

Honing your vision

You wouldn't buy a car without kicking the tires, so it makes sense to take a walkabout in each area where you're considering investing. (We don't recommend kicking the properties, though. That smarts.) Testing your response to these neighbourhoods gives you a sense of how others are likely to respond to them.

To become familiar with a potential neighbourhood, pay it a few visits at various times of day and night. Give yourself a chance to experience it as a driver, a pedestrian, and a transit user. Are traffic patterns unusual? Is it walkable? Are transit connections frequent, smooth, or a hassle? Your experience of these aspects of the community may give you an understanding of why a neighbourhood is hot or not, and may point you to areas within the neighbourhood that are more convenient places to be than others.

A walkabout is a more intensive way for you to gauge several of the factors we discuss in this section. Keep your eyes open for the following:

- **The fabric of the neighbourhood:** This includes the condition of the properties and landscaping. The better the condition of the neighbourhood, the more attractive it will be to potential tenants and the less risk to the condition and value of your own property. Priming yourself with neighbourhood history tells you whether the condition of properties is improving or declining.

- **Local businesses and amenities:** These are important indicators of your fortunes in the neighbourhood. A handful of local businesses serving up staples and a few pleasures is a good sign. Communities that lack a decent grocery store and other basic shops stand to be less favoured by potential tenants and future buyers.

- **Street vibe:** This is an significant factor in making a neighbourhood a place people want to be. Good traffic flows, people who chat with one another, maybe even street-side decorations are all signs of a vibrant neighbourhood. On the other hand, desolate streets where the windows of the homes have bars may not send the right message to people you're trying to interest in your property.

- **Noise and environmental factors:** These affect different people in different ways. Unless you're investing in commercial or industrial property, chances are you won't want to buy something on the flight path to the local airport. Similarly, properties that are downwind from a pulp and paper plant or wastewater treatment centre may not be the most attractive assets.

Be sure to consider the full range of factors at play in the neighbourhoods you're considering! A personal visit may help you make sense of issues local newspapers have raised about the area, or may temper the impressions you've received from others who claim to know what's going on.

Consulting the locals

One of the best things you can do as a potential investor in a neighbourhood is get to know the locals. This gives you a feel for the area, as well as local concerns and attitudes, and further your understanding of the community. You may even discover information about the property you're looking at that may encourage you — or prompt you to think twice about the investment you were hoping to make.

Opportunities for meeting locals abound. Buy a paper and chat up the person who serves you. Stop in to the local coffee shop (if there is one), listen to the chatter and maybe strike up a conversation with the people at the neighbouring table. You may not be good at small talk, but even chatting about the weather can create an opportunity to hear what people are saying about the market.

Dimitri took a more direct approach. He wanted to buy a waterfront home for his young family. He found a home for sale in southern New Brunswick, but decided he would do his research homework and check with its neighbours before he made an offer. It was a wise move. He discovered that rats were a serious problem in the area, and that successive attempts to eradicate them had been unsuccessful. The area was also prone to flooding in spring; though none of the people Dimitri spoke with had ever had water in their own homes, they said it wasn't unusual to find it lapping at their basement doors. Dimitri decided not to scout properties on higher ground, eventually opting for a house in a new subdivision overlooking a lake.

Building relationships with locals is something you can never begin too early. This is especially true if you plan a major development of a property or are considering a rezoning. Cultivating an open relationship with members of the community will help bring them onside with your plans. The goodwill you foster by participating in the community as either a homeowner or business operator is invaluable.

Keeping watch

Having an extra pair of eyes scouting properties is a great help when you're looking for a good investment. And who better to ask than a real estate agent, especially one with access to databases such as the Multiple Listing Service (www.mls.ca) for residential properties or ICX (www.icx.ca) for commercial properties?

Take Dan, for example. An experienced real estate investor, Dan regularly buys properties that need some tender loving care. He fixes them up, puts them back on the market and reaps a profit. To do that, Dan has a long-standing professional relationship with his agent Pam. Dan sets out the type of property he's interested in buying, the location he wants to buy in, and the price he's prepared to pay. Pam monitors new listings as soon as they're listed,

getting the low-down on them even before they've officially hit the MLS site. When a property comes up that meets Dan's requirements, she gets in touch with Dan. Dan quickly checks the properties, and before the market is fully aware of the listing he puts in his offer.

Knowing what you want and developing a relationship with a listing agent who's able to connect you with properties that meet those criteria can give you an edge over other buyers. The properties Dan scouts need lots of work and typically list for the value of the lot, so there's a limited number of competitors for them. Still, without his relationship with Pam, he wouldn't have been as successful as he has been in finding the best deals possible.

Selecting a Property

The property you're seeking in the locale you've chosen may not be simple to find. You have to look for it, or have your broker do so. We discuss strategies for locating potential investment properties in Chapters 1 and 2. After you've selected a neighbourhood in which to invest, you'll want to pull out newspapers, log on to Web sites such as Multiple Listing Service (www.mls.ca) for residential property or ICX (www.icx.ca) for commercial and industrial properties, and keep your eyes open.

Facets of the property to consider include its location, the availability of amenities and services, and the property's potential for appreciation. The criteria are largely refinements of the principles that have allowed you to narrow your search to a handful of properties. By now you should know what you want!

Home sweet home

A house draws out a lot of emotion, regardless of whether you're the owner-occupant or simply a tenant with the option of moving out if it gets on your nerves. You have a lot more conditions you want to satisfy when you're looking for a chunk of residential real estate than, say, a retail unit. Your standards are especially high if you're also planning on living in the house. Any tenants you welcome into the building are there because they've chosen to rent from you and can move on if the place isn't what they expect, but you're going to be stuck with the place as the primary occupant and user. So be selfish and put your own interests first!

First off, consider where you want to live. Price, affordability, and availability each play a role in determining where you buy, but your own idea of what makes a livable neighbourhood also factors into your decision. Being practical won't hurt; what appeals to you may appeal to tenants or future buyers. Being able to tout a feature of your neighbourhood that has been of particular value to you will help the sales pitch you'll make to the next purchaser.

You have many factors to consider when selecting a home, whether for your own use or as an investment. Here are a few questions to ask yourself:

- **What is the neighbourhood like?** A thriving neighbourhood promises to be a great place to live, whereas one where not much is going on could make for dull evenings and weekends. Or, the run-down nature of some of the buildings could mean there's more excitement than you really care to know about. These factors won't just affect your quality of life as residents, either; they could be indicative of long-term trends that will either make it easier or more difficult for you to sell your property in the future.

✔ **What are traffic flows like?** The local highway may be a great feature if you do a lot of commuting, but you don't necessarily want to be living next door to it. Consider, too, the potential health impacts from living next door to a major traffic artery. These factors could limit the resale value of your property, but convenient access to transportation networks could be an asset for some buyers. Research the traffic patterns and impact on property values in any area in which you're considering buying.

✔ **What community amenities are within a 10-kilometre radius?** Nearby schools, places of worship, parks and recreation facilities, transit and shopping can be points in the favour of residential real estate. The closer your property is to amenities, the more you're able to offer others. The higher value of a location can pay itself back if you approach the purchase as an investment rather than simply your own home.

✔ **What does municipal zoning allow for the property?** Favourable zoning can open the door to enhancements that can affect the value of your property. Depending on your neighbourhood, changes may be in the works that will either increase the value of your property or diminish it. Researching what the city plans for a particular residential neighbourhood is an important part of analyzing a property.

✔ **What are property tax rates like?** Taxes are one of the few certain things in life, so make sure you study which direction residential property taxes are heading before you buy. Rates typically differ from city to city, so you may be able to find a property comparable to one you like in a municipality that levies a higher tax rate on homeowners, and thus end up paying less tax.

✔ **What are the prospects for an increase in property value?** Regardless of where you buy, try to make sure your home has potential to appreciate in value! Some of the basic market research you'll undertake to determine a location (we discuss that elsewhere in this chapter) can help you to make the this call.

✔ **What are condo fees and building regulations like?** Don't forget to take condo fees and bylaws passed by the building council into account when you're looking at condominiums. Be sure to review building council minutes prior to buying to make sure there are no ongoing issues of which you should be aware. (We discuss condos in Chapter 2.)

Having chosen a neighbourhood in which to buy, scout potential homes using the Internet. Here are a few sites to check out:

✔ The Canadian Real Estate Association maintains the Multiple Listing Service (MLS) site, for example, which boasts a near-comprehensive set of residential listings across Canada (www.mls.ca). This will give you an idea of the homes available for purchase in a given area, after which you can approach a Realtor to assist your search. You can identify several potential Realtors through listings on the MLS site.

✔ Independent agents also exist who can offer insights and connections regarding the area where you hope to buy. You need to find someone with the experience and skills to serve your needs and with whom you can work — so look around.

✔ A number of services also exist that give owner-vendors a venue for pitching their properties, such as PropertyGuys.com and ForSalebyOwner.com. Although we encourage you to use a real estate agent in your various transactions, it's worth remembering that not all people will. You may find a deal on one of these sites that, given some skillful negotiating, will hand you a bargain.

Accommodating tenants

A home isn't a good investment if you can't achieve a return on it. Although appreciation over time is one means of achieving this goal, sharing your home with a tenant provides an ongoing cash flow. To ensure your experience with a tenant has the best chance of success, you want to make sure the home you buy has certain features.

Ideally, if the previous owner of the house has had tenants, you'll be able to judge the property on its features as both a residence and a rental property. Though you may need to make adjustments to the layout, the structure itself should be flexible enough to accommodate some key features:

✔ Dividing walls, to ensure a more complete separation of your living area from the tenant's

✔ Potential for sharing laundry facilities and other amenities, which could eliminate your need to set up a separate laundry area for tenants

✔ Wiring and circuitry necessary for the installation of a fridge, stove and other appliances

These features make the space less hassle for you to adapt for rental use, and create a more desirable space for potential renters.

Dividing walls are just one element that help ensure a happy co-existence between your family and your tenants. A separate entrance is a primary consideration; this will give the tenants a feel of privacy and decrease the chance their comings and goings will disturb you. But if you're buying a two- or three-bedroom condo and want to rent a room, you may want to put a higher priority on having an extra washroom as well as adequate sound-proofing.

Buying a home located close to a major public transit route will enhance your chance of securing a tenant. A parking spot is another attractive feature.

Not all municipalities allow secondary suites, so be sure to check the legality of having tenants before you buy! Some jurisdictions will turn a blind eye to tenants, but you invite a range of hassles by not complying with the letter of the law. For peace of mind check what local bylaws have to say, and speak to your lawyer.

Attracting purchasers

Gauging future demand for housing in your neighbourhood is difficult, but you can take steps that will position your home to be attractive to potential purchasers in 5, 10 or even 20 years. Some of these will be reasons that you're attracted to the home yourself, such as proximity to schools, parks, shopping areas, transportation and other amenities. But looking at the locale is also worthwhile:

✔ Is it close to major institutional employers with ongoing employment needs such as a hospital or university?

✔ What is the potential of the home to be adapted for other uses, say rental to tenants, home office use, or the like?

✔ Does it have the potential to appeal to buyers completely different from yourself?

✔ Does the local zoning allow expansion or redevelopment of the home? You may not be interested in doing this, but the possibility might attract a future owner.

Location, location, location

Okay, "location, location, location" is a time-worn phrase, but it makes sense! And what would a book on real estate be without it? A property's location isn't something to take lightly, given the potential impact on appeal to tenants, your cash flow, and potential resale value.

Appealing to tenants

Many of us, at one time or another, have had a landlord who's baffled us. The rent was good, but property conditions were such that we didn't have to wonder why we were the ones living in the suite rather than the owner!

Now that you're a landlord, why do the same thing to your tenants? As we discuss in the previous section, choosing a property that's in a location where you would want to live yourself makes sense even if you *don't* live there. That's because lots of other people probably would look forward to finding the place you've found. A decent neighbourhood makes for happy tenants, which makes for stable cash flow and, ultimately, a better return on your investment. (We cover the value amenities can add to a property's location elsewhere in this chapter.)

A property that's attractive to tenants is better than a utilitarian rental property with no cachet at all. Chances are you'll also be able to charge higher rents, potentially securing yourself a long-term advantage that beats buying a larger property in a less attractive neighbourhood commanding lower rents.

Cashing in

The quality of the neighbourhood will affect not only how long tenants stay and the rents they're willing to pay, but also the cash flow the property generates. You'll be able to charge tenants higher rents for suites in well-located properties, and you'll likely face lower operating expenses.

Though you may pay closer attention to the overall appearance of a property that's surrounded by attractive neighbours, the quality of the tenant that a better-groomed property attracts helps your investment property deliver a return. You'll find it easier to secure better-quality tenants — that is, tenants who respect your property — who reduce your maintenance costs. This ensures better margins on the rents you're able to charge.

Trading up

Future buyers will have an interest in the property you've bought if it is in a better-quality location. The chances for appreciation increase if the fortunes of the surrounding area are also on the upswing.

Even if the locale seems to be facing a downturn, a better-quality asset will tend to lose less of its value than one in a poor location in a poor neighbourhood.

Amenities and services

The kinds of amenities and services you hope to have near your investment property varies. Users of residential properties want something different from tenants of commercial and industrial properties. When identifying amenities available to users of the property you're considering buying, you're generally safe to look in a 10-kilometre radius around the property.

Residential

Standard residential amenities include schools, places of worship, parks and recreation facilities, transit links, and shopping areas. The closer a property is to a greater selection of amenities, the more you'll be able to command in rent.

Amenities are also increasingly important to resort properties, with those who want to get away from it all not wanting to leave their urban comforts behind. Ensure that the resort property into which you're buying is well-served with amenities suited to the recreational user.

Commercial

Commercial properties, such as office and retail buildings, have their own unique set of needs. Depending on the size and kind of workforce, selling points can include proximity to recreational amenities and shopping facilities as well as food service. Postal outlets and business supply and service centres are also important.

Infrastructure such as parking areas, proximity to main commuting routes, and transit services can also enhance the value of the assets in which you're looking to invest.

Industrial

Connections to transportation infrastructure are among the most important amenities you can provide industrial users. Because these properties are typically where items are made, stored, and distributed, it's important that users have ready access to roads, and even rail and port connections. In many areas of Canada, quick access to the U.S. border is also a consideration.

Like commercial users, industrial tenants appreciate proximity to food service and retail outlets.

Looking to the future

Here's a startling revelation: No one can predict the future. But based on the amount of research you've put into finding a property, we bet you'll be able to take an educated guess at what the future holds for the ones you're considering buying. Because the main success of your investment will be in its appreciation, you want to make sure the property itself stands to gain in value. You should also have some confidence that the prospects for the surrounding neighbourhood are good.

Looking in

The future prospects for your investment in and of itself depend on the quality of the building, and overall market conditions.

We discuss the various ways to gauge a property's inherent value in Chapter 10, but it's worth pointing out here that your property should be structurally sound. A building with potential for adaptation will also have stronger potential to appreciate in value in future years, as residential and other requirements change. The greater the number of uses to which a future owner can put a property, the greater the chances that it will retain its value, and even become a more valuable asset.

The overall market conditions are something over which you have little control. A glance at the history of the property's value should indicate whether or not it has seen a steady appreciation, or whether it has suffered depreciation in the past. Researching the causes for past fluctuations in value may not reveal the potential for appreciation or depreciation, but such research will indicate whether there were any unusual circumstances behind the fluctuations.

Looking out

The surrounding neighbourhood can sometimes work to lower or raise the value of your property. Although your property is a passive player in the phenomenon, any increase or decrease in the quality of the community could have an impact.

As an investor, you should aim to find a property in a stable neighbourhood with potential for appreciation. Recognizing the warning signs that could indicate the start of a downward trend in value is a skill that should prompt you to sell the property — or stay away from it if you thought it might be a good purchase.

Knowing a Property's Right for You

We have no more business telling you when a property is right than we do telling you who to marry. But, just as with falling in love, you know you've found the right investment property when it happens to you.

But here are a handful of tips and warnings for you to keep in mind.

Make sure the property in which you're interested shows potential to serve your investment goals. Check it against the objectives you've set for yourself, and verify your opinion with those of your advisers. You might be missing something that's obvious to them. Consulting them will ensure you're making the best possible decision under the circumstances.

Your actions in the market aren't the only reason to know about market cycles. The information you glean may help you negotiate a better deal, perhaps even a few concessions from the vendor. Building up your knowledge of the local market and the factors affecting it will make you a better negotiator.

A property valued at above the current market average could narrow your margins, or potentially become a burden to you if the market slips. This is particularly true in poorer neighbourhoods, where you have not only general market conditions to worry about but the conditions of the market in the immediate vicinity of the property.

Poor neighbourhoods aren't always going to have good long-term potential. Knowing the history of an area will help bring to light any long-term negative perceptions that area faces, and the potential for a turnaround. Although many poorer areas in Canada's major cities have undergone *gentrification* — simply put, the process of being made more attractive, more expensive places to live in — and improvement in recent years, many others have experienced periods of prolonged decline. Your investment may be a glimmer of hope among those who wish for a turnaround, but it's not likely to solve the problem by itself.

Many areas in Canada have older neighbourhoods that boast buildings with character and established landscaping and that have become popular following gentrification. Property values could easily double or triple in response to consumer demand as these areas become trendy and desirable places in which to live and work. The Cabbagetown and Yorkville areas in Toronto, and Yaletown and Gastown neighbourhoods of Vancouver are a just a few examples. In Vancouver, for example, the successful sell-out of 536 units in the former Woodward's department store prompted the listing of properties for 25 to 30 percent above their previous prices. Many began moving, despite their location in an area notorious as Canada's poorest postal code, bringing the former owners a windfall many never expected to see.

Chapter 10

Determining Value: Price versus Potential

In This Chapter

▶ Understanding how appraisals work

▶ Assessing your own property

▶ Seeing the best in the worst

*D*etermining the value of a property is part perception, part overcoming perceptions to get at its real worth. Many properties you wouldn't consider worth your own money might be worth someone else's — that of either a tenant or a future buyer to whom you'll sell it. And some real estate is more valuable for the land than anything that's been developed on it.

The question of what you see in the property and what you want to make of it as an investment property is key to what you're willing to pay. Many people are willing to pay more for a property because they think it has value, and gamble on the market following their intuition. Others pursue a more rational approach and back up their investments with research. Successful investors generally do a bit of both.

This chapter is our opportunity to introduce you to basic appraisal principles that can help you assess a property both on its own merits and with a view to investing in something that might not have value now, but will in the future. We also try to help you see the best in areas that may not look great now, but have potential to improve. Opportunities exist in most markets.

Sometimes you'll opt to hire a professional appraiser to provide a more complete picture of a property's value or potential. The tips we provide shouldn't exclude your asking for a professional opinion.

Appraising Properties

When you buy a property, the lender typically wants to have an independent professional appraisal done to make sure the property is worth what is being paid for it. This has implications in terms of protecting the mortgage security on the property. Normally the lender will pay the cost of the appraisal, which averages about $300 to $400. Sometimes the lender will pass that cost on to you.

A basic appraisal is a pretty simple matter of comparing recent sale prices for comparable assets and extrapolating a value based on what the market is likely willing to pay for the asset. Thanks to the wealth of information available in databases these days, the job is so simple that most residential appraisals are now computer-generated.

But a good appraisal is really more complex than a simple comparison. It takes into account a variety of factors, from the construction value of a property to the sale value to intangible factors such as location, future uses, and all-round potential. In this section, we discuss some of the basic types of appraisals, and how you can use professional appraisers to your advantage when scouting properties.

Understanding appraisals

You may not always understand how an appraiser reaches a specific value, but knowing the basic methods appraisers use can help you understand something of the rationale for their calculations.

Here are four primary methods of appraising investment properties:

✔ **Market comparison,** or the traditional point-in-time valuation, by which an appraiser compares several benchmark sales and determines a value for the property you're considering

✔ **Cost comparison,** involving comparison of a property's market value against the cost of buying the lot and constructing a similar building

✔ **Income comparison,** a common method to evaluate the relative merits of income-producing properties as well as attempt to gauge the maximum an investor would pay for a property

✔ **Internal rate of return** gives a measure of the annual rate of return an investor can see from a property

The several kinds of appraisal aren't mutually exclusive. Often, it helps to have a couple of different perspectives on the potential value of the asset you're considering. You'll then get a sense of how to make the most of properties others may consider poor investments.

Comparing values

To compare values, you need other values. Circumstances most conducive to the market comparison approach to appraisals are those in which properties are numerous and sales are frequent. Condominiums, single-family houses, and raw land are the most common types of properties for which to use the market comparison method.

No two properties are alike, of course. Variables include age, location, layout, size, features, and overall quality. Conditions in the market at the time of sale also influence value (the values would never change, otherwise). Special features of the property and the property's location — anything that makes it more or less desirable in the market — also factor into its appraised value.

Because market comparison relies on the existence of similar properties for comparison purposes, you may find yourself caught out by a lack of suitable properties. The motivations of the vendors of the properties is difficult to gauge, too, meaning the prices of the properties you select as benchmarks may not accurately reflect a fair value.

Comparing costs

You may be looking for a home to renovate, but comparing the cost of buying an older property and renovating to the cost of building anew may make you think twice. A cost comparison will help you see what the difference is, and may even give you the tools you need to negotiate a better price than the one you're offered for the property.

To compare costs, estimate the cost of developing a new building relative to the one already on the property. Determine the value of the existing building, taking into account depreciation. Because the land value is stable, you won't need to concern yourself with this; simply compare the value of the existing building to the cost of building anew. If the replacement cost is above market value, or above the list price plus any renovations or maintenance you plan, the investment is probably a good one.

To ensure you've made an accurate comparison, seek an appraiser's assistance when calculating depreciation. In addition, construction costs vary depending on location, supply and demand, and inflation. Consult an appraiser to be sure your calculations aren't misleading you (after all, appraisers do their job professionally, and even the most talented amateurs can make mistakes)!

Renovations often increase the value of a home (see our discussion of the advantages of renovations in Chapter 2). Buying the undervalued property and renovating it increases the chance the future value can repay you handsomely.

Comparing incomes

As the moniker *comparing incomes* suggests, this method is primarily useful in comparing the relative value of revenue properties. Other means of appraising the property's value are important too, but the potential of the property to generate revenue and pay for itself is key if you're buying a property as an income-producing investment.

Comparing the net income of properties indicates not only how the properties stack up against one another in terms of income generation, but also how many years they'll take to pay for themselves. Although you may not hold them this long, the ratio you get is important as a comparable, and it will also indicate how much an investor would be willing to pay for your property.

You can determine the net income of a property by simply looking at its financial history — that is, the annual rental income less all the expenses — to determine whether there is positive cash flow (money into your pocket) or negative cash flow(money *out of* your pocket). Typical expenses include property tax, insurance, mortgage interest, maintenance, repairs, and possibly utilities depending on whether you pass that cost on to the tenants or absorb it yourself. After you know whether the property is generating cash or losing it, you can compare the net profit or loss with other properties to determine which property has the most favourable net revenue profit before income tax.

A $1-million property with an annual net income of $100,000 would take ten years to pay for itself. But if your investment strategy pins you to a seven-year payback time frame, you may want to find a comparable property that generates more income or a smaller, less expensive property for which you can achieve higher rents.

Some investors assess the value of a property based on gross income, but this is an inaccurate method as it doesn't reflect operating expenses. Expenses may vary, and unless the assessment looks at the net income, the true value (inclusive of margins) isn't known.

Comparing returns

The *internal rate of return* (IRR) is a measure of how much a property will return the investor annually on the investment made. It differs from the investor's actual return, which reflects the equity less any debts and sales-related expenses.

An internal rate of return of 25 percent, for example, represents the return an income property delivers on the initial down payment. A $800,000 rental property purchased with an initial investment of $200,000, for example, would boast a 25-percent internal rate of return if the projected net cash flow from the property and the anticipated net sale proceeds averaged 25 percent of the initial investment.

An internal rate of return of 25 percent doesn't reflect the income you're likely to see from the property in each year of ownership! Considering the internal rate of return and ignoring the actual cash flow isn't a good idea. You may find yourself counting on a return far better than what you'll actually enjoy. Nevertheless, the higher the rate of return touted, the better the investment promises to be. (The key word here is *promises* — like a promising relationship, it could go either way.)

The IRR doesn't reflect inflation. Ideally, you want an IRR that exceeds the rate of inflation. To compare the actual IRR of various properties, you should adjust the IRR for inflation. Calculate the IRR for a given period, then subtract the real (or more likely, forecast) IRR for the same period. The current inflation rate is available from the Bank of Canada (www.bankofcanada.ca), which also offers a calculator to show the impact of inflation on your investments (www.bankofcanada.ca/en/rates/investment.html). Because an IRR is only an estimate of the expected return on your investment capital, you should consult your tax adviser regarding specific implications for your situation.

Seeking professional advice

We offer tips on how to select an appraiser in Chapter 4. But what do you do with an appraiser after you've found one? Here are a few ideas:

- ✔ **Determine the most appropriate purchase price for a property:** An appraiser's expertise in comparing property values can assist you in determining how much you should pay for a particular property. You can use some of the insights the appraiser offers regarding the property as you negotiate the purchase price of your investment.

- ✔ **Develop a strategy for increasing the amount of mortgage financing available to you:** An appraiser's assessment of a property's value may flag opportunities for you to develop the property. You may be able to use these to argue for a larger mortgage than you may otherwise receive, as in the case of a residence to which you hope to add a rental suite. (We discuss mortgages themselves in Chapters 6 and 7.)

- ✔ **Appeal your tax assessment:** An appraiser's knowledge of the value of your property and the rationale for the appraisal can help you craft solid arguments if you need to appeal your property tax assessment. This is a lucrative segment of many appraisers' business.

- ✔ **Determine future potential of the property:** An understanding of zoning and other municipal policies that can influence a property's potential enables some appraisers to provide insights into how you can make better use of a property. The improvements can help increase the property's value or at least safeguard its value in the event that market conditions seem set to change.

> ✔ **Identify investors with an interest in purchasing your property:**
> Knowing what makes a property valuable allows an appraiser to suggest
> target markets for your property, based on its various attributes, includ-
> ing the value assigned to it. Read more about selling a property in
> Chapter 16.

Of course, these are just some of the ways in which appraisers can assist
you. You may use any of these and other services appraisers provide as you
hone your portfolio and investing strategy.

Assessing Potential

Potential, by its definition, is something not yet realized. It is a power yet to
be exercised. The potential of a property depends on several factors, from
the fabric of the building itself to operating expenses and demand in the
market for that kind of property.

To ensure the potential of the property you're considering buying is worth the
listing price — and to rein in your own enthusiasm for the property itself —
set some goals. Goals may be both personal and financial, and include operating expenses, potential return as an income-producing property and eventual
sales offering, and perhaps even redevelopment opportunity.

Setting goals

We've all seen it: The cute little property that would be perfect, if only we had
the cash to fix it up — and pay the mortgage, the property taxes, the operating expenses, the . . . okay, well, maybe it's not such a good Idea after all.

The process you go through to dismiss the cute but unrealistic properties
from your list of things to buy applies equally well to all the other properties
that catch your interest as an investor. The criteria they have to meet fall into
two major classes: personal goals and financial goals.

Personal goals: Satisfying yourself

The last thing you want when you buy a property is eventually to lose interest in it. There's no reason investing can't be enjoyable, so why disappoint
yourself with a lacklustre asset? And, hey, in the long run you'll care more
about a property that holds interest for you, whether for aesthetic, cultural,
or mere personal reasons.

Depending on your investment goals, you may be limited to a certain type of property, or a certain price range. But knowing whether you want to have hands-on management of the property, to live in it as an occupant with all the joys of an on-site manager's life, or to buy and renovate the property as a weekend project will make all the difference. It may also determine how much you're willing to spend and whether the appraiser's advice regarding possible upgrades is appealing to you.

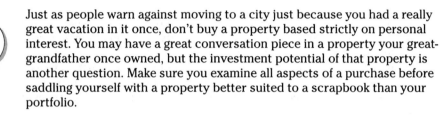

Just as people warn against moving to a city just because you had a really great vacation in it once, don't buy a property based strictly on personal interest. You may have a great conversation piece in a property your great-grandfather once owned, but the investment potential of that property is another question. Make sure you examine all aspects of a purchase before saddling yourself with a property better suited to a scrapbook than your portfolio.

Doug recalls the case of Bob, who had fond memories from childhood of his grandmother's house. When she died, he decided to buy it as an investment. However, he did not get the 60-year-old house inspected. It turned out that it had wood rot and mildew and mould due to poor construction, a leaky roof, and lack of maintenance. Carpenter ants burrowed away in the walls. The electrical wiring didn't conform with fire and building codes and was a fire hazard. To do all the substantial renovations required, all parts of the house would have to be brought up to code standards. This repair estimate was $100,000, exactly what Bob had paid for the property. Because he couldn't rent out the property until he completed the renovations required, Bob's dreams of recapturing his youthful past turned into a textbook case of an investment nightmare.

Financial goals: Satisfying your portfolio

The goal of investment isn't to lose money. The chief criteria for satisfying your portfolio, then, are those that indicate a given property will earn you money rather than cost you.

We discuss various forms of appraising properties and assessing value in this chapter. Whether you're looking at the relative cost to buy and rebuild, the potential for appreciation based on long-term growth trends for the surrounding area, the cost to operate the property, or the property's income-generating potential, you don't want to put yourself in a loss position.

We're cautious, but we do try to think the best of properties. Even if you buy a property on the strength of personal interest, the advisers on your team will probably be able to suggest ways to make it work as a financial investment. Talk to them, and see if they can suggest a strategy to help you find a property that satisfies your personal desires and yields a healthy return.

Operating expenses

Running a standard apartment building in Canada isn't cheap. Rents usually come in at just over double the expenses, which account for between 35 and 45 percent of gross income. Although expenses vary, this is a good rule of thumb. A vendor who suggests expenses are any more or any less may be toying with the facts.

Ask for records and documentation from the current owner for all the expenses, including property taxes, utility costs, maintenance costs, and insurance. That is a good starting point. Your mortgage costs could be less or more than the current owner's, but you're now in a position to estimate the expenses. What was the current owner getting for rental income? Was it a realistic price or considerably under what the marketplace would pay?

You don't need to contract someone else to obtain this information if you can obtain it yourself. However, you need to discuss the information with your accountant, to determine whether the investment will work for you. This is important for three reasons:

- ✔ You receive confirmation of the operating expenses, and be able to understand how the building will fit into your portfolio, what rents you may want to charge, and so forth.
- ✔ You have insight into what a fair price for the asset should be, and better grounds for negotiating with the vendor.
- ✔ An audit identifies areas that may benefit from upgrades and improvements, expenses that you'll want to bear in mind as you negotiate a price for the property but which could make the property more efficient and valuable over the course of your ownership.

An investment property with potential should have reasonable operating expenses. Knowing what these include, and how your management of the property will compare to the previous owner's, will indicate the property's potential to provide a decent return.

The fewer multiples of the net income — that is, rents collected less expenses — required to match the property's purchase price, the better the investment. The more efficient the property's operation — a topic we discuss in Chapter 15 — the lower the expenses. Professional advisers will help you draft a strategy for reducing expenses and making the most of your property!

Cap rates

When you purchase a revenue property, it will have what's known as a *cap rate*. Cap rates are similar to an annual rate of return, insofar as they are measures of the potential cash flow you can expect from the property. In short, the cap rate assumes a property is worth a multiple of its annual net operating income.

Cap rates often drop when markets are strong because more buyers are willing to pay higher amounts for the available assets. The greater the purchase price, the less favourable the net operating income is as a return. The cap rate is important to take into account when assessing a property's potential, because knowing where the cap rate is heading will give you an idea of demand for the asset you're considering buying and what kind of a return you're likely to see on it. Cap rates are hardly a sexy topic, but they're a common indicator of a property's merit.

For example, a cap rate of 6 percent on a $4-million office block indicates that the building annually returns $240,000 in net income to the owner. Had the owner paid $4.5 million or $5 million for the property, the cap rate (and return) would be less.

Should cap rates rise, however — whether because the rents the market will improve or because demand for investment properties decreases — you will enjoy an advantage from having purchased when cap rates were low. You can judge where cap rates are going based on your read of the market cycle, a topic we cover in Chapter 9.

Good neighbourhoods, bad buildings

One indicator of a building's potential is its neighbourhood. You probably wouldn't buy property in a neighbourhood that was heading for a tailspin, because the chances of finding someone to take it off your hands when you want to sell would be pretty slim.

Opportunities await investors who invest in lower-quality buildings in good neighbourhoods, however. Such properties have a potential to deliver steady returns based on the need for affordable product in good locations. Whether you're targeting the apartment or office market, smart management can make a winner out of a building that would otherwise be a loser.

A building may be lower quality for several reasons, including age, decor, maintenance issues, and layout. To make the most of such properties, look closely at what neighbouring buildings have to offer and attempt to match these offerings as much as possible in your own property. This may require you to make some cosmetic improvements, or tweak your marketing strategy.

Living it up

A lack of affordable housing in many better-off neighbourhoods creates opportunities for investors willing to maintain a property that is appealing without being extravagant. Some tenants, including students and young couples, are interested in affordable housing with quirks that make the property memorable, though not necessarily appealing to those able to afford a better-quality apartment.

Making the most of down-market apartments involves basic maintenance. The premises should be clean, the fabric of the building sound, and the apartment should exhibit an overall character that distinguishes it from others on the market. This will allow you to serve a niche market for housing, not with an *ex*clusive property but one that is more *in*clusive. The approach opens up a wider pool of tenants for you, an advantage when times get tough.

Operating costs may be higher for a down-market apartment building unless you make upgrades that ensure the building is energy efficient and won't require constant attention. Regularly inspect the premises to ensure it isn't costing you money to operate.

Working it out

During an economic boom, demand for office space increases dramatically. The top-tier space gets snapped up, shifting demand to B- and C-class spaces that may not have all the features or amenities A-class tenants expect. Tenants for this sort of space always exist, but a portfolio of properties that can cater to both short-term and ongoing needs is something to consider.

The potential of an older office building will increase dramatically through cosmetic changes that make it a more comfortable place to be. Changes to layout can also make it more suitable for one type of tenant over another. Know the market you're aiming for, tailor the space to the user, and market it! An affordable space in a good location will suit many companies, especially smaller start-ups that want to be close to the action but can't pay top dollar.

Renovations versus redevelopment

Gauging the potential of renovating a building versus redeveloping the site is worth doing if you're buying an older property, or one in need of maintenance. Most buildings have a useful lifetime, after which it is more economical to demolish them and start over than renovate them. Unless, that is, you enjoy renovating properties and making something new out of them (if that's your bag, see Chapter 15).

We discuss the calculations required to assess the relative cost of buying as opposed to redevelopment in this chapter under cost-comparison appraisals. Both renovations and redevelopment have their complications as well as benefits:

- ✔ **Complications** associated with renovations include the need to work within an existing building's structure. You have to respect the existing structural elements, potentially raising the cost of the project. You may also need to satisfy municipal requirements. Redevelopment, on the other hand, may make sense financially but could leave you with less than when you began if municipal development guidelines allow you to develop a smaller building on the site than currently exists.

- ✔ **Benefits** of renovating a property include a chance to redefine and reinterpret the existing structure, perhaps making the inner space more flexible and contemporary. You also have an opportunity to upgrade internal systems and create a building that's more efficient to operate. The result could be a building that's worth far more than the old one ever was or could be.

An analysis of the potential a renovation or complete redevelopment has to deliver a return in terms of cash flow, future sales value, and mere convenience will help you to decide whether the expense is worthwhile.

Seeing the Upside of Down-market Sites

Some of the best opportunities for investors lie in areas with the greatest risk. High-risk areas include neighbourhoods where real estate is down at the heel, tired, and worn out. Old industrial districts are examples. Several gutsy investors have been very successful in spearheading the redevelopment of such areas. Take, for example, the revitalization of the Halifax waterfront. Between the aptly named Waterfront Development Corporation Ltd. and

Armour Group — redevelopers of the justly famous Historic Properties complex — hundreds of millions of dollars have flowed into reshaping the former industrial waterfront into a place where people come to shop, wine, dine, and take in the sea breezes. At the other end of the country, in Vancouver, a similar revitalization is underway in the historic Gastown neighbourhood. A new wave of investment in the heart of the city is banking on big returns from an influx of residents. By converting down-market sites into polished residences and playgrounds, the developers responsible for these ventures have made themselves a pretty penny — in fact, a gold coin. Several.

This section highlights some of the opportunities available in down-market areas. Start by listening to the neighbourhood, then see what meshes with your own financial plans. Sometimes you can also make good even when your properties find themselves in areas that slump. Carefully planned strategies can help you cut losses and even turn a profit.

Listening to the neighbourhood

You may wonder what your chances of surviving are when major shifts occur in a neighbourhood — such as increasing criminal activity, a change in demographics, or other transformations that bode ill for the future of the locale. The bad news is that such changes, once started, are difficult to reverse. What you should ask yourself is how significant they will be and how long they will last.

Significant changes and plummeting property values are hardly the sort of thing you want to see. Quebec saw the departure of head offices and an exodus of Anglophones as the province increasingly legislated and implemented a francophone culture during the late 1970s and early 1980s. The neighbourhood in which Peter grew up underwent massive change, raising serious questions about who would buy properties in a province that might declare itself independent. The changes, however, were not permanent. The neighbourhood bounced back, and when Peter's parents retired, their home sold in a few days. Keep in mind, however, that not all changes have such happy endings.

An ability to gauge the future of a neighbourhood — a skill similar to that of selecting a neighbourhood in which to invest, something we discuss in Chapters 1 and 9 — will help you decide the potential a property has to weather stormy circumstances. You may decide to hold the property for the long term or sell in the near term, but understanding the situation you face will make the decision easier.

Holding your ground in a souring neighbourhood is courageous, yet can be sensible if you think the changes taking place are temporary and merely a lateral shift in the local dynamic. In the case of Peter's neighbourhood, life didn't get worse, it just changed. On the other hand, a neighbourhood in which shops are closing and vandalism to properties is increasing may be in for an extended run of bad luck.

Municipal response to the changes and the development of policies to address the issues are key indicators of how the changes may play out. Steps to tackle crime, or the adoption of policies to encourage new economic activities or redevelopment may be all you need to decide not to stick with your investment. Whatever the rationale for your decision, it makes sense to consult with your advisers on the strategy you adopt to survive — or escape — the downturn.

Changing uses

Rezoning isn't the only option in some municipalities; there are also change-of-use provisions. Whether it's the neighbourhood or your property in particular that's spinning its wheels, consider changing the use of your investment. You may do this either through a simple change of use, or by seeking municipal approval to use the property in a new and more lucrative (we hope) way.

Check with your municipality's planning department to see what your options are. The ease or difficulty of the process will vary from place to place, and you'll benefit from having asked questions early on. And don't forget, some particularly obstinate municipalities will take years to allow some activities (we won't name names).

Changing the use of your property has the potential to yield several benefits:

✔ **Makes use of the property you have:** Rather than selling the asset and having to find another in which to invest, you simply change the use and adapt to new circumstances.

✔ **Accepts the viability of the investment:** Just because a neighbourhood has changed doesn't mean you can't make money in local real estate. You just have to identify the kind of property that is doing well, and shift gears to make the best use of the property you've got. Agricultural properties across the country routinely make this sort of change. Farmers seeing diminishing returns from what they usually produce have, in some cases, transformed their farms into tourist destinations. The farms may sell farm produce, such as berries, but fresh berries sell alongside jams, pies, and the tourist attraction. Redevelopment strategies sometimes follow the same principle, knocking down a building of one sort to make way for another serving a different market. The land is fine, but the new building is better!

Redevelopment isn't always the answer. Undertake a cost comparison, and consult with your advisers to see if a change of use makes sense. Consider the following:

✔ **A new use broadens the range of users you can interest.** A property geared toward a greater number of potential users has a greater chance of maximizing its potential than one that depends on a narrow selection of users. Why focus on residential, for example, if you can make over a property to have retail premises on the ground floor and apartments above?

✔ **Broadening a property's potential uses may make it a more valuable asset.** Remember, the greater the cash flow from a property, the greater the amount of mortgage it will support. The greater the potential uses for a property, the more interesting it is to a potential buyer, and if you can demonstrate the potential for greater cash flow, all the better.

Changing the use of a property can help address changes in the surrounding neighbourhood. You may, however, have to make changes to the property itself, which could incur significant costs. Check with your investment advisers to see if changing the use of the property is the best option for you.

Chapter 11

Doing the Due Diligence: What to Watch

*D*ue diligence — the term itself sounds a bit ominous. But it's not a negative thing: When you buy a piece of real estate you can count on due diligence to protect you from troubles ranging from shoddy construction to a bad invest-ment or even fraud. By the same token, undertaking *due diligence* — which is, simply put, the process that allows a buyer to double-check the facts regarding the potential purchase — will reassure you that you're making the best invest-ment possible.

This chapter provides you with the knowledge you need to size up a property and make sure it's all you're hoping for and a few other things besides. We tip you off to some of the dangers that can imperil your investment, given the amount of real estate fraud that takes place in Canada on an annual basis. We also discuss strategies and tools that can help protect you from both fraud and shortcomings in your real estate transactions. Even if you can't identify all the real or potential shortcomings of a property, various forms of insurance are available to safeguard your investment so that it won't end up *costing* you money.

Understanding Due Diligence

Due diligence is unlike the appraisal process, which we discuss in Chapter 10, because it doesn't concern itself with value so much as with the facts regarding a property. The facts may include the appraised value, but they also include the stated condition of the property, whether or not clear title is available, and so forth.

Your job as a real estate investor is to make sure that everything the vendor has said about a property is in fact correct. Performing your due diligence also gives you a chance to satisfy your curiosity on matters that might not be critical, but which could help you gauge the true value of the investment you're about to make.

A careful eye is one of the attributes a good investor brings to real estate transactions. During the due diligence process, you have an opportunity to take a second look at what you think you know about the property, but also at any underlying factors that may create problems.

Buyers typically conduct due diligence after securing a property through a deposit or some other consideration that confirms their genuine interest in completing the transaction (we discuss the sale in Chapter 12). Because it occurs late in the process, buyers generally have enough knowledge about the property to be sure that it's right for them. Whether the due diligence bears that out, however, is another story. Consider due diligence as the final opportunity to review a purchase: Speak now or forever hold your peace!

The due diligence process can last as long as you please. The more complex the deal, the longer it lasts. For a simple purchase, such as a house, it can be as little as 24 hours. For an office tower or industrial building, the due diligence can last months. The less complex the deal, the greater the vendor's expectation of a short turnaround time. You won't find many single-family homes subject to weeks of due diligence!

Due diligence is an important step in the purchase process because it allows for the investigation of issues raised in *subject clauses,* or conditions, in the purchase agreement. These can ensure the deal closes smoothly. If you have lingering doubts about the appraised value of the property, or the prospects for the neighbourhood, due diligence can allow you to conduct further investigation of the property's value and potential. You may also wish to use the time to research the environmental quality of the site (if fears of contamination arise) or to double-check that there are no *liens* (outstanding legal claims) against the property or other issues, formally known as *encumbrances,* that could place you at risk if you buy.

To protect yourself, you can include many of the most contentious issues that could prevent the sale of the property in the subject clauses of the offer to purchase. Should due diligence uncover a significant problem, the subject clauses can give you an exit from the deal. We discuss subject clauses at greater length in Chapter 12.

Generally, due diligence is a means to limit your risk and cut any losses you could suffer when you purchase a property. Due diligence is a priority in three specific areas, which we cover in the following sections.

Sizing up the property

Making sure the property you're about to buy is a good investment is one of the main goals of due diligence. The central part of any real estate deal, the property, should live up to the expectations you have for it. Have you been told the basement doesn't leak during the spring thaw? Call in a specialist to do an assessment. Not sure whether the back portion can accommodate that renovation you're planning? Now's the time to check. (We include additional information regarding property inspections elsewhere in this chapter.)

Confirming the facts about a property, and its potential, can save you from several costly disappointments:

- ✔ You'll know that facts such as square footage are correct.
- ✔ You won't overestimate the property's ability to serve as an investment property.
- ✔ You'll know how the property will perform under various environmental conditions.
- ✔ You won't make the investment with unrealistic expectations.

You may also be pleased to find that the property has more potential, or is even more suitable for your purposes, than you'd originally imagined. Either way, becoming more familiar with a property will allow you to avoid unexpected losses and enjoy greater clout in negotiating financing. This is especially true if you see an opportunity to increase the cash flow possible form the property, and have a plan for maximizing its revenue-producing potential. Lenders will often take the potential cash flow into account when they gauge your ability to service a debt.

Sizing up the vendor

Due diligence is also important in giving you a clearer picture of a property's vendor. We're not necessarily talking personal information here, but rather their reasons for selling and any reasons why you might want to be wary of what they're offering. In short, due diligence is an opportunity to shed further light on what the vendor brings to the table, aside from an asset that interests you (we discuss reasons a property might be for sale in Chapter 12).

Becoming familiar with the vendor is important, because circumstances that aren't readily apparent may be behind the sale. These include several factors that could influence the asking price. Should you dig up information about the vendor that doesn't quite match what you've been told, you might want to seek legal counsel in case there's potential for fraud, which we discuss in this chapter.

Suspicious about a vendor? Checking a vendor's credit rating through Equifax (www.equifax.ca) may tip you off to potential dangers of the sale. You should also make sure every last bit of information in the offer to purchase is correct — down to the vendor's name and company (if included). Inconsistencies can indicate a potential problem.

Sizing up the deal

Due diligence is part of closing the deal, but the deal itself also requires scrutiny.

Two particular areas of interest to you are the financial and legal aspects. Double-crunch the numbers to make sure they work, and fit in with your worst-case scenario for your portfolio. Make sure numbers such as the appraised value, potential return, and similar elements mesh with official figures.

Legal considerations include making sure you can secure clear title to the property, and that no competing claims to it exist. Verify that any renovations you have planned are in accordance with municipal bylaws.

Consult with your advisers to ensure the deal meets with their approval. They have the skills to examine the deal in greater depth than you can, and you should involve them as necessary throughout the due diligence process.

Inspecting a Property

A basic part of any due diligence related to real estate is the property inspection. Professional inspectors are available from several fields. Depending on their expertise, they may be able to provide a general inspection or examine and assess particular parts of the property.

We flag elements to which you may want to pay particular attention, and provide tips that may make it easier for you to determine which parts of a given property require the closest inspection. We also discuss inspection reports, and occasions when you should seek professional advice regarding inspection results.

What to watch for

Depending on the age, type, and size of a property, an inspection could take as little as a few hours or as much as several days. The inspection should take into account the material integrity and soundness of a building and how the material integrity and soundness equip the building to withstand a major event such as a flood, fire, or earthquake. Your attention should focus on three main areas:

- ✔ The building itself
- ✔ Site conditions
- ✔ Servicing and infrastructure

These three elements all play into the future value and potential risks you face if investing in the property.

The cost of an inspection reflects the time required to conduct it and prepare a report, but generally ranges from $300 to more than $1,000 for a residential property. If you're considering a commercial property, the cost will be much higher. Older and larger properties often take more time, resulting in more expensive reports, as more problems are typically present. The qualifications and expertise of the inspector, as well as demand in the market, also factor into pricing. The number of variables means some negotiation on price is possible, but make sure you obtain a written quote in advance.

 You should make a point of being present during the property inspection, to see exactly what was inspected, and if there are problems, what those problems are. It might reveal issues that will make you want to run away from the deal as quickly as possible! When speaking to the inspector, take notes and ask questions regarding the possible cost of repairing any problems found.

The building council minutes for a condominium property should include inspection reports conducted on any part of the property. Previous reports could flag areas that you might want to investigate in any report you commission prior to your purchase.

The structure itself: Building confidence

A building inspection will tell you what's right about a building and what's wrong. The inspector you employ should inspect every accessible part of a building, including the following:

- Interior
- Exterior
- Attic area and roof
- Basement and crawl spaces

Keeping watch

Some of the features a property inspector will watch for are common to several types of real estate, others are pertinent to just one or two. Obviously you won't get an inspection report on an elevator shaft for that suburban bungalow you're buying to rent out, but the elevator might be on the list if you're buying a four-storey apartment property.

To give you an idea of things to watch for, here are a few categories that a property inspector assesses:

- **Driveway:** Condition of the concrete or asphalt, slope, potential for water and debris accumulation
- **Walkways:** Condition of the concrete or paving stones
- **Roof:** Slope and type of covering; condition of the flashing around chimney and vents; presence of skylights

- **Attic:** Condition, evidence of leaking, insulation extent and type
- **Laundry area:** Condition of the laundry tub and machine hook-ups; presence of electrical outlets and number
- **Garage:** Overall condition; type of firewall and condition; electrical outlets; presence of leaks and other factors that may affect overall maintenance
- **Interior rooms:** Overall condition; type and quality of floor coverings, wall coverings, and ceiling; assessment of plumbing, venting, and electrical systems; assessment of toilets, sinks, shower stall, and tubs
- **Basement:** Presence of cracked walls, sloped floor, and condensation; condition of windows and other means of access; presence of smoke detectors and sump pumps; type of electrical outlets

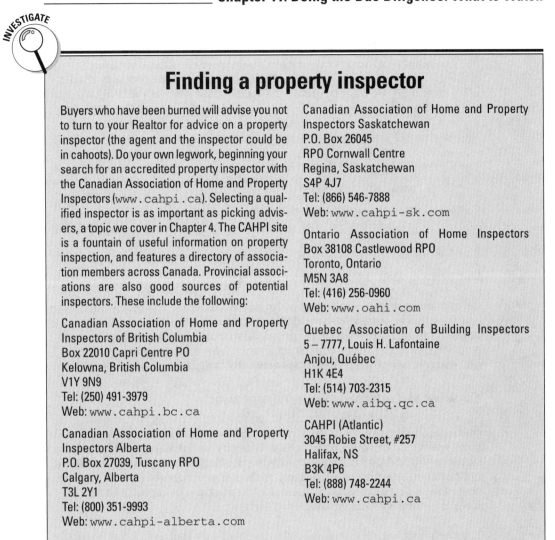

Finding a property inspector

Buyers who have been burned will advise you not to turn to your Realtor for advice on a property inspector (the agent and the inspector could be in cahoots). Do your own legwork, beginning your search for an accredited property inspector with the Canadian Association of Home and Property Inspectors (www.cahpi.ca). Selecting a qualified inspector is as important as picking advisers, a topic we cover in Chapter 4. The CAHPI site is a fountain of useful information on property inspection, and features a directory of association members across Canada. Provincial associations are also good sources of potential inspectors. These include the following:

Canadian Association of Home and Property Inspectors of British Columbia
Box 22010 Capri Centre PO
Kelowna, British Columbia
V1Y 9N9
Tel: (250) 491-3979
Web: www.cahpi.bc.ca

Canadian Association of Home and Property Inspectors Alberta
P.O. Box 27039, Tuscany RPO
Calgary, Alberta
T3L 2Y1
Tel: (800) 351-9993
Web: www.cahpi-alberta.com

Canadian Association of Home and Property Inspectors Saskatchewan
P.O. Box 26045
RPO Cornwall Centre
Regina, Saskatchewan
S4P 4J7
Tel: (866) 546-7888
Web: www.cahpi-sk.com

Ontario Association of Home Inspectors
Box 38108 Castlewood RPO
Toronto, Ontario
M5N 3A8
Tel: (416) 256-0960
Web: www.oahi.com

Quebec Association of Building Inspectors
5 – 7777, Louis H. Lafontaine
Anjou, Québec
H1K 4E4
Tel: (514) 703-2315
Web: www.aibq.qc.ca

CAHPI (Atlantic)
3045 Robie Street, #257
Halifax, NS
B3K 4P6
Tel: (888) 748-2244
Web: www.cahpi.ca

Particular buildings may have other specific areas worth inspecting. Feel free to request an inspection of an area that concerns or interests you. You want to make sure you're comfortable with every aspect of the building, and its suitability for the uses you have in mind, before you buy.

Site conditions: Grounding the deal

Site considerations such as drainage also demand consideration from an inspector, as these could factor into the future value of the property if a disaster strikes or you want to undertake a significant renovation or addition to the existing structure.

Here's what the property inspector will commonly assess:

- ✔ Garage, carport, and garden shed
- ✔ Steps, paths, and driveway
- ✔ Retaining walls separate from the building itself
- ✔ Fencing
- ✔ Septic field
- ✔ Surface water drainage and storm-water runoff

Certain areas of your site may concern you even before you receive the property report. These may fall outside the inspector's expertise or demand the attention of an accredited professional. Advice or a second opinion from an engineer, lawyer, or other consultant simply helps further your knowledge and comfort with the decision you eventually make regarding the property.

Servicing and infrastructure: serving it right

Though not part of the property itself, you should consider investigating the servicing (such as sewer, water drainage, electricity, cable, propane gas, and so on) provided to your property. Age, capacity, and maintenance history are factors worth taking into account as you consider whether disruptions in the operation of your property are likely. Although you may not have to bear the cost of repairing damage to municipal infrastructure, being without key services is extremely inconvenient.

You can check with the building department of City Hall as to what types of municipal utilities or servicing are currently available, and if not, when they will be available, if at all, and what projected costs there might be for users.

Privately delivered utilities such as telephone and Internet connections are worth factoring in, too. More and more areas enjoy high-speed access, but it's still far from universal. The level of Internet service in a particular area may affect how you use the property or position it to potential tenants.

Inspection reports

Any given property report has the potential to deliver good, middling, or just plain bad news. Sometimes the conclusions won't be news to you; occasionally they dredge up more information than you really wanted to know. Beyond basic details such as the property's address, the date, and the extent of inspection, what information can you expect to see in a report? And, more importantly, what do you do with it? As you read the report — typically a point-by-point assessment of the property that can run from just a few pages to hundreds of pages in length — focus on areas of particular interest to you and future buyers. These include the following:

- ✔ **Reason for the inspection**: This is a vital element because it indicates whether the inspection was routine or if a specific concern prompted it. A report conducted as part of due diligence generally counts as a routine report.

- ✔ **Areas not inspected:** As well as outlining the areas of the property that were inspected, the inspector will flag areas the inspection didn't cover. Perhaps the areas were inaccessible, or some obstacle prevented an examination. You may need to hire a specialist to investigate these areas if the inspector considers it beneficial. Some specialists you may need to consider include electricians, plumbers, painters, drywallers, mechanical contractors, and pest control and extermination specialists.

- ✔ **A summary of the property's condition**: The summary is the heart of a property report. It will detail both the good and the bad of the property.

- ✔ **A list of significant problems**: Problems flagged in the summary may require varying levels of attention. The inspector will detail the most urgent. Factor these into your negotiating strategy and your decision to purchase the property. Serious problems may prompt you to decline the purchase altogether.

When to seek professional advice

Major deficiencies in a property flagged in the property inspector's report may require you to contact a professional — a structural engineer, an environmental consultant, or even a tree doctor. Whether you involve a professional will depend on the inspector's opinion as well as your own commitment to purchasing the property. A professional can provide a detailed analysis of outstanding problems prior to your purchasing an investment property. The professional assessment may indicate problems that are too costly to make the purchase worthwhile; likewise, the professional may recommend a solution that allows you to negotiate a bargain price for the property that turns it into a winner.

A professional opinion can help, and may assist you in negotiating a better price in light of the improvements the property requires.

Inspection report to the rescue

The information a property report brought to light proved especially helpful to Cindy and Jack. They had been looking to buy a character house for some time, and eventually found one the current owner had renovated and was offering for sale at an affordable price. As part of their purchase offer, they included a condition that a professional home inspector provide a report on the property within 10 days of their offer's acceptance. The deal's closing was contingent on a satisfactory report.

The report was a real eye-opener. It showed that the current owner had extended the house without first obtaining a local building permit. The renos had extended the foot print of the house beyond the permitted setback distances from the property line, and also gave the house a larger area than that permitted on the lot. In addition, the wiring was inappropriate for the building and a potential fire hazard.

The condition in the purchase offer allowed Cindy and Jack to walk away from the deal hassle-free. By purchasing the property, they could have become liable for the unauthorized building extension (which the municipality could have asked them to remove), and the wiring would have had to be completely re-done to comply with local building and fire codes. The alterations to the home would have meant prohibitive costs, not to mention stress they didn't need.

A favourable report from the initial property inspector rarely requires further confirmation from a professional with specialized knowledge, but you may wish to temper an overly optimistic report with a second opinion.

Protecting against Fraud

No firm data exists on how many fraudulent real estate transactions occur in Canada each year, but even the handful of spectacular cases that have hit the news from time to time are enough to warn potential investors that the risk exists.

Protecting yourself against real estate fraud involves knowledge of the warning signs combined with a keen sense of intuition. Wiser folks than we point out that evil is dangerous because it looks so normal, and the same is true of fraud. Just because it looks legal doesn't mean it is! We hope the tips we offer here will make you a bit more street-wise as an investor, and alert you to schemes you may encounter.

Understanding real estate fraud

In the context of real estate transactions, fraud involves breaches of laws prohibiting passing forged documents or obtaining credit using false identities or pretenses. The opportunities to assume a false identity have increased significantly in our information-rich age. Real estate fraud typically takes two forms:

- **Fraud for shelter,** in which someone uses inaccurate or false documents to secure a property or gain title

- **Fraud for profit,** in which someone uses false documents to achieve an undue profit on the sale of the property or leverage a mortgage well in excess of the actual value of the property.

Taking shelter

Fraud for shelter is particularly dangerous because you may not detect it until after you've bought a property — at which time it's too late to prevent. It typically occurs during discharge of title, allowing someone to gain title by using a false identity or gaining authority to transfer the property to someone other than the legitimate owner.

Peter recalls one story in which someone with a relatively common name was able to secure several properties because her documentation appeared to match that required of the property owners. Her common name allowed her to pose as the rightful owner of the properties, and to develop her own real estate portfolio.

To prevent identity theft, always shred your sensitive documents. Don't release confidential information about yourself to strangers or others who have no business knowing it. And above all, demand proper identification whenever you're engaging in transactions related to your property. Expect the same precautions among those with whom you deal.

Raking profits

More common than fraud involving title is mortgage-related fraud. Mortgage fraud accounts for well over $300 million in fraudulent transactions each year in Canada, according to industry estimates.

Fraud for profit typically allows someone to secure a mortgage that's significantly more than the property's appraised value warrants, and the fraudster secures the extra cash on the sale of the property. Alternatively, a property may be flipped through a fictional buyer for a value higher than the previous purchase price.

Buying the gold mine . . . or shaft?

Raymond found a nice house in his area of choice after several months of property hunting. The property, advertised with a simple "For sale by owner" sign, seemed too good to be true. When Raymond knocked on the door, the man who answered said he needed to sell it "right away," because he was being relocated to another city. He was open to any and all offers. The homeowner accepted Raymond's offer on the spot. Raymond proceeded to sign the necessary paperwork and set about arranging the necessary financing. Just before the deal was supposed to close, Raymond's lawyer called with the news that the deal was fraudulent, and would not complete.

What happened? The property owners, it turned out, were going through an acrimonious break-

up. One partner had left for a month to reflect on his future solo life. The partner Raymond dealt with had done a pretty good job of nearly selling the house during his partner's absence by forging the signature of the vacationing partner on the documents necessary to transfer title. He had hoped to get the proceeds of the sale and skip town in a hurry (that part of his story was true). Needless to say, Raymond's lawyer managed to discover the scheme and thwarted the deed.

Had Raymond bought the property, the deal would have been as sour as the previous owners' relationship. Raymond would have been on the hook for costs associated with the deal, and without the dream property he thought he had acquired.

A savvy lawyer will usually spot, from the circumstances of the deal, when fraud for profit is underway. New regulations in some provinces are designed to ensure that lawyers are not complicit in fraud, by requiring that the discharge of a mortgage occurs within a specific time frame.

Avoiding fraud for profit is important for real estate investors because this kind of fraud skews the value of a property, and hence their portfolios. A fraudster may find it useful — for a limited time, anyway — but an improperly valued property will leave you holding the bag. Rigorous due diligence, including verification of the property's appraised value, helps ensure you don't buy into a property with an inflated value.

Estimates indicate that fraudulent discharge of mortgages happens about four times more often than fraudulent transfer of land.

Spotting warning signs

Several indicators will tip an investor off to deals that may not be as clean as they seem:

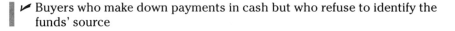 Buyers who make down payments in cash but who refuse to identify the funds' source

✔ Lenders who fail to confirm a buyer's sources of down payments, income or employment

✔ Financial institutions that trust mortgage brokers to confirm information rather than double-checking it themselves

✔ Owners who register a second mortgage without informing the first lender

Some real estate consultants offer to assess the risk of fraud associated with a specific property, but you're safer always to operate under the assumption that the challenge of spotting fraud indicators is your job. The best way of doing this is to obtain independent verification of any data that could potentially be falsified.

Here's some information worth verifying:

✔ **Purchaser's employment information,** to ensure work and salary documentation are genuine

✔ **Statements of a purchaser's equity,** to ensure financial accounts are in order

✔ **Property attributes,** including measurements, zoning, easements and covenants

Misrepresentation of any or all of these points constitutes a serious breach of trust at the very least, and possibly fraud if the purchaser is using the false information for gain through the transaction. The same consultants who will assess the risk of fraud can usually assist you in verifying the information associated with a property.

The involvement of professionals such as lawyers and appraisers in real estate deals has diminished in recent years, according to some critics. The decline has meant less scrutiny of real estate deals by people and more by automated systems. Involving as many individuals as possible to vet your transaction could keep you from becoming another hapless victim of real estate fraud.

Addressing fraud

Regulatory changes in recent years have attempted to stem the growing tide of real estate fraud. But what should you do if you suspect something funny — distinctly not so if you're on the receiving end — is going on?

Report it, of course. Think blue! Not the police — not at this point, anyway — but the Blue Pages of your phone book, where you'll find listings for the government agency in your province that oversees the financial side of real estate transactions. The provincial or local real estate association will direct you to the regulatory body for Realtors in your province, and the provincial law society will help you if you believe a lawyer is at the heart of the trouble.

Because real estate fraud has the potential to undermine confidence in the real estate market, most professional associations with significant interest in property deals have policies regarding real estate fraud. The information available through these organizations will help raise your awareness of the difficulties you face, as well as offer you advice on how to protect yourself from fraud in the future.

If you believe the vendor, a partner, or some other individual has taken you for a ride with your investment, contact a lawyer. Present an accurate record of the alleged fraud and seek a legal opinion as to whether you should prosecute the case. (We discuss selecting a lawyer in Chapter 4.)

Limiting Risk

Due diligence can sometimes put you where you never expected to land. And sometimes it doesn't put you where you need to be. Either scenario makes insurance an important tool to have on hand. It can help protect you from pitfalls you expect as well as pitfalls you didn't expect.

The results of a thorough due diligence exercise may serve to flag types of coverage you should have, while having other types of insurance will ensure you aren't caught short if you need to back out of a transaction because of something you discover. Here are the major types of insurance to consider.

Better disclosure, fewer problems

The better the controls on information required for a real estate transaction, the less chance of fraud spoiling the deal.

For example, the Law Society of B.C. enhanced reporting procedures for lawyers in the wake of the case of a Vancouver lawyer disbarred in 2002 following allegations that he misappropriated millions of dollars in trust funds instead of applying them to the payout and discharge of various mortgages.

A vendor's lawyer in B.C. must now discharge a mortgage and file proof thereof. The purchaser's lawyer must receive confirmation of the filing within 60 days or report the vendor's lawyer. The system lays legal obligations on both the vendor's and purchaser's lawyer, ensuring neither side can evade responsibility should an opportunity for fraud arise.

Property insurance

Property insurance, the basic coverage that property owners have for a variety of protections, covers claims after you take ownership of a property. It generally includes fire, theft, and liability insurance (which protects you from any lawsuits for injury to those who enter on or into your property). Depending on where you live, you may also want to have earthquake or flood insurance. If you are on a known flood plain, you may not be able to obtain insurance, or if you do, it could have high premiums, high deductibles, and only partial damage recovery.

Speak to at least three insurance brokers, and obtain comparative quotes in writing. Read the fine print — it reveals the exact coverage you receive along with any exclusions, limitations, and deductibles. If you don't clearly understand the document, speak to various brokers, and then obtain advice from a lawyer who specializes in insurance law. You can normally obtain a free or nominal-cost initial consultation by checking with your provincial lawyer referral service, provided by the provincial law society or provincial branch of the Canadian Bar Association.

Discoveries during the due diligence process may not always help you. Though being on a flood plain may not be a disaster waiting to happen, discovering the local fire service is a skeleton crew of volunteers is a different story. Depending on the risks of your particular situation, and the chance of what insurers like to call "an event" occurring in your particular circumstance, you may find yourself facing limited coverage or no coverage at all. If insurance is granted, the broker may require a higher deductible or greater premium. Consult your insurance broker to see what coverage is available, and whether the coverage is sufficient to satisfy your concerns.

Just because the property of your dreams wasn't eligible for a certain level of coverage when you first bought it doesn't mean it won't get coverage in the future. Any time you reduce an insurance risk you can go back to the insurer and request a re-evaluation and argue for reduced premiums. Deficiencies discovered during due diligence may be small hurdles you can overcome as you improve the property and make it a more valuable — and insurable — asset.

Title insurance

Title insurance protects a buyer against defects and errors in a property's *title* — the owner's right to a property. The insurance provides coverage from the time you take title until you sell your property. Title insurance will cover the legal fees incurred in defending your ownership of the property, as well as your actual financial losses. (We discuss other forms of insurance, such as property insurance, that are integral to managing your investment, in Chapter 14.)

Problems with title can include

- ✔ Competing claims of ownership or interest in the property

- ✔ Survey errors that pre-date your acquiring an interest in the property, resulting in your not receiving what you were told you were receiving in purchasing the property

- ✔ Outstanding building code issues that render a building on the property non-comforming under municipal bylaws

- ✔ Liens and other encumbrances, such as discharged mortgages that remain on title

The cost of resolving many of these issues falls on the shoulders of the new owner, but title insurance provides coverage against such claims. Many companies in Canada provide title insurance; one of the largest is First Canadian Title (www.firstcanadiantitle.com).

Title insurance also provides protection against forms of real estate fraud affecting title. Similar to other forms of real estate fraud discussed elsewhere in this chapter, these include

- ✔ **Fraudulent refinancing of your property,** in which someone using fake identification and a forged signature offers your property as security for a mortgage you're left to account for

- ✔ **Fraudulent transfer of title,** whereby fake identification and a forged signature enables someone to obtain title to your property

Though many lawyers have mixed feelings toward title insurance, it has advantages in these circumstances. On the other hand, title insurance may postpone the resolution of issues until they become a problem. This may create difficulties when it comes time for you to sell the property.

 Some investors use title insurance to reduce the legal costs associated with closing a deal. Traditionally, lawyers would search a title prior to a property purchase closing. Today, all major financial institutions accept title insurance in place of a title survey demonstrating the prospective purchaser's clear title. However, a full search as part of the due diligence process will provide genuine security that title is indeed clear and free of encumbrances.

New home warranty programs

Several private, third-party warranty programs exist across Canada for new homes. New home warranties — as the name implies — insure new homes against defects for up to ten years. All new homes must carry insurance of some form, usually offered by the developer as part of the sale package.

Although most buyers wouldn't expect defects in new homes, insurance is a useful protection against unforeseen problems that your due diligence won't necessarily uncover.

Depending on the purchase deal, the builder could include the warranty coverage premium in the purchase price, or have it up-front and paid for by the buyer, or split the cost 50/50 with the buyer. If you are buying a two- or three-year-old home that is still covered by the original home warranty protection, you will want to check on the terms of the coverage and make sure you understand them, or ask questions during the due diligence period to satisfy yourself. Make sure everything is in writing in case you need to rely on it.

Resident builder homes, residences built by the future occupant, are among the several types of housing exempted from new home warranty coverage. Beware of homes developed by erstwhile resident builders offered to you directly. They may not have the coverage they legally require, which may not only cause headaches for you but also leave you on the hook for repairs should a defect emerge.

Guaranteeing peace of mind

Some home warranty coverage is offered through the provincial government, and other through private insurers. To locate approved builders and warranty providers in your area, contact the government department or ministry in your province that addresses home owner protection issues. These include

✔ Alberta New Home Warranty Program: www.anhwp.com

✔ Association provinciale des constructeurs d'habitations du Quebec: www.apchq.com

✔ Atlantic New Home Warranty Program: www.ahwp.org

✔ British Columbia Homeowner Protection Office: www.hpo.bc.ca

✔ Manitoba New Home Warranty Program: www.mbnhwp.com

✔ New Home Warranty of Saskatchewan: www.nhwp.org

✔ Ontario New Home Warranty Program: www.newhome.on.ca

Suppliers of private new home warranty programs include

✔ London Guarantee Insurance Company: www.londonguarantee.com

✔ National Home Warranty Programs: www.nationalhomewarranty.com

✔ Residential Warranty of Canada Inc.: www.reswar.com

✔ Wylie-Crump Limited: www.wyliecrump.com

Chapter 12

Closing the Deal

• •

• •

After you find a property you think will be a good investment, you've got to make it your own. In this chapter, we talk about negotiating a deal that fits your investment goals and closes as quickly and as smoothly as possible.

Because each transaction is as different as the people involved, we can't offer you the secret formula for the perfect deal. Instead, we walk you through a range of strategies that are good to have in your back pocket when you're at the negotiating table. (Knowing a few negotiating strategies will also prove helpful if you ever decide to sell your property, something we discuss in Chapter 16.)

Negotiating a deal successfully is just one part of closing on your new purchase, however. To make sure your investment gets off to a good start, you need to clear away the financial and legal details. You also need to make sure the appropriate people are paid for their roles in the transaction. We guide you through the finer points of the purchase, and offer a checklist to help make sure you dot your *i*'s and cross your *t*'s. We also tell you what you need to know about becoming a full-fledged owner as you prepare to manage your investment and enhance its value.

Before the Deal: Understanding the Seller

By the time you decide on a property to buy, you've already done a lot of research. You know the market conditions, what the other properties in the neighborhood are selling for, and what you're willing to pay for this property. So what's the next step?

That's right, more research!

After you know what you want, you need to understand what the other party wants so you can use that knowledge to make your offer more appealing to the vendor. Being able to identify and meet the other party's needs may help you close the deal faster and make it one of those win-win situations people like to say they made happen. Your research might even make you realize that you're better off not pursuing the property.

Discovering the seller's motivations and limits is difficult, however, so expect to do a bit of detective work.

Looking for clues

Typically, your real estate agent plays a lead role in negotiations you undertake for a property. That doesn't mean you're out of the picture, however! Your role is to guide the negotiations, which requires that you keep abreast of what's going on with the property, the back-and-forth that's happening with the vendor, and any factors that might give you (and your Realtor) an edge over any competing bidders for the property.

Preparing to negotiate involves looking for clues that indicate why a property is up for sale. The information you discover will help you determine how to make your offers more appealing to the vendor. In the following sections, we go over common sources of clues.

Digging in

Tax assessments and other public records regarding the property you hope to buy may indicate possible reasons why the property is on the market. The kind of information you're looking for is the size of the tax bill, and any increase from year to year. A sizable increase over the previous year or series of years, or significant changes in the assessed value of the property, could indicate a vendor for whom the tax burden has become too much.

Rising property tax rates may also give you pause, but on the other hand, the property may fit with your investment strategy. You may also have some ideas for the management of the property that will improve its performance, making good on an asset the vendor is finding difficult to hold.

Property tax assessment records are typically available through the local provincial assessment office. Search fees may apply to specific requests, depending on how much information you require.

Reading up

Court records may hold clues to the property's current fortunes, and whether the vendor is facing pressure from creditors. A simple search for references to the vendor, whether an individual or corporate owner, in the database maintained at the provincial courthouse for the area may turn up relevant claims. Many papers run listings of the latest lawsuits in their respective areas, meaning you may just need to do a quick search of the newspaper's archives to find a bit more about the vendor.

The archives of most major newspapers in Canada are accessible for free through public libraries. Court records, while usually open to the public, typically require payment of a search and viewing fee. But the actual search to see if the record exists shouldn't cost you anything.

Logging on

Google (www.google.ca) is often the best, and cheapest method of searching for dirt on a vendor, or anyone else for that matter. The depths of the Internet contain an ocean of information, and while not all of it is true (remember to verify what you find out), you may find some useful clues. The information will help frame your discussion and negotiations with the vendor.

Being savvy is good; being too precocious isn't. Many people will become uncomfortable if you flaunt the fact that you've done background checks on them (unless they've agreed to the check). Be discreet, and, as much as possible, check the accuracy of your information. You don't want bad information to be the basis for a negotiation process that costs you a prime asset.

Of course, clues regarding the seller's motivations may be obvious to you. The condition of the property may suggest an owner unable to maintain or manage it in the manner tenants, neighbours, or the city wanted. Though you may not get to know the vendor personally, you may discover through conversation or through your broker that personal reasons are prompting the sale of the property you hope to buy.

Research isn't high espionage, so don't feel you need to worm your way into the vendor's life to get some real dirt. Often, a broker acting on behalf of the vendor will know the sorts of things you need to make a deal work in your favour. An open, sympathetic, and alert attitude on your part as you discuss the sale of the property can yield information that could prove important to your position. Loose lips sink ships, as the old saying goes. Being a savvy investor means being savvy to the personal and practical reasons someone might be selling, and using that information to your advantage.

You may occasionally find yourself in a position where after selling one property, things didn't quite come together for the new property in which you planned to invest. Perhaps you were the losing bidder, the vendor halted the sale, or some other obstacle came up. No matter; if you can't find an alternative listing, you may have luck putting in an unsolicited offer on an attractive property the owner wouldn't otherwise have thought of selling. The kinds of clues we've discussed in this section are useful indicators of properties that may not have hit the market, but which are potentially good additions to your portfolio.

Understanding reasons for selling

Many of the reasons for selling a property are pretty much the same whether it's a house owned by the current occupant, or an existing investment property. Here are some of the common reasons for selling:

- **Owners' difficulties:** Perhaps the current owner finds the property more difficult to manage than he expected, or has personal reasons for selling such as a desire to invest in a different type of asset or reduce investments in real estate altogether. Or perhaps disputes among joint owners — about 80 percent of partnerships will run into difficulties at some point — require the sale of the property. Providing an answer to the owners' exit strategy presents opportunities to pick up a solid investment property for less than market value, helping the existing owner to eliminate the stress of managing it.

- **Poor management:** Deterioration of a property thanks to poor management may also create opportunities for acquiring a prime investment property at a reasonable price. With a sound management strategy, you can avoid some of the difficulties the previous owner encountered. You first need to consider whether it's worth the work you'll need to invest in fixing up the place (we talk about assessing a property's potential in Chapter 10 and management in Chapter 13).

- **Foreclosures and tax sales:** Properties sometimes find their way onto the market through a court order when the previous owner encounters difficulties paying creditors or the taxman. These so-called *distressed* *properties*, can offer prime opportunities to acquire properties for less than current market value, but this isn't always the case. You'll need your knowledge of the property and local market conditions to guide you in making your offer. Typically, only the top bid is accepted (in fact, almost always, unless other factors such as the reputation of the bidder come into play) because a claim could otherwise come forward alleging that creditors of the previous owner were short-changed.

Property tax sales occur but they are rare. Most owners try to prevent losing the equity they've got in a property on account of the relatively smaller amount owing a municipality in property taxes. They are going to borrow money from a lender or family to pay the tax arrears, or list the property for sale. Many provinces allow seniors to defer their property tax payments until a home sells, with proceeds from the sale going to pay the taxes plus a modest rate of interest.

✔ **Market conditions:** The owner may believe the market is about to slump. This is when the research you've conducted pays off. If you think the market is doing just fine, thank you very much, you may be able to secure a property for a price that reflects the downward trend. If the seller's guess has you thinking twice, try to buy the time you need to double-check your assessment and try to capitalize on the vendor's perception to work the price down. Either way, bid confidently and try to secure the best deal possible.

✔ **Trial balloon:** Some vendors will use you to test the waters for their property, making you party to an exercise in property valuation. This could be because they want to sell but aren't quite ready, or because they're trying to determine their own negotiating strategy. Don't let them waste your time. Weeding out unwilling sellers is an important part of your research. You don't want to waste your time indulging their curiosity about the market, let alone giving them insights into your own plans.

✔ **Time to sell:** Of course, a property may come on the market simply because the current owner thinks it's the right time to sell. Although the reason is straightforward, it could mean negotiations will be more difficult, and you'll have a tougher time drawing up a "win-win" agreement because the vendor's primary motivation is to secure the highest possible return.

Whatever the seller's motivation, you're out to secure a profitable investment. Though the property might appeal to you, make sure your emotions don't carry you away. Respect the investment plan you've developed for yourself, know your limits, and just say no if you can't live with the terms the seller offers.

Savvy negotiating: Understanding motivations pays off

One of our friends, we'll call her Barb, used to live in rural Saskatchewan. She recently bought a condo in Regina where she plans to spend her retirement.

To finance her new home, Barb had to sell her old home. As in many small towns, news travels quickly, and soon most of the locals knew that Barb was heading to Regina and had to sell. One family in the town saw an opportunity to play on Barb's need to buy and thus move into a better-quality home than their own if they could make the best offer of the few buyers interested in buying Barb's home.

Barb eventually sold to the family because she needed the cash to finance her new home. They, in turn, were able to acquire a second property for a price that was fair but slightly less than Barb might have received if her neighbours hadn't known she was under pressure to sell.

Getting the Deal You Want

Finally! You're itching to own and you know that you've found the place you've been looking for. It's time to play *Let's Make a Deal*, a game that — for you — has three rounds:

- ✔ Offer
- ✔ Evaluation
- ✔ Acceptance — you win! — or Rejection — play again! — or Counteroffer — not so quick, mate!

In this section we walk you through each stage, explaining the ins and outs of the process and offering tips to help you get the best deal possible.

Even though you may feel tempted to pretend you're a ruthless real estate mogul, you will reap more rewards through gracious deal-making at every stage of the negotiation process. Deals that work well for you and the vendor may lead to future deals and business relationships. Be serious and professional, but not unreasonable in negotiations.

Don't go it alone! Your advisory team is an important part of the deal-making process (we discuss selecting advisers in Chapter 4). It also helps if you and your advisers meet the vendor face-to-face. Conferences of this sort aren't always possible or feasible, but they can help build a more amiable relationship that gets the deal made.

Making an offer

Making an offer on a property isn't as simple as calling up the owner and saying, "Hey, Doug, I like your place. Can I buy it?" In real estate, an offer is a formal document written up by the prospective buyer's broker and passed to the vendor's broker. It may all seem mighty impersonal, but you have a lot of influence over how the deal proceeds.

Being straightforward is one of the ground rules. Even if you're playing your cards close to your chest, every purchase offer requires a few basic elements:

- ✔ **Who is offering to buy the property:** Are you buying the property as an individual, a partnership, or a corporation? (We discuss the various types of ownership in Chapters 2 and 8.)

  Be completely clear about who you are. Opening the door to an _assignee,_ someone who could take over your position in the deal, may benefit you by allowing you to step back and enjoy an interest in the deal but not necessarily a front seat. Think twice about doing this, however, as the move could potentially create confusion about who the purchaser actually is. Similarly, clearly stating that you're bidding through a corporation may prevent you from bearing personal liability for legal claims if the deal falls through. (We discuss the fine lines between personal and corporate liability in Chapter 8.)

- ✔ **What amount you're willing to pay:** This amount should reflect everything you know about the market, the neighbourhood, and the seller's motivations. An knowledge of the market, and a gutsy willingness to pay top dollar will ensure you have the attitude needed to outwit competing bidders for the property.

  Offer the lowest reasonable price but make sure it's just that — reasonable. Low-balling could turn off the vendor, and may make you seem less than serious about doing a deal. By the same token, be ambitious and start with the ideal price and terms as determined by the market research you've done. The vendor, depending on the rationale for the sale, may find your lower bid attractive. Don't anticipate rejection; if the vendor counteroffers, you enjoy an opportunity to exact concessions. Concessions reflect the nitty-gritty of negotiating.

- ✔ **Any clauses you want to impose:** Your offer will come with strings attached, in the form of subject clauses. These are conditions you choose to place upon the vendor that will have to be fulfilled if your offer is to move to completion. You should state a specific date by which the clause has to be fulfilled, as well as the person whom the clause benefits (this also allows them to waive the condition if they choose). Setting conditions on the deal ensures you get the property you want and can also give you extra negotiating room. Some common clauses in your interest that you might write into the deal include:

- **Confirmation of financing:** You may need time to arrange a mortgage, or may plan to use proceeds from the sale of another property or investments to finance your new purchase. This clause will give you time to make sure you have the funds required, as well reducing your risk should you not be able to secure the financing you hoped to get.

- **Deposit funds:** Your offer should state what happens to any deposit you place on the property to secure your interest. Ideally, your deposit should be sitting in an interest-bearing account, with interest accruing to you in trust until the deal closes. Should the deal fail to complete, you want to ensure you get your deposit back with the interest it was earning.

- **Conveyance of free title:** You want to be sure title to the property you're buying is clear, that is, free of any outstanding legal claims. Ensuring that's the case is typically the responsibility of the vendor. This condition should state what has to be done, and whose responsibility it is, and establish the deadline for clearing the title. A lack of clear title could limit your ability to make the most of your investment. It may require more time to clear the title of one property than another, but you'll want to set a time limit if you can't wait for title to be cleared. Some properties have too many claims upon them to make them worth your while, and a clause requiring free title will allow you to exit negotiations if that's the case.

- **Satisfactory inspections:** You may want to seek a second opinion about the property you're hoping to invest in, whether it's from your business partner, spouse, or an engineer. They may have expertise and insights you don't have. A structural engineer may notice weaknesses in the building that could save you headaches as a manager. Whatever the reason, make sure you set aside enough time to get the opinions you need to make an informed decision about your purchase.

- **Resolution of site conditions:** A growing area of concern for many purchasers is the legacy of a site's previous uses. You may want to stipulate that the vendor remediate site conditions, such as landscaping so that the site approximates its original condition. Soil contamination is a more serious concern that could leave you liable to claims from the owners of neighbouring properties, so it's in your interest to make sure the vendor removes unwanted or dangerous materials (such as asbestos or urea formaldehyde foam insulation) from the site prior to the deal closing.

Condo (strata) units and apartment buildings may require special clauses. For instance, you may want the right to check out an apartment building owner's books to be sure that the building's cash flow is everything you think it is. Or in the case of a condo, you may want to subject the deal to information in the minutes of the strata council and engineers' reports on the integrity of the unit and building. This information could strengthen your bargaining position, allowing you to suggest a lower price than the vendor is asking. The minutes could also alert you to potential structural problems that may need repairs in the future. Knowing the potential dangers helps you make a decision so future assessments, if any, aren't a complete surprise.

The vendor may also stipulate certain conditions that you'll want to take into account:

- ✔ **Removal of conditions in the event of a backup offer:** The vendor may receive a competing bid that seems more attractive. To ensure the vendor has a free hand in the other negotiations, she will ask that you remove your conditions within a set period of time (usually 72 hours).

- ✔ **Confirmation of vendor take-back mortgage:** The vendor may have financed the last deal for the property you're interested in through a mortgage broker. To ensure the financing can be paid off through the proceeds from your purchase of the property, the vendor may ask for time to arrange this with the mortgage broker.

- ✔ **Deposit funds:** Just as you want to make sure your deposit is secure, the vendor wants to make sure the funds you deposited go toward the purchase price after the deal completes. The vendor will stipulate that they're nonrefundable and payable after all your conditions have been met.

- ✔ **Credit check:** Of course, you're an honest dealer. But the vendor may want to make sure that's the case, especially if she wants to pay off a debt with your payment for a property. Give her time to confirm your credit worthiness, so she's confident that you're her best offer.

- ✔ **Legal review:** You may want to make sure that you're buying a solid investment, but the vendor will also want to make sure you're offering a legitimate deal. Make sure you give the vendor as much time as you need yourself to make sure the deal is up to snuff and doesn't include legal loopholes or traps.

- ✔ **Expiry date:** Set a time limit for the evaluation period, usually a minimum of 24 hours, but for more complex deals you might extend it to three or four months. If you're considering purchasing urban land or a commercial property, it may sit under contract for months while due diligence proceeds. Make sure you have enough time to satisfy yourself and close the deal properly. Too short a time frame and you may not be able to satisfy your questions about what you're buying; too long, and the vendor may question your motives.

- ✔ **Closing date:** When do you want this all wrapped up? After your offer is accepted, you need a final date that gives both parties enough time to complete any outstanding due diligence and necessary paperwork. The date should respect both your desire to take possession and the needs of the vendor.

The various elements in the offer to purchase are important because not only will they become the basis for the purchase contract if your offer is accepted, but also you want to make sure they give the negotiations the momentum that helps you and the vendor to reach a satisfying deal.

Evaluating the bid

What are you waiting for? After you've submitted your offer, the vendor will evaluate it and eventually respond with outright acceptance or rejection, or a counteroffer and/or an offer to discuss. While you're waiting for the vendor's response, however, stay cool, but be collected. You'll be doing your own due diligence, enjoying a perfect opportunity to do research that strengthens your negotiating position. The information that you gather in fulfillment of the subject clauses (see above) can help you in the event that you have to respond to a vendor's counteroffer.

Hot markets raise the potential for competing bids, often several on a single property. Don't let your guard down! A willingness to make a better offer, based on both your research and the advice of your advisers, is key to gracious — and professional — negotiating. Your bid shouldn't be so far out of line with the state of the market that you lose credibility, but the early stages of a hot market can see significant appreciation in a property's value during the sales process. Outbidding a competitor, then selling the property further on in the cycle, may net you a healthy profit.

Planning to rent? Think ahead!

Nancy was about to buy her first house in an up-and-coming neighbourhood in Toronto. A single professional, Nancy knew the list price was in her range but she also knew having a tenant would help her job of making the payments that much easier. After Nancy took possession of the house, she searched for a tenant, and wasn't able to find one for three months — three months in which Nancy wasn't seeing rental income that she had been counting on.

Had Nancy been more experienced, she would have made advertising for tenants a condition of her purchase offer. The clause could have allowed her, in agreement with the vendors, to advertise and show the property to potential tenants. The clause would have given Nancy a headstart on renting in what was admittedly a tough market. An abundance of rental properties meant that anyone interested in moving would have to give their existing landlord a full month's notice or end up paying double rent. Since Nancy bought the house early in the month, so automatically, the earliest that any prospective tenant could give notice and be able to move in would be approximately two months after she closed the deal.

Alternatively, Nancy could have included a clause in her offer that set the closing date four days before the start of the month in which she planned to rent the property. This would have been another way for Nancy to avoid losing three months' rental income.

Finding acceptance

Like the moments just before the contents of the sealed envelope are revealed at the Oscars, the time waiting for the vendor's answer is filled with anticipation. But having kept on top of the market and having addressed your concerns about the property during the vendor's evaluation period, you'll be ready to handle counteroffers and maybe even exact concessions from the vendor.

Of course, if your offer is accepted, then you're ready to move on with closing the deal and becoming an owner. But if your offer is rejected, you may want to consider submitting an amended offer that addresses the vendor's concerns. Similarly, if the vendor thinks there is a prospect of a deal, they will counter-offer and set a deadline for acceptance, rather than simply reject your offer and walk away.

Trying again

A counteroffer will test your negotiating skills. Ask your Realtor exactly why your offer was rejected. If you don't ask the question, you won't know the answer. Perhaps the vendor has discovered something about you in the course of the evaluation period that he feels he can use to leverage concessions from you. Perhaps the vendor knows a better offer than yours is in the offing and wants to see how far you're willing to go to secure the property. It helps to be able to provide an argument for the competitiveness of your offer. And whatever the circumstances of the counteroffer, be candid but professional as you hammer out a deal that satisfies both you and the vendor.

Dotting i's, Crossing t's: Financial and Legal Paperwork

Closing can be within a few days of making an offer for a residential property or several months away for a complex transaction. Various changes may have taken place in the market or in financing conditions since the sale, but now's the time to get your papers in order and become an owner.

Wading through the legalese

Your advisers should be able to help you wade through the legalese on the various documents, but here are a few tips that will help you prepare. The most important document is the offer to purchase, as it will become the sale agreement if your offer is accepted. It sets out the terms and conditions between the parties and will become legally binding on the satisfaction of any subject clauses. To help you understand what it involves, we've included a sample form in the appendix to this book.

All contracts must be in writing to have legal effect. Although you may make verbal agreements, always make sure all agreements relating to the purchase are set down in the offer to purchase, and ultimately, the sale agreement. That includes any withdrawal of your offer, which you have a right to do at any point prior to acceptance. But remember, if your offer has been accepted and signed prior to receipt of your withdrawal, a binding contract has occurred.

Tallying the costs

The offer to purchase will include a few financial figures in addition to the sale price of the property you hope to acquire. Keeping track of these figures could play an important role in structuring the deal. We discuss the figures of interest in the following sections.

Paying down the purchase

The cash deposit required to secure the property for you while the purchase completes is an important element of the contract. It usually takes the form of a cash deposit equal to 5 to 10 percent of the purchase price. The deposit makes the sale agreement binding.

Make sure your deposit money goes into a lawyer's or real estate agent's trust account, where it is protected by provincial legislation. Never give your deposit funds to an individual or company that is not a lawyer or licensed real estate agent. Also, make sure your deposit is in an interest-bearing trust account with interest to your credit between the deposit date and closing date or when the funds are returned to you.

Make any purchase offer conditional on various requirements being met to your satisfaction. For example, subject to your financing, home inspection satisfactory to you, review of the condo corporation's financial statements and minutes over the previous two years, and whatever other conditions you care to impose. If your conditions are not met, and a deal isn't reached, you automatically get all your deposit monies back. If you place a deposit and remove all conditions and then change your mind and don't complete the deal, you could lose your deposit monies, plus be sued for any financial shortfall the vendor could suffer, if they can't sell the property for the same price or more to someone else. Obtain legal advice on your rights in advance if you are considering trying to get out of a deal in this type of situation.

Though it is in your interest to offer the smallest possible deposit so that you don't tie up any more money than needed, it is sometimes worth laying down a bit extra to make it clear that you're serious about closing the deal.

Consult a lawyer if you opt to withdraw an offer or proceed with rescission of a signed contract. Several provinces have a rescission period that allows the parties to back out of a deal without penalty, but you may wish to incorporate such a clause in your offer to purchase. This could help avoid litigation regarding non-performance of an agreement to purchase or actions seeking damages for your failure to buy the property.

Court action is costly, however. Costs are currently between 25 to 40 percent of the damages awarded, meaning you need to take a good look at what you're actually going to gain from the time and stress involved in launching a lawsuit. (We discuss liability and court action in Chapter 8.)

Chatting about chattels

Chattels include the moveable elements of a property. Occasionally, however, doorknobs and chandeliers also feature in the list of a property's chattels. Because tax implications are associated with the value of the property attributed to the land, the property, and the chattels, clearly stating what the chattels include is important.

Defining what each of these categories comprises is also a good idea. Chattels can be particularly contentious. A chattel is moveable, but items such as doorknobs and chandeliers that you might assume to be fixtures can be treated as chattels. Generally, fixtures aren't named in the agreement and are considered part of the purchase price. But to avoid future legal difficulties, it's worth stating that all fixtures are included except those specifically excluded in the agreement. You should also include a clause listing chattels.

Some properties have a history, a location, or a reputation that deserves a value in its own right. This is particularly true of commercial properties, less usually of residential properties. The value of this component, known as *goodwill*, should also feature in the offer to purchase. This relates specifically to the allocation of value when buying a property for tax purposes. For example, you could allocate W amount for the market value of the land, X amount for the depreciated value of the building, Y amount for any chattels (such as furniture) included in the building, and Z amount for "goodwill" — the long history of being leased to good, long-term tenants that make the revenue stream more attractive (and valuable to you as an investor).

The purchaser and vendor can enjoy tax benefits depending on the allocation of values to W, X, Y, and Z. For example, based on tax advice, you could negotiate a lower overall sale price for the commercial building to the purchaser, in exchange for a higher value on the land, as the land could have capital gains tax savings. Scott, an investor Doug knows, has a professional accountant review his purchase offer. One of the accountant's strengths is analyzing the tax implications of real estate investments. He usually encourages Scott to negotiate chattels separately from the property itself, to allow for extra leeway when it comes to calculating profits.

Offering a rewarding fee

Any commission owing on the sale of the property, usually a percentage of the purchase price, should appear in the contract to purchase. The contract should also indicate to whom the commission is owing. We talk more about this in the next section.

Paying the piper (and everyone else)

Closing a sale requires paying not only the vendor, but also the various advisers and professionals who've helped you make the investment. To help you keep track of the various payments required, consult the chart of closing costs later in this chapter.

The vendor, not the purchaser, pays the commission owing to the Realtor. If you use a "buyer broker," this Realtor splits the sales commission according to an agreed-upon formula. The vendor and the Realtor will negotiate the commission in advance and confirm it in writing in the listing agreement. The amount of the commission paid is negotiable, and can vary considerably, depending on the circumstances.

The standard fee for legal services for transferring the title of the property and doing the mortgage documentation is also negotiable. You may want to comparison shop, as a considerable variance may exist in a competitive marketplace. The standard fee is 0.75 percent to 1 percent of the purchase price for legal services, but could be higher or lower based on various factors. Taxes and disbursements (out-of-pocket expenses) are extra, of course. Have a fixed quote for all the legal fees confirmed in advance in writing to avoid any confusion. The quotes also make it easier for you to cost out the transaction!

Doug's friend Sam takes a particular interest in watching every penny he spends when buying a property. The attention he gives each deal allows him to maximize his net after-tax profit (with the help of an accountant, of course). One of his strategies is to use the same real estate agent to both buy and sell properties. The solid relationship allows Sam to negotiate an attractive commission on all his deals.

You also have to take several taxes into account:

✔ Sales taxes, provincial taxes, and the federal goods and services tax (GST), are applicable to chattels (making it important to factor the value assigned chattels into the purchase offer).

✔ Though the GST isn't charged on resale homes, it may be owing on substantial improvements to a property.

✔ Provincial property purchase tax, which varies from province to province, will also be due.

A non-resident withholding tax is a special charge applicable on properties purchased from non-residents of Canada. Equivalent to a quarter of the purchase price, it is a safeguard that assures the Canada Revenue Agency that funds are available should the vendor owe capital gains taxes. Because collecting the amount from a foreign vendor might be difficult, Revenue Canada targets you.

Shelling out: What to remember

In addition to the actual purchase price of your investment, you have to pay other expenses on or prior to closing. Not all of these expenses will be applicable. Some provinces may have additional expenses. We provide space (see Table 12-1) for you to keep list the amount you expect to pay on your particular investment.

Table 12-1	Closing Costs	
Type of Expense	*When Paid*	*Estimated Amount*
Deposits	At time of offer	
Mortgage application fee	At time of application	
Property appraisal	At time of mortgage application	
Property inspection	At inspection	
Balance of purchase price	On closing	
Legal fees re property transfer	On closing	
Legal fees re mortgage preparation	On closing	

(continued)

Table 12-1 *(continued)*

Type of Expense	When Paid	Estimated Amount
Legal disbursements re property transfer	On closing	
Legal disbursements re mortgage preparation	On closing	
Mortgage broker commission	On closing	
Property survey	On closing	
Property tax holdback (by mortgage company)	On closing	
Land transfer or deed tax (provincial)	On closing	
Property purchase tax (provincial)	On closing	
Property tax (local/municipal) adjustment	On closing	
Federal Goods & Services Tax (GST)	On closing	
New Home Warranty Program fee	On closing	
Mortgage interest adjustment (by mortgage company)	On closing	
Sales tax on chattels purchased from vendor (provincial)	On closing	
Adjustments for fuel, taxes, etc.	On closing	
Mortgage lender insurance premium	On closing	
Condominium maintenance fee adjustment	On closing	
Building insurance	On closing	
Life insurance premium on amount of outstanding mortgage	On closing	
Moving expenses	At time of move	

Type of Expense	When Paid	Estimated Amount
Utility connection charges	At time of move	
Redecorating and refurbishing costs	Shortly after purchase	
Immediate repair and maintenance costs	Shortly after purchase	
House and garden improvements	Shortly after purchase	
Other expenses		

It's All Yours: Taking Possession

Assuming ownership of your new investment property is a major accomplishment — congratulations!

But the work isn't over yet. Before you get down to the business of managing your new purchase, you need to take some legal and practical steps.

Arranging the final details

On the legal front, your lawyer confirms that the deal has indeed closed and send you a letter with all the documents relating to the purchase, including an accounting of the fees and disbursements that you provided in trust. Your lawyer also obtains and registers the various discharges of mortgages that were paid out of the purchase price, unless the vendor's lawyer is taking care of these matters. Your lawyer also ensures that all other commitments regarding the property have been satisfied.

Closing the deal

When the time comes to close the deal for your investment, you have a lot on your plate. Keep in mind a few key elements that will help make the process easier:

✔ **Devise an appropriate budget for closing the deal.** Be sure you know what the fees and disbursements associated with the property transfer, mortgage and associated closing costs will total. Then be sure you have the finances in place to cover these.

✔ **Get your documents in a row.** You may buy groceries without a shopping list, but we don't recommend you buy a property without a list of the documents you need to receive from the vendor when the transaction closes. Keep the documents you receive in a single place in some sort of logical order. Knowing what you need and keeping them in one place will help prevent essential paperwork from going astray at the last minute. The agreement of purchase and sale should itemize most of the documents you require, so there shouldn't be any surprises for either the vendor or you.

✔ **Visit the property you're buying when the transaction closes.** Buying real estate isn't like some folktale in which the treasure disappears as soon as the hero thinks it's secure, but this step is necessary to confirm that you're receiving the property in the condition you expect. If it's not in the condition you expected, talk to the vendor.

✔ **Kiss a few babies.** Flash a smile and press the flesh with the current tenants if your purchase is a revenue-generating property. A few simple gestures will help get the relationship off to a good start.

Follow up any concerns with the vendor immediately, just as you would with any other purchase that might not seem up to snuff. After the property has been registered in your name and you've taken full possession, you're ready to begin managing the property as part of your investment portfolio. We tell you how in Part IV.

Part IV
Building Value: Managing Your Investment and Seeing a Return

The 5th Wave   By Rich Tennant

I know renovations can add to a property's value, but don't you think this might be a little excessive?

In this part . . .

Knowing how to successfully manage the property you buy is almost as important as understanding the fundamentals of investing. Knowing the ropes gives you more flexibility in terms of the properties you can consider, and thus helps diversify your portfolio.

The following pages offer lots of background and tips aimed at helping you to manage your property smoothly — and see the kind of returns you're striving for.

Chapter 13

Managing Properties

· ·

· ·

*B*ecoming a property owner means becoming responsible for all that goes with the property, from the maintenance to any tenants that you inherit. Perhaps you've never managed anything in your life and see property as a lucrative investment option. Maybe you've been a manager but always avoided dealing with people (not everyone's a glad-handing gadabout — or wants to be one).

Becoming a property owner means more than just making a cash investment and hoping for a return. In this chapter, we discuss the finer points of property management. Ultimately, as the property's owner, you're responsible — and if you choose to contract out management duties, you're responsible for the people acting on your behalf.

We help you decide whether to manage a property yourself, and how to foster good relations with tenants. We also discuss how to attract tenants who will pose the least problems for you; after all, management isn't just a one-way affair — you can only work with what you've got. We also discuss the rights and responsibilities landlords and tenants owe one another, and ways to defuse disputes that arise. Things don't always go smoothly, even in the best of relationships; establishing ground rules from the start will go a long way to ensuring things stay civil.

Building connections

Don't be afraid to ask for help! Regardless of the type of property you've got, several organizations can support you in your efforts to become a better manager. You might want to consult your local apartment owners' association if you own a residential property, or the Building Owners' and Managers' Association (BOMA) if you own a commercial property. Professional help of various sorts can help you improve your people skills if you're good at managing assets but come up short when dealing with people.

Choosing a Property Manager

You've invested in real estate because you want to make money. One of the keys to doing that is to buy in the right neighbourhood at a good point in the real estate cycle. But being a smart and prudent manager is also an important part of the equation. What's that? You're not a good manager? Well, you can always contract out the job.

We discuss some of the considerations surrounding property management in this section, and whether you should opt to be the property manager yourself. Many novice landlords eventually put their properties up for sale, frequently at a loss, likely due to their lack of property management knowledge and skills. Investors sometimes gets tired of the chronic frustration, stress, and time involved in dealing with the problems created by their own poor management.

Good management isn't just about making the executive decisions that create value in the property. A host of other, secondary decisions go into creating value, from selecting tenants to managing vacancies, maximizing revenues, and minimizing expenses. Grasping the impact each of these factors has on the property's long-term value is an integral part of a property manager's job.

To self-manage or not to self-manage

That is the (potentially million-dollar) question! As a property owner you'll have to deal with any number of tricky issues:

✔ Late-paying tenants

✔ Disruptive tenants

✔ High vacancies

✔ High turnover

✔ Vandalism

✔ Sporadic cash flow

✔ Disputes with tenants

✔ Regular complaints, real or frivolous

✔ Never-ending maintenance costs

If you'd rather perform your own root canal than deal with these sorts of things on a daily basis, then you have an important option to consider: farming out your dental . . . er, property management . . . duties to somebody who *is* well-suited for the job.

To decide whether you should manage a property, take a good honest look at the attributes of the property, your own skills and interests, and the potential benefits you'll enjoy from contracting out the management responsibilities.

Filling the property manager's shoes

Worries and challenges aren't the norm for an investment property. If they were, we could recommend lots of other places for you to put your money (and if you're still wary, we discuss some of them in Chapters 1 and 2). More important, if you buy a well-run property expecting a certain cash flow, you don't want to find yourself slipping into a situation where headaches are constant, cash flow suffers, and your investment isn't the deal you thought it was.

To gauge whether it's a good idea to manage your property yourself, take these factors into account:

✔ **The type and number of properties you have:** One revenue property is likely easier for you to manage than a handful, and a portfolio with a half-dozen investment properties may not leave you with as much attention as you would like to devote to your new residential property. Knowing your limitations is important.

✔ **The size of the property:** Some residential properties really require a manager even if they're your only investment, simply because their size warrants it. On the other hand, a warehouse property twice as large as your apartment block may be easier to manage because there's just one tenant.

Typically, a property with more than eight tenants warrants its own manager. We discuss selecting a manager elsewhere in this chapter.

✓ **Your interest and experience in management:** Chances are, if you're not a people person and have little experience in a management role, you'll be better off contracting out the management of your property. The amount spent hiring a qualified manager will return to you in the form of fewer headaches and hassles, and a property that may require less attention and improvement when the time comes to sell.

Your time and peace of mind is worth at least as much as you'll spend (once you've shopped around, of course!) on a manager who can do a job you're not interested in.

Choosing self-management

Now that we've given you a few caveats about the risks of managing your investment property yourself, you're probably wondering under what circumstances you *should* try to manage a property. We're glad you asked!

Small revenue properties, those with fewer than eight units, often benefit from the owner's direct involvement in management. Single-family homes and duplexes typically come under the supervision of the owner, who selects the tenants, and handles maintenance and many of the other chores required for his own home. More complex properties require the attention of a dedicated manager, however.

Even if you manage a property yourself, don't feel obliged to take care of routine maintenance such as landscaping, snow removal, and the like. You can easily contract out these services, especially if you have a handful of properties. You may also wish to give the tenants responsibility for these services in exchange for a small reduction in rent, cutting your expenses while giving them a stake in the upkeep of their home.

Self-management, regardless of your capabilities, may be necessary if you're outside a metropolitan area. Professional managers are not always available in smaller communities, and people willing to manage your property may not pass muster with you. The positive side is that a revenue property with no suitable managers is probably small enough for you to handle yourself.

Many colleges and apartment owners' associations offer basic courses in property management. Even if you've never managed anything or anyone before, take the opportunity to learn something new and expand your expertise!

Soliciting outside help

Two options exist if you decide to contract out management of your property. For a residential property, you can choose a *resident manager* — possibly one of your tenants — to oversee the daily affairs of the property. Alternatively, you could contract a *professional manager,* either an individual or company, who would add your property to a portfolio of properties under management. The option you choose will largely depend on the complexity of the property and the value you expect to see from employing a third-party manager.

Generally, only apartment buildings with eight suites or more can justify the employment of a full-time resident manager. Crunch the numbers to be sure your investment in a manager is worthwhile.

Tenants as managers

Contracting with a tenant to manage your property has its advantages. You may grant the resident manager a cut in rent in exchange for services, an arrangement that can sometimes be more economical than contracting with a professional manager. The tenant lives on site, is familiar with the building and has a stake in making sure the building is in good shape. Often, a married couple makes a great resident "manager."

Look for the following qualities in a resident manager:

- ✔ Honesty and integrity
- ✔ Conscientiousness and a willingness to do the job, not just take a cut in rent
- ✔ Ability to assume the responsibilities required
- ✔ Pleasant and easygoing personality
- ✔ The time and skills needed to monitor the property and undertake basic cleaning and maintenance

The responsibilities of the resident manager can vary, but generally include the following:

- ✔ Collecting rent
- ✔ Making deposits
- ✔ Keeping the grounds neat and clean
- ✔ Making minor repairs and maintenance
- ✔ Showing vacant suites and signing up new tenants
- ✔ Keeping records
- ✔ Promptly advising you of any problems and serving as your representative to other tenants

And how much you pay a resident manager will vary depending on several factors, such as the following:

- ✔ The duties and responsibilities you assign her
- ✔ How many units she is looking after
- ✔ The degree of maintenance and upkeep required
- ✔ The amount of interaction with other tenants required
- ✔ Reporting and record-keeping requirements

A salary could vary from a break on rent of 10 to even 100 percent. Or, you may wish to pay the resident manager in addition to a break on rent. You need to decide how much the manager's services are worth to you?

The resident manager of a smaller property should command the respect of fellow tenants. A resident manager who isn't respected or who incurs the envy or bad feeling of tenants isn't the best person for the job. In such a case, you may be better off contracting out management, or selecting another tenant.

Property managers, good, bad, and . . .

Property management comes in many forms, whether you're managing your own home, a rental property, or a commercial property such as a restaurant. Peter has his share of anecdotes gleaned from a lifetime of watching people, working under them, and even taking a lead role himself.

He remembers, for instance, one of his first experiences of managing a property — taking care of the homes of neighbours when he was a teenager. It was part of a fledgling property services business he ran in the summer. The home of one client bore the ravages of a Great Dane, the door jambs and other elements showing signs of wear and tear. He quickly understood why so many landlords don't allow tenants to keep pets. He also learned the value of not letting wear and tear get out of hand. He wasn't being paid to give advice back then, but he knows what he would have recommended.

A few years later, Peter found himself the resident manager of an apartment building in New Brunswick where he did a fair to middling job taking out the garbage, cleaning house, and generally making sure the landlord heard the tenants' perspective (and vice versa). By taking care of the property, he aimed to make sure tenants didn't have to worry about it.

The worst management story he can tell, however, regards a roadhouse he worked at one winter along the Alaska Highway. Management of the property was delegated to a confident young manager who wound up costing the property owner much more than the owner expected. The manager was confident but lazy. When the owner came back after the winter, he had to fix ailing equipment and restore order to the operations of the property (a motel). The moral of the experience? Regardless of how hard good help is to find, it pays to get someone with the experience needed to manage your property so that it runs smoothly, costs are kept under control and tenants remain happy.

Companies as managers

Owners of properties with over 12 units (or the equivalent number of tenants in several properties), as well as absentee owners, manage their properties through a professional management company. You'll pay a fee for the service — typically 2 to 5 percent of the property's gross monthly revenue — yet have the advantage of working with a company far more experienced in management than you are.

Specific advantages of contracting out management to a professional firm include the following:

- The firm will have established bookkeeping procedures, accounting practices, and management systems, reducing hassle for you.

- The firm typically has access to suppliers who can provide bulk-buying discounts and good service.

- You'll avoid worrying about the selection of tradespeople for maintenance, as the management company will usually have a roster of contractors with whom it works.

- Tenant relations will be the firm's responsibility, including showing apartments, selecting tenants, and negotiating tenancy agreements and leases, though you'll set the ground rules (such as no pets, no smokers, and the like).

- Collecting rents, paying bills, and maintaining relevant records will be the manager's job, with your involvement limited to review of the monthly statement to ensure operations are running smoothly.

Because the management company will handle only the tasks as you assign to it, you may also authorize the appointment of a resident manager if you believe you should have someone on site. As with any business arrangement, have a written management contract that clearly defines the role of the management company and the resident manager, if applicable. And make sure your lawyer reviews the contract before you sign it!

Becoming an employer

Hiring an individual rather than a management firm as a property manager means you're effectively acting as an employer, if not formally then certainly insofar as you've got someone reporting to you. To ensure the relationship goes smoothly, it helps to follow a few basic principles in choosing and working with the manager:

✔ Give the manager a job description clearly outlining his or her management responsibilities.

✔ Develop a basic policy manual so that the manager knows what to do in the event of an emergency, dispute with tenant, burst pipe, or other unexpected event. Your lawyer and another competent professional should review the manual, however basic, to ensure it doesn't open you to legal claims and also reflects current best practices for the type of property in question.

✔ Have a contract with the manager stating payment terms, notice time in the event you wish to terminate the arrangement, and so forth.

Otherwise, hiring a property manager is not unlike contracting for any other type of service, except that you may find yourself in contact with the property manager more often than with other contractors with whom you deal.

Attempt to short-list at least three desirable candidates for the position of manager before making your decision.

Property managers in Canada may have the Certified Property Manager (CPM) designation, awarded to those who complete a set of courses prescribed by the Real Estate Institute of Canada (www.reic.ca).

"My Roof, My Rules": Smoothing the Transition with Tenants

To ensure the change in ownership goes smoothly, and that your relationship with tenants gets off to a good start, we recommend that you make introductions promptly, state clearly any changes you hope to make, and work to develop a solid relationship with existing tenants. This section will consider these various recommendations in greater detail.

The first rule for a smooth transition: Bear in mind that when their home changes hands, many tenants will have concerns about their new landlord's intentions. They may have questions regarding potential redevelopment or a change in use. Or they may wonder if you'll raise their rent, or if you have plans in the works for major renovations. Some may even hope — either secretly, or very, very vocally — that you'll sink a bit more cash into upgrading the property than had been done in the past.

The right stuff

Certified Property Managers pursue a program that combines education and experience. Candidates for the designation learn to analyze a property's physical status and fiscal performance, to draft and implement policies and procedures designed to improve the short- and long-term value of properties, and to manage and improve relationships between tenants, residents, and employees. In addition to financial training, candidates must complete a rigorous ethics course, and agree to abide by a code of professional ethics.

An ownership change that goes poorly may make it more difficult for you to secure tenants in future. Tenants will not hesitate to warn their friends from renting from a landlord they consider unprofessional.

Making introductions

Whether you manage a property yourself or through a third-party, it pays to introduce yourself to tenants. Some landlords prefer to remain low-key, in part because of the risks of being known by tenants who may later become dissatisfied and become a problem. On the other hand, a personal relationship can help forestall difficulties, especially in smaller properties.

If you plan to employ a property manager, it makes sense to introduce the manager at the same time that you introduce yourself. This reinforces the authority of the manager and ensures a smooth transition.

In addition to introducing the manager, you should introduce a few others. You could include a regular maintenance person if he's likely to be a regular visitor to the property. Too many people, however, and the tenants are likely to feel overwhelmed!

Any introductory visit should be brief and to the point. Try to arrange a time when tenants are least likely to be disturbed. Post a notice in the building's foyer indicating the time of the proposed visit. For those you can't visit, prepare a short letter of introduction.

Think a personal touch is reserved for small properties? Peter knows a major property developer who follows up with residents of his projects when there's a concern about the quality of workmanship. Often, his suites are occupied for several months. The personal touch reinforces the personal concern the developer takes, and makes the residents feel there's genuine interest in their welfare. The same attitude can work for landlords, too.

Making changes

Depending on the property you buy, you could have plans for major changes, or for simple adjustments that tenants will hardly notice. Regardless of the scale, make sure you communicate clearly and promptly with tenants regarding the proposals and any work schedule.

By law, you have to let a tenant know at least 24 hours in advance if you have to access their suite for any reason. The better your relationship with tenants, the less notice you'll likely have to give, so treating tenants with respect in this regard will pay off in making life easier for you in the future!

Here are some typical changes that require special attention:

- ✓ **Common-area housekeeping:** Even if you only let the tenants know once, it tells them what to expect and whether they should be concerned about the strangers walking through the building.

- ✓ **Major maintenance or landscaping:** Tenants shouldn't have to see a ladder outside their kitchen window before they know you're putting new siding on the building! They will be less than impressed with your approach to landlording. Major work to the grounds or the building itself is something tenants should be informed about.

- ✓ **Service to the building infrastructure:** Tell tenants if you have to turn off the hot water or test the fire alarm system. Cutting services without notice, or creating an unexplained disturbance, is hardly the way to win friends, though you may influence people — alas, not in your favour!

Whether you're talking film shoots in the neighbourhood or street repairs or the start of a construction project on an adjacent lot, telling tenants that things are happening, and being willing to discuss their concerns, will go a long way to building a relationship with them. And it'll ensure they stay *your* tenants, and don't become someone else's!

Building relationships

Cultivating an ongoing relationship with tenants, especially if you're not the most outgoing person, may be difficult. A range of traditional and creative options exist if you're looking for means of developing better relationships, however. Consider the following possibilities:

✔ **Send greeting cards:** Do you know when your tenant's birthday is? Perhaps Christmas or New Year's is approaching. Whatever the reason you choose, acknowledging special days in the calendar can further your relationship with them and make them feel you actually care. Just as with any other business, it makes sense to pay attention to your client when things are going well (not just when they have complaints). You can nurture much goodwill this way.

✔ **Jazz up the common-area decor:** Does the lobby of your building look drab, with only your licence to operate an apartment building breaking up the monotony of the builder-beige walls? You may want to consider adding a bouquet of flowers or some other decoration that livens it up a bit, and makes it more welcoming. Even if you have a single-family home with a granny flat, making sure your place has a welcoming feel can go a long way to ensuring a positive attitude about your role.

✔ **Hosting a meet-and-greet:** Ever considered a tenant appreciation event? Many other businesses show their appreciation for clients, but property investors seem less prone to hosting events that build goodwill. Of course, you face several limitations in hosting such an event — it may not work if you don't already have a good relationship with tenants, and you'll face limits on the kind of event you host. A gala dinner is out of the question. But even a morning "open house" style event with coffee and pastries where tenants can mingle and chat may be enough — do it in your newly jazzed-up lobby!

No matter how simple the gesture, it will help boost both tenant loyalty and your reputation as a reputable landlord with the interests of tenants at heart.

Regular communication, no matter the reason, will foster open, respectful relationships. We aren't suggesting a message in the lobby every week; indeed, too many messages and tenants may ignore them! Still, not telling tenants what's happening in their building — and it is their building as much as yours, possession being nine-tenths of the law — risks alienating them.

Attracting New Tenants

Sooner or later, a tenant will leave and you'll have to replace him. Finding a new tenant who will respect your property and stay for the long-term requires a judgment call on your part.

Before you get to the stage of choosing among specific potential tenants, however, you'll need to assess what kind of building you've got, the kind of tenant mix that suits it (and suits you), and the best means of advertising.

Knowing your building's dynamic

Take a look at the tenant profile in your building. Chances are, if it's mostly professional couples you probably won't want to throw a pair of first-year male college students into the mix. It just wouldn't suit the building dynamic. On the other hand, if you've got a building where the tenant mix is exclusively short-term renters, you may want to take steps to diversify to ensure greater stability in cash flow.

Consider the following factors in sizing up your building and determining the kind of tenant that will work well:

- **Current tenant mix:** Who are your tenants at present? Are you happy with 24-hour party people, or would you rather have a less rambunctious crowd? The neighbourhood in which you've invested may be suited to the tenants currently in the building, and you may be happy with it, but if you want to make a change, you will want to start with selecting new tenants as the opportunity arises.

- **Current length of tenancies:** A building with short-term tenants as the norm could benefit from the addition of tenants who commit to staying for the long term. On the other hand, if your building's tenants haven't changed for a decade, you will need to show sensitivity to the concerns of the existing tenants.

- **Current building atmosphere:** Most landlords favour quiet tenants rather than partiers, but whatever the dynamic, you'll want to make sure an equilibrium exists that everyone can tolerate. Add a profoundly different kind of tenant to the mix and you could put the entire tenant base at risk.

- **Proximity to amenities:** A building close to transit routes may have one type of tenant, while another that's located within walking distance of a hospital is likely to attract health-care workers. Knowing who your target market is will help you select the tenant that's right for the building.

Considering your advertising options

Should you put the word out via the Internet or the local paper? Would you do best with a simple "for rent" sign outside the property, or a banner down the side of the building? How and where you choose to advertise your vacancies will go a long way to determining what kind of applicants you attract.

Soliciting tenants will create work for you, but it isn't a make-work project. Targeted advertising reduces the number of applicants who aren't suitable or have limited interest in renting from you. And the sooner you find a new tenant to fill a vacancy, the less cash you lose.

Several resources exist for advertising a vacancy, some of which may be better suited to certain segments of the market than others. Common advertising venues include the following:

- **Newspaper advertisements:** This is the time-honoured venue for apartment rental ads, for both landlords and tenants. A classified ad is probably the best value for your money in terms of reaching the broadest number of people in the shortest amount of time.

    Don't limit yourself to daily newspapers when placing an ad. Community newspapers that publish on a weekly or semi-weekly basis are also good options. Don't forget newspapers targeting a specific segment of the population, such as student and institutional papers.

- **Online advertisements:** A number of community Internet sites offer venues for posting apartment rental ads, while the much-larger Craigslist.org is a popular venue that exists globally but serves locally (to turn a phrase). Many newspapers will also offer to post your advertisement online as well as in print.

- **Bulletin board:** A simple ad with pull-off phone numbers (you know the type) at a popular coffee shop may attract tenants, especially in student neighbourhoods. The advantage of this kind of ad is that it puts your listing in front of a focused market; the disadvantage is that it could get lost in a crowded bulletin board.

- **Signage:** Many prospective tenants walk around neighbourhoods looking for vacancies. Posting a sign announcing an opening in your building is a great way to attract tenants who are seriously looking for a suite, want to be in your neighbourhood, and are diligent enough to walk the streets to find a place. On the other hand, you may also get a lot of calls from people who see the sign but have nothing more than a passing interest . . . so to speak.

    Signage inside your building, if it has several units, may help you find a tenant not unlike the ones you've got. This could help preserve a balance in the building dynamic, ensuring stability and fewer hassles for you. Offering your existing tenants a "finder's fee," either in the form of cash or some other desirable prize, may also help.

- **Tenant agencies:** Some tenants will sign up with an agency that matches tenants with landlords. This reduces the legwork the tenant usually does to find a suite, and an agent can also give the landlord a better chance of finding a tenant who suits a particular property.

No single advertising method will guarantee you the tenant that will suit your property. Rather the focus on one medium, use a mix of advertising that attracts a good assortment of applicants, but not more than you can handle.

Checking references

Knowing who you're dealing with is an crucial to any business transaction, and it's most important when you're renting your property to a complete stranger. You want an assurance they won't jeopardize your investment, and also that they're a good risk so far as regular cash flow.

The standard rental form asks tenants to provide various pieces of information that helps you to verify who they are, what they do, and whether they're a good risk. Common information required includes the following:

- ✔ **Rental history:** Knowing how long a tenant was at a previous address and the reason for leaving, and knowing who the previous landlord was helps you to determine whether a tenant is a good risk. A tenant who left on poor terms with a previous landlord may create problems for you. Try to understand as much as possible about the previous situation.

- ✔ **Employment history:** Knowing where someone has worked and for how long will give you a sense of whether they're able to handle the rent at your place and if they'll be a good fit for your building. Tenants with several jobs may not be the best bet, but remember to balance employment information with credit checks and rental history. Relying on employment history alone could prejudice you against the self-employed or the independently wealthy!

- ✔ **Credit checks:** Running a credit check on prospective tenants through Equifax (www.equifax.ca) or TransUnion Canada (www.tuc.ca) can reveal shortcomings in a person's financial history worth knowing. Whatever the outcome, it will confirm the applicant's trustworthiness or highlight an area of concern. Because credit checks will cost you, it's worthwhile to reserve a credit check for a short list of applicants.

- ✔ **Personal references:** Some people, especially newcomers to a city, have few local personal references to offer. But if you can't size up a person yourself, it's always good to speak with two or three of the applicant's supposed friends to see if the prospective tenant is all she claims to be.

You *can't* ask some personal questions, depending on the provincial legislation, or personal privacy legislation. Check with your lawyer about restrictions in your market.

A property owner has discretion regarding the choice of tenant. An owner does not have to give reasons for declining to rent to a particular tenant; doing so is, in fact, unadvised. This prevents an unreasonable person, or someone with a negative attitude, from making your life miserable simply because you didn't lease a unit to him.

Renting and repenting

Wendy, a busy young professional, bought a house for investment purposes. Her advertisement for tenants was pretty standard — no smokers, no pets, and no more than two children. Several people contacted her. One couple, who seemed very nice and friendly when she showed them the apartment, had two young children but didn't mention any pets. Because the interview had gone so well, and Wendy had entered a busy period at work, she bypassed the reference check she would otherwise have done. Everything seemed on the level.

There weren't any complaints or apparent problems in the first five months of the tenancy. But the cheque for the sixth month's rent bounced. Wendy drove over to the house one evening to see the tenants and, she hoped, resolve the issue. Wendy discovered three dogs outside — two pit bulls, and a young Rottweiler. On the verandah, her tenants were smoking and surrounded by four children. The renters, it turned out, had been living common law and had a blended family; the other two children had been visiting their grandparents at the time of the initial meeting with Wendy.

Wendy opted not to surprise the pleasant domestic scene, and instead called her tenants.

They gave her several excuses for the bounced cheque, some of which even seemed legitimate. A replacement cheque was in the mail, they promised. But things rapidly went downhill. For the next several months the rent was either late or the cheque bounced. Finally, Wendy went to a lawyer for advice and to her province's landlord–tenant relations office. Four months and $1,000 in legal fees later, the tenants were evicted. The house was a mess, requiring maintenance far in excess of the damage deposit she had collected. Wendy's lawyer advised that it would be prohibitively expensive to try and collect the outstanding debt for rent from her former tenants, leaving her with little recourse but to swallow her losses.

For her next tenants, Wendy made a point of checking lease applicants' references thoroughly, and the successful tenants signed a tenancy agreement prepared by her lawyer. The lease agreement clearly stated her policies and limited how many full-time residents could occupy the suite. The agreement stated that any breach of the agreement conditions would be grounds for eviction, subject to the provisions of provincial tenancy legislation.

Accepting a tenant is ultimately a judgment call on your part, and no matter how much research you do, surprises are always possible. When unpleasant surprises happen, act promptly and professionally to address the issue (we discuss resolving complaints elsewhere in this chapter). When positive surprises happen, celebrate!

Fostering Good Relations and Responsible Tenants

To help you prevent bad feelings on the part of your tenants, and to resolve matters when they do, in this section we take a moment to discuss the various rights and responsibilities inherent in the landlord–tenant relationship.

Provincial, not federal, laws govern landlord–tenant relations. Most provinces and territories have some form of tenancy act. Regardless of what we say, it pays to familiarize yourself with provisions of the legislation in your province or territory. The Canada Mortgage and Housing Corp. offers information on renting a home at (www.cmhc.ca/en/co/reho/index.cfm). In addition, municipalities may have specific bylaws regarding rental accommodation.

Understanding tenant rights

Generally speaking, Canadian legislation works to protect tenants' rights by defining the landlord's obligations, but of course, the landlord–tenant relationship is to some degree reciprocal. A landlord has a right to collect rent from a tenant, for example, but not until the tenant has received a signed copy of the lease agreement. Providing the lease agreement is the landlord's responsibility.

Some of the basic defined in legislation include the following:

- **Right to know:** A tenant has a right to know the name of the landlord who owns and operates the rental property, how to communicate with the landlord, and so forth.

- **Right of refusal:** A landlord has the right to limit or refuse subletting or assignment of a rental suite. Usually subletting terms are included in the rental agreement.

- **Right to privacy:** Tenants have the right to quiet enjoyment of their premises, or at least 24 hours' notice prior to entry of the landlord for whatever reason. Depending on the landlord–tenant relationship, a shorter period of notice is possible, particularly in emergency situations.

Knowing your responsibilities

The sensitive nature of rental relationships may be one reason why legislation emphasizes the responsibilities landlords and tenants bear to each other. Key provisions of most legislation includes the following:

- Tenants must give at least 30 days' notice prior to vacating a suite; the landlord must give at least three months' notice if asking a tenant to vacate a suite.

- Landlords are responsible for providing documents concerning the tenancy, providing means for tenants to contact the landlord, and making themselves available in the event of significant issues.

- Landlords are responsible for maintaining a property in good repair and providing the services they've agreed to provide.

- Tenants are responsible for maintaining a clean unit and paying for the repair of any damage to the property that they cause.

- Tenants are also responsible for the conduct of guests and anyone who sublets their suite.

Neither the landlord nor the tenant should harass the other; the relationship should be as professional as in any other business transaction.

Rights and responsibilities enshrined in law are a great safeguard against abuse by either the landlord or tenant. Social chatter is often a factor in a smaller centre that can effectively serve the same purpose. Buzz about a landlord who treats tenants badly circulates easily in small or tightly knit circles of tenants, such as university students. Although word of mouth is the best advertising, not all publicity is good publicity.

[Dis]respecting agreements

Three months into a lease agreement, you discover the tenant you've leased that non-smoking, no-pets unit to is a binge smoker with long-haired cats that have shed (or worse) all over the apartment. Do you have the right to evict her (or him)?

In a word, yes. Providing your tenancy agreement doesn't conflict with provincial tenancy legislation, and your agreement has been prepared or approved by your lawyer as being compliant, than you can rely on it as a legally binding document. That means a contractual relationship exists between you and your tenant. If your tenant breaches the terms of the agreement, you have a right to demand compliance, impose financial penalties, or even evict them (with notice, of course).

Resolving disputes

When relationships sour with tenants, landlords face all sorts of risks. Tenants may

✔ Damage your property, or otherwise create inconveniences that delay the fresh rental of the suite

✔ Engage in subtle harassment, especially if you manage the property directly rather than through a corporate entity

✔ Lodge a complaint with the appropriate local or provincial body that addresses tenants' rights or oversees landlord–tenant relations

You can follow a series of steps to attempt to resolve tenant disputes:

1. **Speak to your tenant.** A respectful attitude with a view to solving the problem can go a long ways toward dealing with the issue. This could be followed up by a letter confirming the problem's resolution.

2. **Refer to your written tenancy agreement.** A written agreement clarifies and gives a legal framework for your expectations and requirements — after all, it is your property and your investment at risk.

3. **Check with your provincial landlord–tenant government office.** In most cases, they have a mediation option to clarify and resolve disputes.

4. **Seek arbitration.** Formally complain to the provincial landlord–tenant government office, and ask for an arbitration decision.

5. **Launch legal action.** If the above steps do not satisfy you, your lawyer can launch legal action against the tenant for breach of contract.

We discuss business disputes with regard to property, and their resolution, in Chapter 8. Many of the same principles apply when resolving issues with tenants.

Happy Tenants, Happy Landlord

Sound property management doesn't require you to bow to every request from tenants, but a rule of thumb is to give each tenant the respect they deserve — whether they are going about their business, or railing about a dripping faucet. In short, it pays to make sure you do everything you can to make sure your building meets the needs of your tenants, and to listen carefully to tenants when they have a concern.

Treading lightly

If you're new to managing a property or working with tenants, we can suggest a few things to avoid that will help you avoid problems:

- ✔ **Unreturned phone calls:** Respecting tenants means being responsive to phone calls and other forms of communication. Sometimes phone calls don't come at a convenient time; sometimes you're swamped with them. Make it your policy to return phone calls within 24 hours. Doing so is not only professional, it may attract tenants who hear from their friends that you're a responsive property owner who cares about tenants and their concerns.

- ✔ **Unannounced visits:** Tenancy acts across the country typically require you to give at least 24 hours' notice prior to a visit, except in emergencies. Unannounced visits, or frequently checking in on tenants, will make you seem overbearing or intrusive, slowly damaging the relationship you have with them. And speaking of intrusive, keep maintenance and other tasks likely to disturb tenants to reasonable hours. Although you can't always build a work schedule around your tenants, be flexible enough to avoid creating bad feelings.

- ✔ **Disrepair:** No one likes coming home to a property that looks like the Addams family are the landlords. A rental property in good shape limits tenants' resentment about their rent payments (and will allow you to lease the property for more to happier tenants). We discuss some common maintenance issues elsewhere in this chapter.

- ✔ **Disrespect:** Avoiding communication with tenants is one thing; being surly or overly demanding of them is another. Peter recalls a landlord who drove a tenant to a bank machine one evening to ensure that he received his rent on the day it was due. The landlord may have suspected the tenant was liable to default, but escorting the tenant to a bank machine was a step beyond helpful. The buzz this incident created among the other tenants was less than favourable toward the landlord.

- ✔ **Maximum rent increases:** Regularly increasing rental rates to reflect changing market conditions is sound management. Raising rents as often as the law allows, regardless of necessity, is plain greedy. You will likely enjoy a more stable income over the long term when tenants have a stable rental environment. Raising rents gives tenants a reason to look for better deals elsewhere, and compare what you're offering to what other landlords can provide. We encourage you to raise rents to ensure positive cash flow, but avoid giving reliable tenants a reason to move.

Becoming familiar with hot topics in landlord–tenant relations in your area can help you identify potential problems and devise appropriate strategies that minimize the chance of them becoming issues for your tenants.

Coming out on top

Respecting tenants is pretty much a matter of the Golden Rule. You may own the real estate, but the property is their home (or office, in the case of commercial properties). So treat them as you would want a landlord to treat you — and then go a little further, in order to enjoy the following:

- **A stable cash flow:** Dissatisfied tenants may pick up stakes and leave, disrupting your cash flow and increasing operating costs for the property. This narrows your margins, invites headaches, and generally cuts into your returns.

- **A good reputation:** Avoiding bad relationships with tenants boosts your stock in the rental community, potentially increasing the number of tenants willing to rent from you and reducing costs associated with finding tenants.

- **Good karma:** Bad things happen to good people, but bad deeds often return to haunt their perpetrators. Don't give a bad relationship with a tenant a chance to return in the form of lawsuits or general bad will.

Managing Multiple Properties

You may decide to buy just one property for real estate investment purposes. It could be a second recreational property that you use for lifestyle, possibly seasonal rentals, or with a view to taking advantage of appreciation in the property's value over the long-term. Maybe the one investment property you buy is a single-family home or condo for your children to use while they go through university.

However, after you've bought one property, you may have the urge to buy another, then another. Many Canadian real estate investors have acquired significant real estate portfolios this way over time. If you think this possibility may be in your long-range business plan, here are some points to consider:

- Hire a strong real estate advisory team, such as a real estate lawyer, a tax accountant, a financially experienced and savvy Realtor or Realtors, an insurance broker, and a mortgage broker (we discuss selecting advisers in Chapter 4). You want to be able to call upon any member of your team at any time, and know that they are familiar with your total real estate investment picture. After you have a relationship established, you can phone anytime you have a question.

✔ Get strategic tax advice from a business adviser (you can find some under this heading in the phone book) on the structure of your real estate investment portfolio. You may wish to incorporate a company to hold some or all of your real estate portfolio for various reasons — generally to minimize your personal liability exposure, or limit exposure to your other investment properties, if some financial misadventure occurs with one of your properties. For example, if an apartment building you own burns to the ground and people were injured in the blaze, you will want protection that limits the extent to which people can seek damages from you, personally, if there is sufficient insurance to cover the rebuilding but insufficient coverage for personal liability claims.

✔ Get tax advice on writing off home office expenses for managing or marketing your various properties. You may consider hiring your spouse, partner, or children to assist you in your property enterprise, steps that will also require appropriate tax advice.

✔ Specialize in specific types of real estate with which you're comfortable, as this will make the best use of your extensive research and developing expertise and knowledge.

✔ Determine whether you are suited to manage your own expanding real estate portfolio, or whether at a certain point it is smarter to hire an expert property management firm to do that for you (we discuss this choice elsewhere in this chapter).

✔ Have a short-term, medium-term, and long-term investment strategy, and an exit plan.

Negotiate everything, because everything is negotiable. The more money you save, the more money you make. Because you have an ongoing relationship with all your advisers, ask them how they can save you money, through economy of scale, or multiple real estate acquisitions. This includes the Realtor commission, the legal fees, and the accounting services — and many other elements.

Obtain advice from a lawyer who does will and estate planning law, to make sure that you have all your financial affairs in order, and that you are applying strategic legal and tax planning to your full advantage. Update your will and review your estate planning yearly. Have an integrated team approach with your lawyer and tax adviser to optimize your planning.

Above all, maintain a balanced life, making sure your real investment portfolio isn't all-consuming. If you find your real estate investments are taking over, you may want to consider scaling back your holdings.

Maintaining Your Property

Part of keeping your tenants happy and giving them a reason to stick around is ensuring your property is maintained, from major weather-related issues right down to everyday wear and tear. This section considers some of the most common issues you'll face as a property owner. Ongoing maintenance of your property and prompt attention to problems that arise will also improve the property's allure to potential tenants. (We tell you about the *other* side of the coin — the risks you can face if you ignore necessary items of maintenance — in Chapter 14.)

A property that looks good will attract its share of attention, and develop an appeal even when people aren't considering it for a home. When people find out your good-looking property has a unit for rent, half your sales job to prospective tenants is already done!

Keeping water at bay

Water is a major problem for many homeowners, whether in the form of bad caulking, old pipes, or a leaky roof. Don't let maintenance costs give you a good hosing-down! Take a regular look at the following areas:

- **Caulking:** Whether around the tub, shower stall, or an exterior wall, faulty caulking allows water to penetrate and create rot from the inside out. Research indicates three-quarters of all homes lack adequate caulking in the bathroom, and 15 percent of homes have inadequate exterior caulking. Rotten walls are costly to repair, not to mention the adverse health impacts of mould. In the case of exterior walls, you also face drafts that increase your heating costs.

- **Plumbing:** The water-supply valves under sinks and faucets leak in half of all homes. Rather than solve the problem with duct tape and a bucket, as many property owners do, replace the valve and take a load off your mind and your tenant's. The alternative can end up costing you thousands of dollars.

- **Roofing:** If you're in a part of Canada that experiences heavy snowfalls in winter or freeze–thaw cycles, you may wish to inspect your roof annually to ensure shingles are in good condition and that is the roof provides adequate protection against water ingress. One of the worst things is a trickle-down effect that damages your home from the top down. Repairs may end up being quite extensive. Clearing snow from your roof, when possible, also limits the chance of seepage through the roof.

Ensuring good air flow

Making sure your building has proper sealing helps reduce operating costs by improving heat retention. Buildings with good sealing may also enjoy better air quality. Here are the areas to consider with regard to air flow:

- **Doors and windows:** Weather-stripping around doors and windows helps block drafts, but only if it is tight enough to do the job.

- **Furnace filters:** A good air filtration system will enhance indoor air quality. But up to 80 percent of homes have furnace filters that need replacing. Dirty and clogged filters not only make furnaces work harder, they also filter dirt air through dirt, increasing the chances that particulates will circulate through a building. You may be saving money, but don't expect residents to breathe easily.

- **Exhaust fans:** Bathrooms without windows depend on exhaust fans to remove moist, humid air conducive to mould growth. But a third of homes have fans that don't work, leading to mould formation and deterioration of walls and flooring — a rotten situation.

- **Attic vents:** Keeping unwanted drafts out of a home is important, but a completely air-tight home is no picnic, either. When adding insulation in attic spaces, be sure not to block vents. Blocked vents can create moisture build-up, mildew, and rot that's no more helpful in the attic than in the bathroom.

Doing those outdoor chores

Outdoor maintenance can have a significant impact on your property. We're not talking about landscaping, but a host of outdoor chores that can prevent wear and tear on the fabric of a building. Here are some of the issues this maintenance can address:

- **Settling:** Many homes tend to settle and shift over time. Typical causes include heavy rainfall and erosion from overwatering shrubs placed too close to the house. But sometimes the ground simply settles. If water pools near the foundation, the building's foundation could become weak. Preventing pooling and subsequent structural problems is often a matter of simply adding a few wheelbarrows of dirt around the foundation and planting shrubbery that will absorb excess water. If you're watering the existing shrubs too much, cut back on the irrigation!

✔ **Clogged gutters:** The gutters and downspouts of many buildings become clogged with debris and dead vegetation. Ensuring gutters and drains are clear will prevent water from backing up on the roof, reducing the risk of water ingress and preventing the roof from deteriorating faster than it should.

✔ **Overgrowth:** No matter how romantic an ivy-coated wall is, too much of it can damage the mortar and remove siding. Have you ever noticed how historical ruins frequently appear covered in ivy? Don't let your investment be among them.

Chapter 14

Managing Risks

· ·

· ·

As a property owner, you are your own boss, and the freedom can be pretty exhilarating. But you're not all footloose and fancy-free. Owning a property — especially a rental property — brings with it a whole heaping of responsibilities and duties. It's not just your creditors you need to keep happy — keeping tenants satisfied and making sure the property doesn't put them at risk are as important as maintaining good cash flow. A property that's a liability in personal as well as financial terms puts your investment, and your investment success, in peril. As we discuss in Chapter 6, many lenders have good reason to demand that you keep a property in good shape as a condition of financing your investment.

Ensuring your finances, files, and other documentation associated with your property are in good order is a basic aspect of managing risk. But other risks require your attention as well, including maintenance issues and the security of your property with regard to both crime and disaster. In this chapter we discuss each of these areas, providing you with tips that can ensure a property doesn't disappoint your tenants, your banker — or you.

Keeping Records

Personal idiosyncrasies often shape how we keep records. The veritable totalitarian who keeps catalogued and indexed records with unerring diligence and rigour, never caught out when someone asks to see something, stands in sharp contrast to the easygoing (and often equally reliable) person who prefers to keep documents one on top of the other, chronologically (that is, the most recently referenced file lands on top).

Regardless of your personal filing preferences, however, you must maintain accurate records of your property no matter how small your investment. The file for a land investment may be as simple as deeds and records of taxes paid. If you rent out property, the file will be much larger and include the following:

✔ Bank records

✔ Invoices

✔ Receipts

✔ Sales slips

✔ Contracts

In this section, we discuss the reasons why record-keeping makes sense, and some of the options you have when it comes to keeping your records in order. We discuss record-keeping for insurance purposes elsewhere in this chapter.

Keep the numerous documents you accumulate regarding your property in an order that makes sense not just to you but also to your book-keeper, your accountant, and — horrors! — any potential auditors. A filing system that doesn't make sense may enhance your privacy by making sensitive information more difficult to find, but it also stands to boost the cost of accounting services when you hand over your books for scrutiny, create headaches for associates and relatives trying to make sense of your holdings in the event of an illness or your sudden death, and annoy the auditor sent to figure out why you claimed an obscure expense on your tax filing four years ago.

In Chapter 11 we talk about the due diligence you do when you're buying a property. Some accountants also recommend property owners undertake due diligence to ensure their properties have a better chance of selling. Part of that involves keeping proper records that can help you manage your property better, and help you make an argument for selling it when the time comes to do so (we discuss selling a property in Chapter 16).

Of course, keeping accurate records may be sound practice, but it helps to know there are benefits to what you're doing. We discuss both practice and the practical benefits of record-keeping in this section, tipping you off to some of the opportunities accurate records present for managing your real estate investment.

Making sense of record-keeping

Some people are natural pack-rats and some people aren't — it's as simple as that. But if you're a property owner with creditors, the government, and tenants (to name just a few) to satisfy, you'll want to be sure you have a clear paper trail for your property that shows

- ✔ What you've done
- ✔ When you've done it
- ✔ Why you've done it

The information may seem mundane and maybe even obvious in the moment, but it may have a different meaning if someone sees the record without knowing the property in question. Accurate records will ensure financial protection as well as protection from claims that you didn't do something you did in fact do.

If you replace locks on one or several apartments, record whether it was a routine refit or in response to security concerns. Similarly, it may be important to keep a sheet that tenants initialled on receipt of new keys, safeguarding you from allegations that you changed locks without notice.

Records come in several forms, including the following:

- ✔ **Financial,** those relating to the finances of the property and its cash flow
- ✔ **Contracts,** such as tenancy agreements and associated records
- ✔ **Maintenance,** including maintenance schedules, when repairs were made, and fire equipment checked
- ✔ **Administrative,** including business licences, protocols regarding safety procedures, sign-off sheets for receipt of keys and other items

Here are some reasons to keep records:

- ✔ **Government regulations:** Various federal and provincial rules require you to keep records regarding your investment property. Tax requirements are a primary reason to keep records, but Statistics Canada and other government departments may also request information regarding your business activities.

The federal Income Tax Act requires you to maintain records and books in an orderly manner at your place of business or your residence in case of a review or audit of your filings. You must maintain all records and supporting documents for at least six years from the end of the last taxation year to which they relate. If you filed your return late for any year, records and supporting documents must be kept for six years from the date you filed that return. The Canada Revenue Agency permits computer storage of records as long as those records provide adequate information to verify tax claims.

✔ **Financing and lender requirements:** Accurate, accessible records help you develop and support a bid for financing, helping document your credit worthiness to potential lenders, highlighting improvements you've made in your portfolio and other information.

✔ **Insurance requirements:** Establishing a property's value when it becomes the subject of an insurance claim is important to maximizing the payout you see from the insurer. Being able to document a claim with records of improvements, photographs, and other information helps you make establish a better claim for compensation.

✔ **Maintenance requirements:** Having set maintenance schedules and being able to document that these were followed in the event of an accident leading to legal action or damage to the building requiring an insurance claim allows you to prove that everything was in order (or not). Schedules will also help remind you when various tasks need attention.

✔ **Sale opportunities:** Knowing how a property has improved, what its appreciation in value has been, and what it costs you to operate is important in assessing when to sell it. The same information could also help a Realtor or potential buyer understand the property's potential, possibly allowing you to seek and receive a better price.

Considering the advantages of organized record-keeping

Ideally, keeping organized records will help you manage your investment more effectively than if you just toss everything into a shoe box. Actually *using* the information to improve the performance of your investment is up to you.

Solid record-keeping gives you an edge over investors who don't maintain accurate and accessible records in several ways:

✔ You have better information regarding the financial position of your investment that allows you to make faster decisions.

✔ You find it easier — and, often, cheaper — to complete tax returns because your bookkeeper or accountant will have less to wade through.

✔ You have a basis for evaluating the condition, efficiency, and operation of your property.

✔ You find that you can more easily assess the property's place in your portfolio vis-à-vis your short-term objectives and overall goals.

✔ You're able to easily analyze and prepare projections for cash flow, income, and expenses.

Often, a well-designed accounting software package can help you better manage your financial records. Whether you buy an off-the-shelf package or have one tailored to your specific requirements (especially if you have manifold business interests), software is adept at crunching the numbers you require at the punch of a button. All going well, you'll know where you stand with regard to your property investments within seconds.

Far be it from us to recommend an accounting software package to you. Rather than promote a specific company's product (hey, we're not getting commissions on the sales), we simply encourage you to investigate the several that are available — some, even, especially for Canadians. Intuit's QuickBooks package is probably the best-known among small businesses in Canada but other options exist. Some software consultants may even be able to customize an off-the-shelf package for your particular circumstances. Running at about $100, the price of the basic QuickBooks accounting package compares favourably to tailor-made programs costing several hundreds or even thousands of dollars.

A records system of your own

The systems available to property investors for keeping records range from simple, inexpensive manual ledgers to more complex software packages. If you are investing in a single-family house, you may require only a simple system that keeps track of inflows and outflows. As your real estate investments expand in terms of numbers and types of properties, you will likely want and need to use one of the excellent computer software programs available.

A file folder or records box is a convenient way to keep long-term records that require a signature or to which you refer frequently, such as tenancy agreements and maintenance schedules. Some of these can be maintained with the assistance of a computer that will prompt you when certain tasks need attention (such as mortgage payments or fire inspections). Several software programs can help bring order to your financial records. Here's a list of typical elements in financial accounts that need tracking:

- ✔ Cash receipts
- ✔ Accounts receivable
- ✔ Accounts payable
- ✔ Disbursements
- ✔ Credit purchases

Fortunately, an investment property is a relatively simple business in terms of record-keeping. You won't have to do an extensive search for software that needs an expensive customization job. However, be sure the accounting software you choose is the right package for you. Talk to other users and identify any oddities of the program, try out the package if possible, and verify that it can do what you want it to do. If real estate investment is part of a larger portfolio or business for you, see if the accounting program also meets the needs of your other ventures.

Consult your accountant regarding the most efficient record-keeping system for your portfolio.

Managing Maintenance Costs

We outline the basics of maintaining your property in good repair in Chapter 13. Adequate maintenance can ensure a home stays in great condition over the years, significantly reducing ongoing maintenance costs while simultaneously increasing resale value. Our focus in this chapter is on how you can save on maintenance costs while reducing the risks you assume as an owner. Key areas that typically hold the most potential for reducing both costs and the risk of losses include a building's energy efficiency and its ability to withstand water. Pest prevention also requires your attention, as does fire prevention. Preventing fires is a particularly significant issue — yes, a blaze can wipe out your entire investment and potentially those of your neighbours, but take comfort in the knowledge that a handful of simple maintenance procedures can reduce the possibility of a conflagration consuming your property.

Even if you employ a property manager to whom you've delegated oversight for some aspects of maintenance, as an owner you're responsible for staying in touch regarding maintenance. Don't just leave maintenance to the manager; inspect the property yourself on a regular basis — weekly, monthly, or quarterly — so you know what's going on with your investment. You still want to be on top of what needs to be done. In fact, if you have a property manager you should be more on top of what needs doing than if you don't have a property manager. The information you receive should allow you to better manage maintenance costs and budget for future upkeep.

Protecting yourself from escalating energy bills

The early 1970s saw a push toward energy efficiency in response to the oil crisis of the day. Today, energy efficiency is driven by environmental concerns backed up by the promise of cost savings. Whatever your motivation for wanting to improve the energy efficiency of your property, you've got lots of scope for action.

Many consultants recommend first undertaking an assessment of the property to identify where the greatest savings from improvements will be. Why spend $5,000 to cut energy costs by $1,000 a year when you can spend $7,500 and save $2,000? Before proceeding with improvements, consult one of the growing number of renovation companies across the country that specialize in improving the energy efficiency of buildings. The Canada Mortgage and Housing Corporation (www.cmhc.ca) or local affiliate of the Canadian Home Builders' Association (www.chba.ca) should be able to help you if the Yellow Pages don't turn up a suitable contractor.

Start by taking a look at the following:

✔ Upgrading building insulation

✔ Sealing leaks in the building envelope

✔ Improving sealing of doors and windows

Insulating an investment from risk (and rodents)

The amount of insulation you need and the kind you need are both points to ask an expert. Don't forget to ask about the *R factor*, a measure of the insulation's resistance to heat flows. The pink batts of fibreglass insulation that come to mind when most people think of insulation come with varying degrees of resistance. The greater the R value of the insulation installed, the more energy efficient your building will be.

Typically, a higher R rating also indicates a higher resistance to sound, though the soundproofing ability of insulation (important to consider in rental properties) is properly measured by the *STC rating*, or sound transmission coefficient. The higher the rating, the better the insulation is in insulating your building for noise.

A cost-effective alternative to fibreglass insulation in warmer climates is cellulose, a material used since the 1800s to insulate homes. Essentially shredded newspaper treated with fire retardant and Borax (which helps control rodents), cellulose insulation boasts insulative and soundproofing properties equal to and sometimes greater than either fibreglass or foam products. Cellulose is blown into attic and wall cavities, enabling it to fill hard-to-reach spaces without removing sections of wall. Its density also makes it effective in blocking drafts.

A handful of water-based foam insulation products can also reach nooks and crannies without removing a wall. Some forms can reduce the load on heating and air-conditioning systems by as much as 50 percent.

Urea formaldehyde foam (UFFI) and *asbestos* are two kinds of insulation to be avoided. UFFI gained notoriety in the 1970s and early 1980s on account of *off-gassing*, which caused a variety of health concerns. Equally nasty, the carcinogenic quality of asbestos prompted its removal as an insulative material from many buildings. Some older buildings still have it. Due diligence, which we discuss in Chapter 11, should bring to light the presence of either of these materials. If present, these substances could be the subject of clauses in your offer to purchase that make the sale conditional on their rectification. As an investor, you may be able to negotiate a deal that widens your potential margin on the future sale of the property.

Licking a leaking envelope

The *building envelope* — the elements of a building that ensure its innards stay on the inside — is perhaps the least-considered source of heat loss. Most people feel a draft and look to the door or window. As often as not, the draft may be coming through the very fabric of the building. Think of a well-worn shirt or sweater: It may have been cozy when it was new, but several years on it's getting pretty threadbare. Refer to the sidebar "Powering up to power down" for some tips on how to tackle the job of finding and eradicating these drafty spots.

Caulking, available in several formulations, is a simple way of sealing the building envelope. Deteriorated or missing caulking on exterior walls is a common problem in 15 percent of buildings. It helps to weatherproof a building, preventing decay, rather than actually blocking the airflows that can come through the worn and damaged fabric of a building. To ensure your caulking continues to perform as you expect, review it annually.

Similarly, interior caulking helps prevent air loss. Although not a substitute for sound construction, it plays a role in preventing air loss through cracks in the envelope.

Sealing's the deal: Doors and windows

Doors and windows require rough openings in the exterior wall of a building, and if not sealed properly, create opportunities for the exchange of air with the outside. Caulking is an important means of closing the openings around doors and windows. A skilled installer will ensure that these gaps are sealed prior to completing a job.

Weather-stripping is an important tool in preventing heat loss, but to reduce maintenance costs associated with its replacement, choose one that's appropriate to the volume of use (and abuse) it will receive as well as local environmental conditions.

The spaces around doors and windows aren't the only spots you should attend to. Don't forget to take into account the doors and windows themselves! The material that makes up a door may be more or less conductive, allowing heat transfer. So-called "low E," or low emittance, coatings help reduce heat flows through windows and boost the comfort, energy efficiency, and overall value of a building.

Though they are more expensive, many utility companies offer incentives to replace single-pane windows with these new, technologically advanced windows in efforts to promote energy conservation. A common standard for energy-efficient windows and doors in Canada is the Energy Star rating (you'll also find the Energy Star rating on several other things these days, including appliances).

The size of windows and doors raises the potential for heat loss. Ensuring they are energy efficient will not only keep your energy costs down, it will limit the use of your furnace and air conditioner. Less use means a longer life span and lower replacement costs for the systems that regulate the temperature of your building.

Reducing leakage

Water always seeks its own level. Which in itself is fine — no point in challenging Mother Nature, after all. However, the unfortunate thing is when water wants to be in your basement, or in your walls.

The two forms of leakage to watch for are

- Leaks in the plumbing
- Water ingress through the building envelope

Limiting leakage in either of these areas will improve the life span of your property, maintaining its value, and in the case of plumbing, help reduce operating costs.

Leaky plumbing

Burst pipes are bad, regardless of what they carry. We stick to talking about water pipes, though the principles that help prevent leaks in water pipes also applies to some other forms of pipes.

Here are some basic strategies to prevent leakage:

- **Maintaining valves:** Checking valves and joins to make sure piping under sinks isn't leaking should be a no-brainer for most people, as should noticing any leaks that occur. Still, about half of all buildings have this kind of leak at any given time. Resolving valve issues can both limit damage to a building as well as save on water usage, an important consideration in homes that have metered water.

- **Preventing corrosion:** *Aggressive water* has solvents that can corrode copper pipes. Typically, the less acidic the water, the less aggressive it is. If the building in which you've invested has copper piping, monitor the piping for signs of failure and, if necessary, replace it with plastic piping resistant to corrosion. Older piping that has developed a calcium carbonate scale on the interior tends to be resistant to the aggressive compounds in water that can cause corrosion.

- **Insulating pipes:** Preventing pipes from freezing reduces the potential for a burst pipe. Insulation is always the first line of defence in this regard, and in the case of hot water pipes, can also help ensure the water arrives at its destination having lost less heat. Investing in adequate insulation for water pipes not only saves you the cost of repairing damage in the event of freezing, it also saves your tenants from the inconvenience of being without water.

Whatever the cause of the leak or burst pipe, damages can run upwards of $1,000 or more, depending on how long the leak has been ignored and the extent of the damage.

Leaky buildings

Aggressive water is one problem for pipes. A different form of aggressive water is a problem for the roof and envelope of your building. Regular inspection of the fabric of the building can help prevent water ingress from becoming a problem.

Monitor the following areas:

- **Exterior walls:** Cracked or inadequate caulking along joins in the building, or cracks in the foundation, can cause water seepage that can lead to major headaches. Annual monitoring of the building's walls, especially around the base, can help identify areas that may need extra attention. Though you can't change weather patterns that may increase the wear and tear on a building's weatherproofing, you can take steps to ensure the area around the foundation is as dry as possible. These steps include ensuring proper drainage around the foundation (often with the assistance of landscaping) and positioning of storm pipes such that water doesn't pool at the base of the house.

- ✔ **Siding:** Old or loose siding, whether wood, vinyl, or aluminum, can allow water to seep into the building envelope where it can promote rot and the development of moulds. Seasonal monitoring of siding can ensure a prompt response in the event some siding does become loose, either through age or adverse weather conditions.

- ✔ **Roof and shingles:** Roofing material is prone to allow water ingress as it ages. In addition to regularly monitoring the roof, consider replacing asphalt shingles every 10 to 15 years.

Preventing pests

No one likes uninvited house guests, least of all the four- and six-legged kind that go about their own business wondering what you're so upset about. Not all uninvited visitors will cause damage, but you should know about a few that are worth watching for and simple steps to deal with them.

We don't blame you if you'd rather leave pest control to the professionals. Depending on how badly your investment property is infested, it may make more sense to contact a professional. They have the tools and experience needed to do an efficient job, and are also familiar with the provisions of local pest control bylaws.

Furry fiends

Squirrels, rats, and raccoons top the list of unwanted house guests when it comes to the kind with fur. Making sure walls are properly and adequately sealed can help prevent them from getting into a building.

Grey squirrels are particularly troublesome. And yes, we *are* singling out the grey ones — far from considering these animals the cute, nut-nibbling darlings of storybooks, many homeowners consider them rats with bushy tails. Often, grey squirrels chew their way into eaves and attic spaces where they may damage insulation and electrical wiring — small acts of vandalism that can push up heating costs, cause short-circuits in your wiring and even fires. Scratching and the pitter-patter of tiny feet in early morning may be clues to their presence.

Half-inch wire mesh under the eaves will help ward off squirrels. Equally important, ensure tree limbs and vines are well pruned and don't afford access to eaves or ventilation ducts where squirrels may try to make nests.

Rats are also problematic, for reasons similar to squirrels. They also have a more nastier reputation, from the days of bubonic plague through to the old camp song about "rats, rats, as big as alley cats." Some landlords have been known to fit ground-level toilets with special closures to prevent rats from swimming up and entering buildings, given the vermin's hardiness and determination.

To reduce the chance rats will make your corner of the neighbourhood their favourite new hangout, be sure to keep it clean and free of waste. Open compost will draw these scavengers, who will feast on egg shells and much else. Wire mesh around openings at ground-level and under the eaves will help prevent rats from entering buildings (a quarter-inch mesh will also help keep out mice). And don't forget to close your doors and windows, especially pet doors.

Raccoons can also be troublesome. Not only will they dig up your garden, but they often take refuge in sheds or cavities in the walls of homes. The most determined won't just settle for cozying down in your chimney; they'll tear off shingles and boards to make their way into your attic. The need to ward off unwanted animals is a good argument for not only keeping your door locked, but clamping your aluminum siding down tight.

Feathered fiends

Pigeons and woodpeckers can cause problems for property owners — one with its penchant for roosting above and fouling the entrance to your rental property, the other with the damage it can cause to siding.

No doubt you understand the importance of maintaining a clean and attractive property. Pigeons can easily undo your efforts if you give them a chance to habituate themselves to roosting in a particular area. To prevent them from taking up residence, use wire mesh to deny access to eaves or place tiny spikes along ledges where they might otherwise make themselves at home. Also, sweep regularly to prevent them from being attracted to any scraps of food.

Woodpeckers may be rare and distinguished-looking visitors but they can also *tap-tap-tap* away at the siding of your building in search of grubs. Make sure you maintain siding in tip-top shape such that it doesn't attract grubs or invite woodpeckers to try their luck at finding some.

Six-legged fiends

The mere idea of insect pests strikes fear, or at least a vague discomfort, into the hearts of owners and tenants alike. (Did you get the heebie-jeebies just reading that?) Many more insect pests exist than we have the space to cover here, and most often they deserve the attention of a professional exterminator. Before you call in the professionals, however, you might as well know what you're calling them about.

The most common house pests on six legs in Canada include the following:

> ✔ **Cockroaches:** Cockroaches may not *do* structural damage, but their presence is a symptom of structural shortcomings in your building. Getting rid of them is the first step to creating a more pleasant environment for tenants; making sure cockroaches don't come back is the next step. Prevention includes ensuring pipes don't leak; making sure the building envelope is sufficiently sealed to prevent access to moisture and the dark spaces cockroaches and their broods favour; and regularly cleaning common areas.
>
> ✔ **Carpenter ants:** Carpenter ants destroy the fabric of a building but are also a symptom of pre-existing decay. Borers but never boring, they further a problem that's already started. They typically establish nests in wall voids and eaves, in ceilings, and under insulation in attics and crawl spaces. To get rid of them, ventilate damp areas and repair damaged wood.
>
> ✔ **Silverfish:** Common in older buildings, silverfish seem harmless but can cause a great deal of damage to wallpaper and drywall. Attracted to damp, dark environments with starchy materials, these pests are difficult to eradicate without professional help.

High moisture levels and darkness are elements that commonly attract most insect pests. They love a milieu of decay. To help prevent them from becoming established in your property, you should undertake improvements that maximize natural lighting in the interior spaces, seal the building envelope, and limit the chance for moisture to seep into or accumulate in the fabric of the building.

On a drier note, termites are a problem in southern Ontario, and particularly Toronto. The warmer climate of the region makes it the best spot in Canada for the creatures, which have been in the area since the late 1930s. The major danger they pose is to the fabric of your building, by eating away at the wood and potentially causing structural instability. The most common means of treating termites is through intensive doses of highly toxic pesticides that not only cost a lot but also aren't the best for your health or the environment. While sand and sheet-metal barriers can help prevent an infestation, after a colony is established you face a lengthy — perhaps interminable — battle to eliminate the pests. For help, turn to the Urban Entomology Program at the University of Toronto (`www.utoronto.ca/forest/termite/termite.htm`).

Unfortunately, as with most invaders, you often don't know a problem exists until one of your unwanted guests makes an appearance. By the time the population of critters is well-enough established, however, it's often too large to eradicate and you have to focus on controlling the pests and whatever damage they may cause. Pest control specialists (which we're not) are able to counsel you on strategies for the control and potential for eradicating some species but with silverfish and others you'll have to submit your property (and any tenants) to a regular regimen of pesticide treatments. Whether the effort and expense is worth it, however, is something you should consider carefully. Silverfish, for example, are not the most pleasant housemates but most landlords leave them alone (silverfish can damage a tenant's belongings but don't to much harm to a building).

Protecting against fire

Writing clauses into lease agreements that limit the potential for a tenant to engage in fire-friendly behaviours is one way of preventing fires in your building, but ensuring your building is in good repair also plays a part. Even a small fire can cause extensive water and smoke damage, traumatizing tenants and potentially disrupting your cash flow if you have to temporarily relocate tenants and undertake renovations.

Preventing fires may be as simple as asking tenants to sign a lease that prohibits them from smoking indoors or using space heaters. This both establishes ground rules and encourages them — and hands them the legal obligation — to do their part to prevent a fire.

Four areas are of particular concern with regard to fire-prevention maintenance:

- ✔ Wiring and fuses
- ✔ Heating
- ✔ Fireplaces and chimneys
- ✔ Fire extinguishers and alarms

Some jurisdictions require an annual review of fire policies, equipment, and procedures for rental properties. Check whether any such policies apply in your area. Even if none exist, establish a protocol for your properties to make sure you — and your tenants — know what to do if a fire erupts. It could save your investment, and maybe some lives.

Wiring and fuses

Whenever an electrical system requires work, consult a professional. Perhaps we're more handsome than handy, but without any training in electrical work we would rather let a professional handle all matters related to wiring.

Similarly, don't cut corners where fuses are concerned. These are the safety valves in your circuitry. They prevent wires from overheating. If a fuse keeps blowing, pay attention: Your circuit is overloaded. Never try to circumvent blown fuses using pennies or foil! Call a qualified electrician.

Heating

Seeing that your building is working at maximum efficiency and leaking a minimum of air will help ensure a comfortable interior environment. It will also prevent tenants from being tempted to crank up a space heater, which invites the risk of fire.

Fireplaces and chimneys

Providing a fireplace screen to tenants of homes with fireplaces is important, but regular maintenance of the feature is also vital. You may wish to offer an ash removal service. You should also undertake to clean the chimney every one to two years to prevent the build-up of creosote deposits. Creosote is flammable; the hot gases from your fireplace may be just the thing to set it, and the rest of your property, ablaze.

Fire extinguishers and alarms

Each tenant should have access to a fire extinguisher with a valid use-by date. The extinguisher should be of the ABC class, with chemical suppressants designed to combat A (paper and wood), B (oils and other flammable liquids), and C (electrical) types of fire.

Equally important is inspecting and maintaining an alarm system in your building. Even if a tenant signs a lease that prohibits smoking, that doesn't mean he won't disconnect the smoke detector during a party or a cooking adventure that goes horribly wrong. Be sure to check the smoke detector at least once a year, if not more often.

Developing a Security Plan

You can never predict the unexpected, but you can at least prepare for it by developing appropriate policies ad protocols. Savvy management requires that you know what to do when disaster — or even a minor unfortunate incident — occurs. As a responsible property owner, your best interest is to provide leadership when something happens to or on your property.

You may not have progressively serious levels of alert, or a surveillance program in place to ensure the security of your property (though many commercial property owners do hire private security to protect tenants' interests), but you should know what to do or how you'll respond in the case of a robbery or assault, a vehicle accident involving your property, and so forth.

Home safe home: Preventing property crime

Your home is your castle, or so the saying goes. But when a break-in occurs, confidence in the security of the premises disappears and the bad taste can take months, even years, to go away.

Steps can be taken to protect tenants from the trauma that comes with property crime — not to mention the property damage commonly associated with a break-in:

- ✔ **Provide proper locks and ensure that all doors and windows can be secured.** This is a no-brainer! Even in communities where the doors are always unlocked, the doors still *have* locks. No matter how simple the means you provide, priming tenants on the crime in the neighbourhood and the means by which they can secure the property helps them as much as it helps you.

- ✔ **Keep entrance ways well-lit and trim shrubs to eliminate hiding spots.** Lighting is one of the most effective means of safeguarding tenants, especially single women. Ensuring that doorways can be seen from the street also raises the chances that passersby or neighbours will be witnesses should something unfortunate happen.

- ✔ **Keep ladders locked up.** Why make it any easier for an intruder to reach the second level, or otherwise gain access to your building? Removing portable ladders and any other tools likely to cause damage or injury is common sense. Similarly, be sure to review your property periodically to check for potential entry points.

- ✔ **Ensure that windows and doors are secure but still accessible.** You may not want people to come in by windows or doors, but in the event of a fire or some other misfortune, you *do* want occupants to be able to escape a building quickly. Making sure windows and doors open smoothly is as important as making sure stairs or a ladder can provide escape from upper levels of the building.

Regulations governing fire escapes vary from community to community. Check the policies in your jurisdiction.

Whatever you do can only *help* tenants defend themselves against property crime. You're not responsible for what happens, or for insuring their property against theft or loss. It's in your interest to remind tenants of this fact, and encourage them to take out some form of apartment insurance.

When disaster strikes

Unexpected emergencies, no matter how small or large, create stress. To ensure you keep your wits about you, establish a foolproof, intuitive protocol for addressing such events. Know it by heart, and if you have a property manager, make sure he or she knows it, too. Being able to act responsibly in a stressful situation, whether break-in occurs or a flood or fire strikes, could win you the respect of the community.

A well-crafted response procedure that identifies concrete steps for your building manager and tenants to follow in the event of trouble encourages an orderly response that could limit losses to your property. You may, for example, wish to post an evacuation route for tenants in hallways or stairwells, or post emergency contact numbers in a visible place so that people know who to call. A resident manager will require this information as well, in order to provide clear leadership.

Insurance information

Contacting your insurer with as much information as possible is paramount when something goes awry. The sooner you file your claim, the sooner you'll receive a payout (if it's deemed you've got one coming to you).

Most insurance companies will ask you for a statement of losses, and it's in your interest to make this as complete as possible. You should maintain an inventory of everything that you are likely to claim, and submit the relevant articles when making a claim. Often, photos of what you have lost will help support your claim. From a business point of view, you should maintain a record of major purchases backed up with pertinent receipts. Storing this in a place separate from your property, such as a safety deposit box, is a good idea in the event your loss is the property itself, as in the case of a fire. (We discuss other forms of record-keeping, and their advantage, earlier in this chapter.)

Update your inventory of personal effects and major equipment or business possessions annually to ensure you have the most current information in the event you need to make a claim.

Chapter 15

Accounting for Gain

· ·

· ·

*F*ew people, even among property investors, take a strategic view of their real estate holdings. For many, real estate is an investment bought, passively managed, and eventually sold for (one hopes) a profit. Rarely do people consider properties an integral part of their overall investment or business plan.

As a budding real estate investor, approaching your investments strategically and knowing that real estate investing is more than a money play can yield significant benefits. After all, you need to do a lot more than simply buy in a promising neighbourhood at the right time to make sure real estate delivers the return you want to turn a profit.

Don't worry if this kind of approach hadn't occurred to you, though — we can help. In this chapter, we talk about some of the things you can do to enhance the value of your investment property while you're waiting for it to appreciate. For example, you can spend money on its maintenance or even undertake renovations that will help you garner the maximum return at tax time. You can also strategically manage expenses and deductions so that they also serve your interests. Similarly, balancing allowed capital depreciation against the property's real-time depreciation in the marketplace may work in your favour.

Talk to your accountant for some guidance on drafting and implementing a strategy to address the considerations of your specific property portfolio. The advice will help you manage and operate your business interests.

Building Property Value

Appreciation of property, and in turn your portfolio, doesn't have to be a spectator sport. Developing a strategy that allows your properties to rise beyond their natural value in a market is part of wise management.

Strategies either can involve hands-on involvement or be part of the general management of the property. For example, the decisions to invest in maintenance or even do a complete overhaul of the property are examples of strategic decisions that can boost the property's value. On the other hand, improving the tenant mix, raising rents, and giving tenants greater responsibility for utilities and services (topics we discuss as part of "Managing Expenses," later in this chapter) are management strategies that involve taking a look at your books to see what can improve the property's performance.

We could remind you to check with your accountant (never a bad thing), but keep in mind as well that consulting firms exist that can help you devise a strategy to boost your property's value and overall performance. Many appraisers also handle this kind of work, so talk to your local chapter of the Appraisal Institute of Canada (www.aicanada.ca) for references. The real estate firm you deal with may also know consultants with the expertise you're seeking. A simple Internet search for "real estate consultant" brings up people with diverse skills, so finding a consultant who can serve your needs may require networking until you find the one who's right for you.

Ongoing maintenance

In Chapter 13 we give you some tips on maintaining your property, and in Chapter 14 we focus on how maintenance allows you to minimize risk and ensure the long-term value of your property. So what's left? Well, maintenance expenses also factor on the return you file with the Canada Revenue Agency, so it makes sense to understand how they'll affect the amount of tax you pay now and in the future.

One of the most important distinctions your accountant will make when it comes to investing in maintenance is the difference between

- *Current expenses,* which you can write off for the tax year in which they're made, and
- *Capital expenses,* which you must deduct through the capital cost allowance for depreciation.

Your accountant can tell you the dollar threshold at which a simple expense becomes a capital expense. Knowing the basic distinction between the two allows you to schedule maintenance and renovations in a way that delivers the best return on your investment through write-offs and the like.

Current expenses

Current expenses are the minor costs of operating a business. In the case of an investment property, they can include

- Phone charges
- Advertising
- Cleaning and maintenance supplies
- Maintenance and landscaping services
- Property insurance

Major equipment purchases and direct investment in the property itself, such as renovations, are capital expenses.

Typically, current expenses are inescapable. Although you can economize on various operational costs, items like property insurance are annual costs that are difficult to avoid. You either have them or you don't. By the same token, greater control over current expenses will give you a better handle on your overall cash flow.

Knowing where your cash is going — and when — helps you assess your cash flow. Analysis of your spending habits could prompt you to economize in some areas and boost spending in others. Accounting software packages, a topic we discuss in Chapter 14, can help you crunch the numbers.

Scheduling regular payments so that you aren't hit with a load of expenses at any one time can help you achieve a stable cash flow with fewer strains and hiccups. No sense letting bills pile up only to deal with them later, or to leave yourself open to a massive run on your bank account. Paying all your bills at once may be a cathartic experience — and we won't deprive you of it if that's the case — but paying your bills gradually allows you to develop your savings steadily and bring greater discipline to your investing habits.

Current expenses are great when tax time comes around because you can use them to offset income earned. Although you have to pay for them out of cash flow, in the case of a rental suite in your home the expenses related to the operation of the rental suite may completely offset the income you derive from the suite. This may sound like a bad thing, but considering the rental suite is in your primary residence, the result is actually a more economical residence for you!

Even if expenses don't completely offset taxes owing, they reduce what you have to pay even as they make your investment property that much more viable to operate. Not claiming current expenses is the easiest way to leave money on the table at tax time.

Keep accurate records of expenses related to your investment property. If you don't you'll risk missing out on deductions you're entitled to claim, which could hurt your investment's bottom line significantly.

Not all current expenses are eligible for deduction, however. Be especially careful if there's a personal component to any of the expenses you hope to claim, and consult with your accountant to be sure the expenses you're claiming are legit. Claiming deductions the taxman later disallows will increase the taxes you owe, but also raises the risk you'll be paying interest on unpaid taxes — a potentially hefty amount if the deduction is disallowed several years after you file the return.

A market that's leaning in the buyer's favour may require you to do more to a property in order to sell it than you had expected. Ongoing maintenance helps you show the property at its best. Fresh paint, new siding, and even landscaping each help your property make a better impression on buyers and potentially boost the return it delivers. And, you may be able to deduct the entire cost as a current business expense on that year's tax return. (Not the siding, however — read the section on capital expenses in this chapter for what doesn't qualify as a current expense.)

The principle we advocate here isn't unlike the pyramiding strategy we discuss in Chapter 1. Strategically upgrading a property over the long-term ensures stability of cash flow by ensuring something receives attention every year, rather than leaving everything to be done all at once.

Spending wisely pays off

Just because you seem to be having a good year isn't necessarily an excuse to spend wildly at the end just to rack up current expenses. The strategy may work in business environments where this year's spending justifies next year's budget allocation, but it doesn't necessarily mesh with the sound and sober spending principles that make for a successful business.

Instead, we recommend that you plan your spending to meet your needs and seek alternative methods for reducing your taxes. Any spending should be on an as-needed basis, with a view to meeting the property's needs while continually upgrading the fabric of the property. Ongoing maintenance and attention in general to the property will prevent the need for a spending spree just because you're flush with cash. Reinvest those extra dollars in a vehicle that bears interest — and we're not talking about an eye-catching vintage convertible!

Capital expenses

Capital expenses include major expenditures for the structural improvement of a property, such as new siding, windows, and insulation, as well as major equipment purchases. Your accountant can provide the most current information on what qualifies as a capital expense.

The investments you make in a property help enhance its value to potential purchasers. Regular upgrades ensure the property is in a condition to sell no matter when an opportunity arises. A poor market typically presents the best time to invest in your property, however, for two reasons:

- ✔ **Low tenant demand:** A market that's seeing little interest in the kind of property you've got because of low demand from tenants offers an opportunity to invest in upgrades because you may be disturbing or displacing fewer tenants. Similarly, a building hit with higher-than-usual vacancies is a chance for you to make improvements that could attract new tenants, or to reassess the current tenant mix and reposition the property to target a new kind of tenant.

- ✔ **Potential for appreciation:** A buyer's market is a great time to prepare for a seller's market. Upgrading at a low point in the market cycle may allow you to make cost-effective improvements that could better position your property to take advantage of an improvement in the market when it happens. The greater the appreciation, the better the return on your investment.

TIP

Adding to the value of your assets during a poorer period in the market increases their ability to provide leverage for purchases in the future. A general upswing in the market will tend to raise the value of all properties. You'll be glad you've enhanced your equity in a property when the price was low.

REMEMBER

By definition, you can't claim capital expenses in a single swoop; you can only deduct them gradually in accordance with the rules of the capital cost allowance. Making a huge capital investment in the hope of writing it off in the first year will result in an unpleasant surprise come tax time. You'll end up paying more tax than you had expected, and have less money with which to do it, crunching your cash flow.

Capital expenses help ensure a property remains a good investment, above and beyond the everyday maintenance you have to do as a landlord. Thanks to depreciation rules, capital expenses provide ongoing opportunities for deductions that promise to offset your investment income from the property for years at a time.

On the other hand, strategically deferring capital expenditures can allow you to make investments in a property at a time when the capital expense will do you the most good. For example, when cash flows are tight, upgrading a property can offer a significant first-year deduction against limited rental income, reducing the tax payments required of you. As income improves, partly (we hope) due to the upgrades, you'll have more cash to pay an increasing amount of tax but still be able to claim a significant amount of capital expenses.

Reserving capital for improvements may also allow you to diversify your investment portfolio. It pays to consult with your accountant on a proper strategy for deferring maintenance. If the roof's leaking, no sense painting your building just because it's looking a bit drab. Although both could improve the appeal of the property, the roof is clearly a more urgent matter than the paint job.

As with current expenses, it pays to make regular capital investments both to ensure the property is always in tip-top shape, and also to prevent the hit to your cash flow.

Renovating for fun and profit

For some, renovating properties and reselling them is a way of life. When it comes to revenue-generating investment properties, however, you may have other considerations.

An established tenant base may make renovations difficult, for example, or perhaps you've just bought the property and are trying to stabilize its cash flow before undertaking major improvements. Perhaps the market is hot enough that improvements aren't required to keep tenants. Any mix of reasons may factor into your decision to renovate or postpone such improvements.

We discuss in this section the main considerations you face in the course of deciding to renovate an investment property — everything from deciding which fixer-upper makes a good investment to drafting a strategy that delivers you the return you're aiming to get. We also discuss how to work with tenants, always a consideration if you're trying to upgrade without losing cash flow.

Before undertaking a renovation, make sure what you're proposing works out in terms of payback (see Table 15-1 for an idea of the scale of benefit you can expect from some common procedures). It doesn't make sense to undertake a renovation that allows, for example, a rental suite in your home if the cost is going to outweigh the rental income or resale value of the home. Talk to your accountant and other advisers for their opinion on the situation before you undertake a renovation project.

Table 15-1	**Recovery on Renovation Costs**		
Renovation Project	*Recovery on Resale*	*Renovation Project*	*Recovery on Resale*
Adding a full bath	96%	Adding insulation	65%
Adding a fireplace	94%	Adding a room	62%
Remodelling kitchen (minor)	79%	Re-roofing	61%
Remodelling kitchen (major)	70%	Adding a wood deck	60%
Remodelling bathroom	69%	Adding a greenhouse	56%
Adding a skylight	68%	Replacing windows, doors	55%
Adding new siding	67%	Adding a swimming pool	39%

Snagging a deal

Fixer-uppers offer classic opportunities for contrarian investing. Buying in a neighbourhood that's at the bottom of the market but which your research — and gut feeling — indicates is set for a rebirth, can potentially secure you a significant return on your investment (for more on doing this kind of research, see Chapter 9). Be prepared for the possibility that your hunch may not pay off, however, and that you'll be left with a gem of a property somewhere that still has a long road to recovery.

A more promising approach, and one that appeals to many renovators looking for a return on their time and energy, is the challenge of renewing an older property. Whether it's a heritage home or one that simply needs updating, the opportunity to add value in creative ways to an existing structure is appealing. These kinds of properties are often available in established neighbourhoods, increasing the chance you'll find buyers willing to move in. And depending on the approach you take to the renovations, you may be able to find buyers willing to pay a premium for your work.

Making changes

Do-it-yourself renovations are rewarding, but if you're not a do-it-yourselfer, consider using a design firm that specializes in renovations. It gladly assists you for a fee, and is often well worth the price. Professional advice can help you determine the scope of the work you want to undertake, as well as assist you in setting priorities. If you're new to the game, this can ease the anxiety of renovating a home.

Any contracts you sign should meet professional standards, clearly outlining the scope of the work required, start and finish dates, payment schedules, and holdbacks. A *holdback* is a set amount withheld from your payment to the general contractor in order to pay subcontractors. A holdback is critical if you've undertaken the renovation to an investment property, because if the general contractor you've selected doesn't pay for supplies or services, its creditors have the right to file a lien against your property for the money owed. That not only puts you on the hook, cutting into your returns, but it could also prevent you from marketing the property as quickly as you had hoped. Holdbacks typically represent a tenth of the final cost of services, materials, and labour on a given project, but be sure to consult local authorities for the specific regulations in your province.

Renovations may be subject to municipal regulations, particularly if you plan to make changes to the basic structure of the building. Don't forget to check your plans against local bylaws — you don't want to get hit with a stop-work order and fines. This could significantly delay or prevent you from completing your renovations. Complying with the local building code is also important because not doing so could jeopardize your right to coverage under your home insurance policy should you file a renovation-related claim.

Several elements of the renovations you plan may be eligible for government funding, especially if you plan to make changes that improve the energy efficiency. Restoration of heritage properties can also be eligible for grants, though these typically have exacting requirements concerning the work you plan to do. After all, heritage societies will expect a restoration rather than a reinterpretation of the original form!

Getting your return

The renovations you complete may include a suite suitable for renting to a tenant, and a tenant will provide an ongoing cash flow. But the alternative — selling — will let you recoup an immediate return from your property and give you the capital needed to move on to your next investment project. Selling the home differs little from selling any other property, a topic we cover in Chapter 16.

Substantial renovations — those involving 90 percent or more of the house — may be eligible for tax rebates. (This typically excludes minor additions such as a porch, sunroom, family room or bedroom, or the construction of more than one room.) The Canada Revenue Agency allows you to claim a rebate on GST/HST paid on costs related to the purchase of the land and construction, providing the fair market value of the home after the renovation is $450,000 or less (this amount may change, so be sure to check with the Canada Revenue Agency). Keep in mind that you won't be able to sell the remade home without charging GST, however, as the substantial renovations you've completed put the property in the same class as a new home.

Doing renovations to your primary residence is a good way to boost the resale value of your home — added value on which you don't have to pay capital gains tax. And if the renovation is of a property other than your primary residence that you've been using for rental income, renovation expenses reduce the taxable capital gains you'll realize when the property sells.

Take a rental property, for example: When a renovated property sells, renovation costs are tallied with the property's original purchase price and the sum is subtracted from the sale proceeds. What's left over is the capital gain, which is taxed at 50 percent. For a $150,000 home renovated at a cost of $25,000, the sum is $175,000. But if proceeds from the property's sale total $200,000, you've realized a capital gain of $25,000 — half of which you have to hand over to the government. This may sound bad, but if the renovations weren't taken into account you would be paying capital gains on $50,000!

Renovation frustration

Pat and George had long-planned to renovate their older home. With the real estate market on the upswing, the time seemed right to sell the property and use the proceeds to buy a larger house with a two-bedroom rental suite in the basement.

Since Pat and George had a limited budget of $30,000 maximum to pay for the renovations, they found the name of a renovator in the phone book who said he could do the job for $25,000. They didn't ask for references, let alone check the company's standing with the local home builder's association or Better Business Bureau. Because they were in a rush to get the job done and the price was right, an initial interview was enough to win their trust that the contractor was the one for them.

Costs soon rose to $50,000, and Pat and George were concerned, to put it mildly. The renovator provided a revised estimate that pegged the final costs at $100,000 plus taxes. He said Pat and George "should have known that renos always cost two or three times more than originally planned," adding that if he wasn't paid for the work he would file a lien on the property and proceed with legal action.

Pat and George were shocked. Since they hadn't received the initial quote in writing, it was the contractor's word against theirs. To cover the added costs, they obtained a bank line of credit. When the renovations finished, they quickly put the house up for sale. Unfortunately, the work had added just $20,000 to the value of their home because it upgraded the house but didn't reposition the property to take advantage of what buyers were looking for.

Needless to say, Pat and George weren't able to afford the bigger house with a rental suite they had planned to buy; they had to reduce their expectations and settle for less than what they had hoped.

Timing a makeover

A variety of factors may influence your timing of a renovation:

- ✔ **Market considerations:** Property improvements could help make a property more attractive to potential tenants or purchasers. Undertaking improvements at a low point in a market in anticipation of increased demand is a common strategy that can position your investment to deliver a decent return.

- ✔ **Tenant considerations:** Depending on the scope of renovations you plan, you may have to work around tenants or terminate their leases altogether by invoking the *demolition clause* in the tenancy agreement, a clause that gives you the right to evict them when substantial upgrades are planned. Limiting disruptions to your tenants whenever possible is probably in your interests.

- ✔ **Material and labour considerations:** The availability and cost of materials and labour may prompt you to accelerate or defer renovations in an effort to control costs and maximize the return on your planned investment. at the time of writing this book, a heated construction market in many parts of the country has created shortages in labour and driven up both wages and the cost of building supplies. This is prompting many projects to be deferred, while others are scaled back and accelerated to meet the limitations of available financing.

Thoroughly assess the various time-sensitive factors that could affect your project, such as the factors driving the need to renovate by a certain date, increases in construction costs and market conditions. You may discover that you don't need to complete the project right away, or, alternatively, that you should get to work as soon as possible. As the rabbi Hillel famously asked, "If not now, when?"

Renovations typically require municipal approval. Approval times can range from days to months, depending on various factors. The nature and complexity of your renovations are two considerations. The more complex the makeover, the more time the municipality will take to review your documentation for the work. Municipal staff may also face a backlog of applications if renovations are booming in your community; your project may not be their first priority! The skill, experience, reputation, and connections your architect or contractor possess may also expedite (or retard) the processing time. Be sure to research typical approval times in your municipality and account for these — and potential delays — in your makeover plans.

Working with tenants

Announcing a major renovation to tenants requires tact. Some tenants may be threatened by your plans, others will accept it. Your goal should be the least disruption possible in the daily lives of tenants, and your cash flow.

Here are some key tenant concerns:

✔ **Eviction:** You may not want to lose tenants, and tenants also want to avoid having to find new quarters. Clear and open communication — making sure tenants know from the beginning whether they will be asked to leave — will smooth the way. Where evictions are necessary, be sure to provide plenty of lead time so that tenants can find new accommodation, put their affairs in order, and generally conduct an orderly move.

During a major renovation, consider not leasing units as tenants leave or providing short-term housing in an alternative rental property you own. Such an approach not only maintains cash flow from the property, it saves some tenants the hassle of having to find new digs.

✔ **Debris and noise:** Renovations that don't require evictions may prompt tenant concerns regarding the amount of construction activity that will be taking place. You don't want tenants to feel they're living on a construction site. Good construction managers will try to ensure a limited amount of dust and disturbance, but making sure tenants are comfortable with what's going on is equally important.

✔ **Rent hikes:** Renovations cost money. You may choose to hike rents when you lease up vacant suites following a renovation, but carefully consider the question of rate hikes for current occupants. It may be part of the goodwill you offer existing tenants that rents remain the same as they were before the renovations to ensure the loyalty of long-term tenants whose lives may have been disrupted by renovations, even if the makeover improved common areas such as the foyer or laundry room.

Making overtures to tenants to maintain goodwill during a renovation project is essential to preserving your cash flow. It also makes good business sense. When planning a complete overhaul of a building, for example, see if existing tenants have an interest in leasing in the renovated property.

Working with the property

Properties can be polymorphous, assuming different shapes as the market or tenants require, or the whim of owners dictate. A renovation is an opportunity, within local zoning limits, to enhance, or in some way tweak a property's existing use to better take advantage of market conditions.

To maximize the value of a property renovation, you should take into account several factors:

- ✔ **Property history:** Knowing a building's history may allow you to play up its character and outfit the interiors to appeal to a specific aesthetic. You may also want to reinterpret the building's form to suit new users, as has happened with warehouses that have been broken up into office or residential units.

- ✔ **Tenant mix:** A property may not have the potential to attract a better-paying tenant without renovations. Tailoring a renovation to give a property an appeal among a better-paying pool of tenants can deliver solid top-line returns in the form of higher rents, wider margins, and eventually a better resale value. (Buyers like properties with good income flows.)

- ✔ **Highest and best use:** You may wish to change the use of a property, or add an additional use to improve the cash flow of a property. Walk-ups on a busy commercial street may have potential as a mixed-use project with retail at grade and residential above. Even a simple change like this, depending on local bylaws, could make the property a winner if the reno is done right.

A makeover just won't work for you if no one is around to take advantage of it! Thoroughly research potential markets for a property prior to renovating. You may discover an opportunity for its use that wouldn't otherwise have come to mind. You should be able to build on the knowledge you gathered prior to purchasing the property to gauge uses that would likely appeal to the local demographic.

Speak with your accountant to confirm the tax implications of the renovation, both in the immediate aftermath and when you want to sell the property. A significant renovation, usually to over 90 percent of the structure, can incur taxes that wouldn't apply to a standard resale, because the property will be considered equivalent to a newly built asset.

Flipping: A note

Let's talk flipping. What does it conjure up in your mind? No risk, high rewards? Or high risk, unknown rewards?

When Doug thinks of flipping, he thinks of Paul, a TV addict who was always looking to make a million dollars on the weekend for no money down, just like he'd seen on late-night "infomercials." Paul was especially enthusiastic about the idea of flipping real estate. He thought that if he could buy a property for no money down, find another buyer who would pay $50,000 more for it before the deal closed, and walk away with the gain, he could retire wealthy by the time he was 30. Paul soon found that no one would sell properties to him without a down payment, and he couldn't find anyone to pay him cash to take on the agreements he hoped to enter.

Simply put, real estate doesn't offer any easy route to riches. For many would-be flippers, the best advice comes from the age-old phrase, "Act in haste, repent at leisure."

Flipping real estate means buying and selling real estate:

- ✔ Before you close a deal and transfer of the property occurs, or
- ✔ Not long after (usually within days, occasionally within months) for a greater-than-average profit.

Flippers aim to get in and out of a hot market (characterized by rapidly rising prices and high demand), without the expense and hassle of financing the acquisition or getting renters. That makes flipping less a question of real estate investment than real estate speculation, with all the inherent risks and rewards speculators the world over face. Speculation always assumes the market cycle will continue going up rapidly. That may be true, but as we all know, real estate, business, or investment markets don't keep going up forever. Any type of market is cyclical (have a look at the discussion on market cycles in Chapter 3), and what goes up will come down in time — or at least slow down and plateau.

Flipping before closing

Let's say you locate a buyer for the agreement of purchase and sale of the property you've agreed to buy before you close the deal, but after you remove any subject conditions. You would assign your interest to the buyer, who closes the deal. You would receive money for the assignment in this example, which would include your down payment, plus the extra money you negotiate for the assignment. In this example, your plan is not to close the deal and have to arrange financing, but to have a buyer already arranged (or in the wings) who will take your position in the deal. A relatively long closing date — say four to six months for an existing property, or maybe a year or longer for a pre-sold property that's under construction — gives you the opportunity to find a buyer while real estate prices rise, potentially allowing you a greater return than if the closing time was shorter.

Certain risks are inherent in this option. You may not be able to find someone willing to take your position, either because of the price you're asking or a skepticism about the deal you're trying to arrange. More important, the vendor may not agree to the assignment (after all, the seller originally negotiated the deal with you). And of course, the real estate market could lose momentum, interest rates could start to increase or buyers get cold feet. The result could be more than mere inconvenience; you could find yourself in a deal you don't want as well as out of pocket. Or the vendor may sue you for breach of contract. This kind of flipping is not for the faint of heart.

Don't forget to read the fine print! Some condo presale agreements prohibit you from assigning your unit to another purchaser prior to completion, or selling within a certain timeframe after completion. The prohibition is meant to discourage speculation and to encourage a stable community of residents that set the tone for the development. If you intend to assign your unit, make sure the sale agreement allows you to do so!

Flipping after closing

Some vendors will not permit assignment of sale and purchase agreements, precisely because they don't want to be party to a flip. But after you've closed the deal, you can either hold it or put it back on the market.

It all sounds legitimate, but if you don't have a strategy for the property, you face the same risks someone buying with the intention of assigning the deal does. In addition, you may face carrying charges you didn't expect because you're saddled with a property you didn't plan to keep. You may also end up paying a commission to the broker reselling the property — a commission that could eliminate your profit because you were going on a short-term appreciation in market value rather than a long-term increase in the value of the land and improvements.

Managing Expenses

Given the number of current and capital expenditures you potentially face as a landlord, the strategy you draft for your property should seek to effectively manage — ideally, minimize — the money flowing out as well as maximize the money coming in.

Every property has its costs, so a key decision you need to make as owner and operator of a property is who will pay for the cost of running the property. If you're the primary user, you won't have a lot of other people willing to cover costs stemming from your use. But if you lease out the building to tenants, you have opportunities to share costs and thereby increase your margins.

In this section, we discuss opportunities for you to lower operating costs, explore which items you can manage alone, and identify expenses that you can legitimately ask tenants and building users to cover. We also discuss other opportunities to make good on expenses through savvy tax filings and wise negotiating when the time comes to sell a property.

Distributing costs

The skill of knowing where to cut costs and how to spend wisely goes by the old-fashioned name of prudence. And it's a virtue, especially when you're confronted with many costs and perhaps too little time to assess them all as much as you would like. A prudent investor (that's you) knows which costs to watch, which ones to cut, and which ones to pass along to others. Your goal should be to allocate costs in a way that makes the most sense for everyone, without shirking your duties as landlord (we discuss some of these in Chapter 13).

For example, many landlords pay for heat and hot water, but leave electricity to their tenants. Why? Although different tenants have different comfort levels when it comes to heating, it doesn't make sense for every unit to have its own heating system. At least with electricity, a separate meter can track energy consumption. Heating is a lot more difficult track, unless of course the radiators run off electricity.

What to watch

A simple assessment of your building can highlight the various expenses it faces each month, or on an annual basis. For example, property taxes and insurance, utilities, and garbage pickup are hefty charges that require attention. Maintenance, repairs, and landscaping (including snow removal) have to be addressed. Although some of the costs are fixed for the long term (which can be as little as a year), others crop up in the regular running of a property. Tenancy legislation typically requires you to cover the replacement cost of anything that was in the suite when the tenant moved that later breaks down, whereas the tenant has to cover the cost of repairs (hence the safeguard of damage deposits). Landlords are legally on the hook to replace items they've provided in the suite that wear out, but most tenants won't call their landlord if a light bulb blows or a similar small items need replacing.

Damage is another matter, which is why *damage deposits* — typically a half-month's rent that covers damage a tenant may inflict on leased premises — exist. The laws governing landlord–tenant relations in your province set some basic ground rules for these, so familiarize yourself with them. Most jurisdictions also have free booklets in lay language explaining these types of things. The information is typically available online through your provincial government Web site.

Due diligence prior to your purchase (something we discuss in Chapter 11) should provide a clear picture of the average annual expenses associated with the property. This information, combined with a consultation with your accountant, should highlight areas where you may want to make changes. Perhaps you'll decide to pass along some of the costs to your tenants, or a review of your expenses may flag areas where you're spending more money than necessary and need to economize.

What to absorb

Typically, the more an expense applies to tenants as a whole or the common cost of operating your property, the more reasonable it is for you to cover it. For example, garbage collection is usually handled on a per-building basis rather than tenant by tenant. It makes sense for you to cover the costs associated with garbage collection, but electricity, gas, and high-speed Internet are items best left to the individual.

Making it clear that the rent you're asking covers certain utilities may make your suite more attractive to potential tenants who don't want to deal with bills. You may even be able to charge a premium for the suite. Make sure you're stating a competitive rate for the utilities, however. Don't, for example, argue that the apartment is $750 a month and utilities $50 a month when a standard electricity bill in your area is typically closer to $25 a month.

Just because you pay up front for utilities and the like doesn't mean you have to actually bear the cost! Tallying your average monthly operating expenses and dividing the total by the number of tenants in your building is, after all, one way of determining the rent to charge. The expenses should work out on a per-suite basis to something less than the average annual rent in your area. If not, you need to either seriously question the viability of the investment, or make upgrades that allow you to charge more.

What to pass on

Of course you can pass along the entire cost of operating a building to tenants, but it isn't usually advisable. The tenant of a suite in your basement is unlikely to be willing to pay a rent that reflects the sum of your property taxes, utilities, and other expenses. Similarly, if you've invested in a strip mall with five bays of varying sizes, you may want to divide garbage collection fees equally but pro-rate property taxes according to unit size.

Key items to pass along to tenants directly are regular, recurring metred utilities such as hydro and natural gas. Unless you're able to track the consumption of utilities on a per-suite basis, however, handing the responsibility to just one tenant is probably not a good idea. Peter recalls living in a duplex where the natural gas, which powered the hot water tank, was cut off because his neighbour didn't pay the bill. The mistake of one caused distress to many. The situation took several hours to resolve, embarrassing the landlord and prompting Peter to think owning his own home might not be such a bad thing.

Natural gas-fired fireplaces are appealing, but not everyone is as attentive to them as they should be. Unregulated use can end up consuming a great deal of natural gas. The result is that many property developers are ensuring each suite has control and responsibility for natural gas consumption. This prevents individual building users and tenants generally from bearing the cost of someone else's profligacy.

Determining how much gets passed along may be part of the bargaining process with prospective tenants, particularly if you're a landlord with commercial property. You may have a basic asking rent in mind, but by negotiating other elements of the lease you may be able to secure a deal landing you a long-term tenant and stable revenues.

Recouping expenses

Developing a strategy for recouping expenses has something to do with passing along costs, but it also has to do with tax planning and knowing something about the marketing of your property. You may not be able to recoup every cost immediately, but knowing the opportunities can help you plan to take advantage of opportunities when they come up in the future.

From tenants

Typically the go-to people when expenses rise, many landlords opt not to raise rents on existing tenants and instead look to boost income received from new tenants.

On the one hand, limitations typically apply to increases made to rent during the tenancy term, but the usual limitations on rent increases don't apply when a lease is negotiated afresh. The new lease agreement allows you to boost rents immediately to reflect current costs.

Minor upgrades to units can justify a rent increase beyond that which current expenses indicate you should charge. By increasing your margins, you make the property a better investment with an operating income that's more desirable to future owners of the property. They'll want, after all, to get a piece of the pie you've been enjoying.

From the taxman

Seeking higher rents from tenants boosts your income, but structuring your expenses strategically allows you to offset a fair amount of your income.

More important, your accountant can advise you on tax mitigation strategies that may allow you to recoup cash during the ownership of the property and on its sale. We're not tax experts, so we leave it to those who in the know to steer you in the right direction.

From purchasers

Negotiating a good deal for a property whether you're a buyer (see Chapter 12) or a seller (see Chapter 16) should include attention to the operating expenses and the investment a property requires to keep it in top shape.

An owner who's worked hard to bring down a property's operating costs through sound management and investments in its operations may ask a prospective buyer for more than the property alone is worth. As a vendor, being able to tell the story of the property, where it's come from and how much its performance has improved, can significantly boost the return. A buyer, on the other hand, may argue for a discount that reflects shortcomings in a property.

Being in both positions — both as the buyer negotiating a discount and the vendor talking up the price of a property to reflect your achievements — is where you want to be. Recouping the costs associated with a property from the time you purchase it is part of the strategic buying and selling investors have a chance to do.

More Is Less: Maximizing Deductions

Deductions are great for reducing taxes, but because you're paying for them up front, they also have the potential to break the bank. So don't go overboard!

Deductions typically include the cost of operating the property, including current and capital expenses (see the section on these kinds of expenses elsewhere in this chapter). Deductions reduce the income you claim as taxable when you file your taxes.

If you choose your deduction opportunities wisely, less can sometimes be more. Take time to consider where you'll get the most bang for your deduction buck. What we're talking about isn't necessarily a competition between current expenses and capital expense deductions, nor is it a question we expect to answer in a few paragraphs. Situations and scenarios vary across the country, so be sure to consult with your accountant.

However, we would like to offer a few ideas that may help you discern where the best deductions lie:

> ✔ **Compare the value of deductions.** Reducing operating costs is a great strategy for freeing up capital, but for what? Know what you'll do with the cash once you've got operating costs down. Though you'll be reporting few capital expenses, the savings can be put toward a capital investment that will add to the efficiency or value of your property and deliver significant deductions for years to come. The ongoing benefit of the capital expense deduction will outweigh the value of a host of one-time deductions you might otherwise be making.

✔ **Take advantage of regular deductions to help control costs.** You may spend a significant amount each year on spontaneous deductions, such as door knobs, light bulbs and general fixtures that contribute to the upkeep and appearance of your property. These can easily account for upwards of 20 percent of your total deductions that you can count on to reduce income from your revenue-producing property. Zeroing in on regular costs such as electricity, for example, may allow you to reduce your overall costs and invest the money rather paying it out with a view to reducing taxes.

✔ **Defer deductions until you need them.** Sometimes you may be able to postpone major spending at the end of the year until the new calendar year comes in. This can allow you to beef up your expenses to offset increases in revenue from your properties. Because saving up expenditures can only work for so long, the strategy is practical only for larger increases in income, such as when you sell a property.

You're not obligated to use the full amount of a capital deduction in the year in which you made the investment. You may defer taking advantage of the deduction, effectively allowing you to store up deductions until such time as they're needed. Your accountant can advise you on the best strategy.

Managing Depreciation

Ideally, your investment property will appreciate in value and deliver you a handsome return when the time comes to sell. But you also have the chance to claim *depreciation*, an amount by which the Canada Revenue Agency deems your property to have *fallen* in value each year based on wear and tear. It applies only to the building on a property, not the land.

The key advantage of claiming depreciation of assets under the Capital Cost Allowance (CCA) provisions of the CRA is that you can use the annual depreciation portion to offset income. You will have a declining claim for depreciation each year for the particular asset category you are depreciating.

Claiming depreciation on a home office if you derive rental income from your home could require you to pay capital gains on the property if you later sell the house. You could also be subject to *recapture* — having to claim as income — the depreciation previously allowed on the sold property. You can do without the complications and hassles of recapture. The bottom line? Don't claim depreciation on your principal residence home office. Lots of other, hassle-free expenses are available to you.

Additional information on managing depreciation (and lots of other useful tax tips) is available in *Tax Tips for Canadians for Dummies* (Wiley).

Chapter 16

Trading Up, Trading Out

. . . .

. . . .

*A*ll good things must come to an end. And, thankfully, so must the bad. Whatever your reason for selling, the time has come to wrap up your investment.

Much of what you'll have to do as a vendor you've already done at least once, as a buyer. This time, however, the tables have turned and you're employing in reverse the strategies we discuss in Chapters 11 and 12. Whether you're providing the information that tells potential buyers why your property is right for them (and, therefore, worthy of the asking price), or negotiating with buyers to achieve an appropriate return for a property that no longer suits your portfolio, many of the same lessons apply.

Being a vendor is also quite different from being a buyer, however (we get into the nitty-gritty of buying in Chapters 11 and 12). As a seller you can play hard-to-get, but being a buyer is more about finessing a deal. This chapter is our chance to share with you tips that help you decide when to sell a property and how to prepare to enter the market. We also discuss how negotiate and manage the sale, and offer some suggestions on reinvesting the return your wise management has earned you.

Have a gander at Part III of this book when you're preparing to sell; it offers useful reminders of how buyers approach a property. And review Chapter 12's discussion of negotiating strategies — it's handy information to have as you prepare to review offers for your property.

Reasons for Selling

Any number of reasons may motivate you to sell a property — or your entire portfolio. Making sure your decision is the right one for the moment is important. Just as a right time can be identified to get into real estate, a right time can be identified to trade a property and reinvest the proceeds in a new property or another investment vehicle.

In this section we consider a few reasons for selling, with the aim of helping you think about your decision critically, strategically, and successfully. Whether your motivation is a desire to balance your portfolio or a change of heart toward real estate, we hope you find the information here useful. Another common reason for selling is retirement, which we look at in the next section.

Balancing the portfolio

A common motivation driving many investors to sell is the desire to balance their portfolios. Even if you have only one or two properties, they may have maxed out their potential or built up enough equity to allow you to move into another neighbourhood with better potential, or a different class of assets. Your aim may be to

- **Trade up:** Perhaps you've built up enough equity in your current property that you're ready to consider a new one that will garner even more revenue. Trading up gives you a chance to realize the value of one investment and put it to work in a new investment that will generate not only a greater cash flow but also give you access to a greater equity base.

- **Trade out:** Maybe you're looking to retire, or want to explore alternatives to real estate investments. Or perhaps the local market is in a tailspin and you're wanting a breather. Whatever the reason, trading out allows you to reinvest the gains you've made investing in real estate in something that better suits your current requirements.

- **Just plain trade:** Maybe you need a change of scene, or are hankering to shake up your portfolio with a new purchase. Providing you can make a reasoned argument for it, nothing's holding you back from selling one property and buying another. We trust you to justify to yourself — and your advisors — why you're ready to sell and buy somewhere else. We hope it's to improve your portfolio, but we won't diss you if it's simply to give it a breath of fresh air.

The danger in trading properties is that the next investment may not perform as well as the one you just sold, but chances are you're not trading to be comfortable. You're trading to improve your portfolio's performance, and garner a better return on your capital. Still, to do it right you have to start at square one in terms of selecting an investment — or at least take a look at Part III in this book!

Make sure trades occur at an opportune time. The factors that make it a good time to sell one asset may make for a poor time to buy another. This may complicate matters. An ideal time to trade up is when balanced market conditions prevail, though you may also choose a seller's market to sell and locate a buyer's market in which to reinvest. Of course, regardless of general market conditions, opportunities always exist for the savvy investor.

Seeking other investments

Your real estate investment may not have been a happy one, or perhaps you're just ready for a change from real estate. Here's hoping you sell at market-topping prices!

If things have gone well, you'll likely have little trouble attracting potential purchasers; on the other hand, if you're selling to cut your losses, you may have a harder time drawing top-notch offers. Understanding your reasons for selling, and presenting them as a benefit to yourself and potential buyers, is a challenge with which your team of advisors can help you.

You also want to have a sense of where to put proceeds from your property sales. We detail some of the alternatives to real estate in Chapters 1 and 2, but you should also consult with your accountant and financial planner regarding the specifics of your situation. You may wish to divest your assets gradually, or find a buyer willing to purchase the lot.

Circumstances may not always allow it, but developing an exit strategy that takes into account both your assets and the tax implications of their divestiture is important to the success of your investment venture. You may wish to transform your portfolio gradually from one generating revenue into one that's banking land, with a view to selling a set of well-located properties to a developer. Alternatively, your accountant may suggest a strategy for divesting yourself of your properties and reinvesting the proceeds in such a way as to minimize the tax owing on the proceeds. And when it comes to those proceeds, don't forget to check out the latest edition of *Personal Finance For Canadians For Dummies* by Tony Martin and Eric Tyson (Wiley) for a few tips on what to do with your hard-won cash.

Thinking about selling

When you feel the time's right to sell your property, you need to make sure you've got a valid argument for the sale. Here are some factors that could justify a decision to sell:

- ✔ The market is reaching its peak and the pace of sales could soon slacken.

- ✔ The property hasn't got a lot of room left for appreciation, and may even have begun to fall in value.

- ✔ You don't expect the property to bring in much more income than it already is.

- ✔ Your return on investment is decreasing.

- ✔ Capital expenditures are set to increase.

- ✔ The area shows signs of stagnation or decline, socially or economically.

- ✔ Property management has become more trouble than the property is worth to you.

- ✔ The property has served its purpose in your portfolio.

Review these indicators with your accountant, appraiser, and other advisors and if, together, you think the time has come to sell, make your move!

Retiring

For many people, an investment property is the promise of a comfortable retirement. When the day comes and the gold watch appears, few people harbour the urge to mark time by caring for a property. True enough, a handful see an investment property as something of a retirement project. Others are happy to contract out management of the property, but most consider retirement a time to begin selling off their portfolio.

We discuss some potential strategies for transforming your portfolio into an ongoing source of retirement funds in Chapter 1. Selling may be part of that strategy, but bear in mind that you don't need to sell immediately. As with the disposition of any other investment, you'll want to take a strategic approach and sell when the market is most in your favour.

Now isn't too soon to plan for retirement! Given the typical five- to eight-year length of real estate cycles, you may want to begin grooming your property portfolio to bring you an independent living a decade before you intend to retire. Should optimum market conditions occur during that period, you'll be ready to sell, rather than selling into a poor market later on just because you need funds.

Common options include a reverse mortgage, a line of credit, a sale and lease-back arrangement, and a living trust.

Reverse mortgage

First offered in Canada in 1986, reverse mortgages give you access to the equity that's in your house. If you're 62 or older and own your home outright, they're one means of tapping into the value of your investment. Because they're loans rather than income, they're tax free. The loans made to you are recouped when you move (or, um . . . die).

Reverse mortgages don't let you to tap the full value of the house, however. Typically, you can access only 40 percent of its assessed value, a measure that ensures the lender receives both the value of the house and interest owing even if the property declines in value.

Reverse mortgages are available through major banks across Canada, as well as several credit unions.

Line of credit

The value in your home can also serve to secure a line of credit, which lets you take out only the amount of money you need at any one time. Interest is calculated on the total amount withdrawn, so you pay for only the amount of equity you draw. Lines of credit are best suited if you have short-term financial needs and can repay the loans relatively quickly.

Sale and lease-back

A common practice in commercial and industrial real estate, selling your property to an investor and then leasing it back for your own use, can be an effective tool for financing your retirement. Although you need to have a strategy in place so you don't find yourself without a home if you happen to outlive your rent payments, sale-lease agreements allow you to access the value in your home, finance living expenses, and invest the remainder in investments more accessible than a piece of real estate.

Living trusts

A living trust places your portfolio in the hands of an independent manager, usually a trust company, with family members as co-trustees. The trust receives your investment portfolio and the trustees manage it such that you receive a stable income for life, similar to an annuity. The remaining capital is distributed to family members on your death. The provisions of the trust agreement should provide instructions for the financing of your care should you require long-term medical attention.

Making the most of an exit

When David was 35 he decided he wanted to invest in property in British Columbia's fashionable Whistler ski resort. For eight years, bought a chalet a year. He had a clear business plan and applied a formula that worked for him very well. He signed a five-year lease with a British ski company that allowed him to rent out his chalets for the five-month ski season each year. The British company then used the chalets to provide fully-catered ski packages. During the other seven months of the year, David contracted a property management company to find short-term tenants for his properties.

David made a point of limiting his investment to 10 percent and obtaining a five- to seven-year fixed-rate mortgage for the rest at the lowest rate possible. That way he could budget his mortgage interest costs easily. Since property values in the resort were going up 10 to 20 percent a year, David was able to leverage the increasing equity of his initial property purchases to pay down payment on subsequent chalet investments. The bank was pleased to give a mortgage, as the annual revenue from

the contracted rentals paid for all the debt servicing costs while leaving David with 70-percent positive cash flow. David put the profits toward paying down his chalet investments. Due to the increasing equity for all the chalet properties each year, the bank had lots of security.

Ten years after making his initial investment, David finalized his exit strategy. He sold his chalets over a three-year period when the marketing timing was optimal, keeping one chalet for his own use. The average market value of his chalets had risen to $2.5 million each. At the age of 48, David accepted a retirement incentive package from his employer after 30 years of service as a fire fighter. He bought a beautiful boat and took his wife and three young children around the world for 3 years.

David netted about $6 million from his property sales, proving the benefits of a focused plan for not only entering the real estate market but getting out. Through diligence and resourcefulness, David was able to retire comfortable and treat his family to the adventure of a lifetime.

Trust companies charge fees for their services, and they do the job. But the main requirement for trustees, is that they be competent, independent parties who will manage your affairs in your best interest. Trustees can be trusted associates with no financial interest in your affairs. To reduce costs, consider whether you really need a trust company to do the job.

Knowing When to Sell

Just as you can increase your potential gain by buying when the market's low, you can improve your return by selling as the market's rising. Gauging when your returns are as good as they're going to get is difficult, however. (We discuss market cycles in Chapter 9 — check it out if you need a few tips.)

An investment not only helps you to make more of your resources in the present, but also promises to help you do more in the future. Many investors invest with a view to funding their retirement, so devising a disposition strategy that helps achieve your financial goals is integral to the financial plan you develop.

Major reasons for disposing of assets include rebalancing your portfolio in favour of more liquid or higher yielding investments, and securing funds for retirement or in accordance with your estate plan.

A standard strategy is regular renewal of your portfolio, either through maintaining existing assets or trading up to new or higher yielding properties. Consider the strategy of pyramiding. Not to be confused with pyramid schemes, *pyramiding* involves the purchase of one or two select assets on a regular basis, and the sale of others, ensuring that your portfolio constantly renews itself and doesn't become stale. Pyramiding also provides an opportunity to review your investments and assess how your financial plan is helping you achieve the goals you've established.

When you're looking to sell, you may face some added incentives to move a property that could affect your judgment of what constitutes a good return. These include the following:

✔ The desire for a prompt sale, for personal or business reasons

✔ A need for proceeds to finance other investments

✔ An inability to finance repairs or improvements to the property

✔ A slowing market that could make it difficult to sell a property in the future

Striking a realistic balance between your needs and the state of the market improves your chances of securing a return that satisfies you.

Gauging your needs

Here's our best advice whether you need cash to finance a new business venture, are preparing to retire, or simply wish to end the investment and put your money elsewhere: *Know your goals.* These may dictate your willingness to accept a range of offers, the degree of variation you'll accept, and how far you're willing to go to strike a deal.

For example, if you're selling a piece of property to finance a new business venture, you may wish to sell only so much as will garner you the amount you need. Or, if you're selling an entire property and that isn't enough, you may want to consider a more creative deal structure. You may own a property that's also a business, such as a bed-and-breakfast or a gift shop. You may consider selling the property but striking a deal that allows you to stay on as manager until you've recouped the amount you hoped to secure.

The urgency of your needs may also prompt you to accelerate a sale, taking a lower price for a property than you might have hoped because a better opportunity awaits or the cash flow on the operation isn't panning out for you. Divesting yourself of the property may deliver a better return than holding it till you receive a better offer.

Sonny, a streetsmart investor friend of Doug's, includes the tax implications of any capital gains possible from a sale in his marketing plans. Sonny strives to sell properties on which he expects significant capital gains in a year where he has seen significant losses on other investments. The losses offset any the capital gains on Sonny's real estate investments, ensuring even bad investments deliver a benefit.

Gauging the market

As we discuss in the previous section, your circumstances may dictate that you can't wait until a market turns favourable to turn your property over. Ideally, you want to sell during a *seller's market*, when buyers are plentiful in relation to the supply of available properties and prices are rising with demand.

The cyclical nature of the real estate market means a seller's market won't always exist, however. Gauging when to enter the market takes research, something we discuss in Chapter 9, but if you're serious about selling you may want to test the waters to see what the market will bear. An appraiser can help you judge the several market factors that could come to bear on your property, and the Realtor you enlist to handle the sale can flag the property to potential buyers and see if any bite. Any offers received during these preliminary forays into the market could go firm.

Regardless of when you go to market with a property, whether it's a case of soft-peddling it or a full-on market blitz to find a buyer, don't forget to be professional. Bringing a property to market too often can give it a well-worn scent that doesn't wash with buyers. In fact, you may need to wash off the scent of disinterest before a sale actually takes place! If that's the case, be prepared to give the property a dramatic facelift, or more simply, wait till the market's forgotten its previous inability to sell.

Waiting out the market

When the market's not in your favour, as a seller, you can take several steps to make the most of your time (and investment). Here are a few suggestions Doug offers:

✔ Boost the so-called "curb appeal" of the property through inexpensive steps such as painting, minor landscaping, and the like to improve its appeal to prospective buyers.

✔ The small improvements may allow you to increase rents over the normal annual increase limit. This ensures that you maximize the cash flow from the property before you sell. You're responsible for making sure you're getting the most revenue from the property you can, while you've got the opportunity!

✔ Look for ways to decrease expenses on the property. For example, maybe you can arrange for the tenant to cut the lawn or do other maintenance work for a reduction in rent, which would cost you less money than if you paid an outside contractor to do the ongoing work.

✔ Reduce your debt-servicing costs if possible. For example, your mortgage may be coming up for renewal. Negotiate the lowest possible mortgage rate with a mortgage broker, taking out a long-term mortgage at the more favourable rate and extending your amortization period to 30 or 35 years to reduce your monthly payments (see our discussion managing mortgages in Chapter 7).

✔ Monitor trends and surveys to get a sense of when the market appears to be going up again, and be ready to sell. (We discuss sources of reliable information in Chapter 17, and elsewhere throughout this book.)

 If you're unsure about market conditions, it probably makes sense to bring a property to market gradually. That doesn't mean moving it closer to the street or selling it one brick at a time; rather, it's a question of building interest in the property before you begin marketing it in earnest. You might opt for a bit of gentle marketing, for instance, treating the initial offers seriously so that potential buyers have the sense you know what you want. This helps to discretely build momentum around a property until a deal actually comes together. People may talk about how long it took the property to sell, but they won't be able to gainsay your discretion and handling of the deal.

Managing the Sale

Securing a great deal for a property is just as complicated for the seller as the buyer. Although the vendor holds the right to reject any purchase offer, the only offers coming forward are what the market is willing to pay.

Handle with care

Property investments may be bricks and mortar, but they're also pretty fragile in the wrong hands. A wrecking ball isn't the only thing that will knock down an investment's value. Take the example of Fred and Alice, who were preparing to sell their home after 30 years of proud ownership. They wanted to buy a condo for retirement, and have some extra cash from the sale. They thought they would save on commission fees to an agent by selling the home themselves.

Unfortunately, the sale did not go smoothly. The market was slow, the asking price Fred and Alice set reflected their own needs rather than market conditions for their area, and negative comments about the property from visitors during the open houses they hosted were discouraging. And, of course, bids on the house were low compared to the price Fred and Alice had set. The experience was frustrating for Fred and Alice, who felt insulted and increasingly bitter towards their prospective purchasers.

Fred and Alice eventually decided to list the house with a real estate agent. However, the market had slowed considerably and the average price for a home comparable to what Fred and Alice were trying to sell had dropped 15 percent. Fred and Alice eventually sold their house but the final price was 25 percent lower than their original asking price. Although professional sales assistance made a difference in the sale, it would have made a greater difference had it happened earlier.

The one bright spot in the gloom was that the general downturn in real estate prices had also affected the condo they eventually bought, so it ended up going for a low price, too.

Given these conditions, managing a sale is just as important to the vendor as negotiating skills are to a potential purchaser. The vendor can position the property and spark demand for it if buyers respond to the narrative woven around the property and the basic fundamentals of the property are strong.

In this section, we explore the sale process from the perspective of the vendor (that's you) and tell you how to achieve the best deal possible from your real estate — even when you're cutting loses because the property or the surrounding neighbourhood is experiencing a downturn.

Becoming a vendor

You may have spent your entire investment career buying properties. Now the time has come to sell. Making the transition to a vendor requires turning the tables and being as respectful, yet hard-nosed, with buyers as you were with the people who sold you the properties.

In Chapter 12 we advise against buying a property without the assistance of a Realtor. Naturally, here we advise against selling without a Realtor's assistance. A Realtor's expertise can save you a lot of time, stress, market exposure, potential legal difficulties, and a host of other troubles.

Avoiding personal exposure in the market may be one of the best reasons to work with a Realtor. A Realtor helps shield you from excessive scrutiny, especially if you're trying to sell a less-than-desirable property in your portfolio. A healthy measure of anonymity may also be an advantage as you review and assess offers.

On the other hand, the deal may be such that a face-to-face meeting benefits the negotiations. Your Realtor can screen offers and select the candidates most likely to buy from you.

Whatever the case, maintain an open attitude even when working through a Realtor. Your negotiating style sets the tone for the discussions. Your mission as vendor is to move the property, not hold it forever.

Preparing the property

Buyers may have the burden of due diligence, but as vendor, you've got the challenge of preparing the property to look its best. You may be able to contract out elements of this to *stagers,* consultants that transform properties to look better to a target market, but the ultimate decisions are yours. The real estate firm with which you're dealing may have people in-house who can help you stage your home; or your community may have one of the growing number of firms that focus on home staging. Some home stagers are represented by the Canadian Redesigners Association (`www.canadianredesigners association.org`).

Preparing to sell a property involves three basic steps:

1. Research the market, particularly comparing similar properties

2. Identify the property's prime selling points, and the value you believe these add to the property

3. Enhance the property's appearance and appeal to potential purchasers

Researching the market

Knowing the kinds of properties available in a given neighbourhood or market area helps you position your property to prospective buyers. The research isn't much different from what you would do as a buyer (see Chapter 10), only this time you're looking at the market from a vendor's perspective.

You may have a one-of-a-kind home, a piece of land in a locale where others have sold for an elevated price, or a commercial property in an area that's booming. Or, recent sales information and a conversation with your Realtor may prompt you to downgrade your expectations of your property's worth.

Knowing the features of your property that will appeal to the typical buyer for your area is also important. Research the following to develop an argument why a given buyer should snap up your property:

- ✔ **Demographics,** which may have changed since you purchased the property and bear re-examination
- ✔ **Site conditions** may make renovation or redevelopment of the property an option for the next owner
- ✔ **Buyers** scouting properties in your area may require you to position your property in such a way that it appeals to their interests, motivations, and investment goals, and allows you to achieve an appropriate return.

Getting the scoop on these elements is key to meeting the market — and your buyers — where they're at.

Identifying selling points

The features of your property that appealed to you or worked for users may not strike a chord with the next owner, but they're what you know. Use the aspects of which you're most proud as starting points for the pitch to prospective buyers that you'll craft with the agent selling your property. Your agent may know what's appealing to the current market, but you know your property better than your Realtor and can provide a list of advantages. These talking points help the Realtor frame the property for potential buyers. We discuss several of these from the buyer's perspective in Chapter 9; they're worth keeping in mind as you prepare to sell your property to others.

Your inventory of selling features should include recent improvements and any major renovations or upgrades that support the asking price. Recent landscaping, a new furnace or heating system, or even new carpeting all deserve a mention. Don't forget to mention intangible improvements too. A reversal in a rental property's stagnant occupancy rate indicates a significant improvement in overall cash flow that highlights how you have enhanced the property's stature since purchasing it.

Neighbourhood amenities such as transportation links, shopping centres, and public amenities including schools, parks, and playgrounds warrant a reference. In short, anything highlighting a property's worth helps your Realtor weave a compelling narrative to attract potential buyers.

Grooming the property

We've all seen sad-sack properties with lots of potential that somehow just don't grab us. You don't want your property to come across the same way. To improve the "curb appeal" of your property, make it as attractive as possible. Inside and outside, the home should appeal to the prospective buyer — enough to command a decent price in short order.

Knowing the kind of buyer to whom a property most likely appeals is only part of your focus in making an appropriate presentation. Getting rid of unnecessary possessions that detract from a sale is also effective. Many people like their surroundings to be filled with familiar items, no matter how unattractive or impractical, and they underestimate how unappealing their personal effects are to complete strangers. The decor and detritus of your life could be a complete turnoff to buyers.

Rather than getting rid of personal effects completely, simply remove them during the sales period and keep them in storage until the sale is complete. (Although if the sales process has also inspired you to cull your stuff, we won't discourage you!)

Various property staging services have set up shop across Canada in recent years specifically to help ensure properties look their best prior to a sale. Often, staged properties sell for 10 percent or more above the asking price. No need to pass up that kind of premium when help is available! Stagers typically charge either a set fee or a cut of the final sale price. Whatever the amount, it's well worth the cost if you're no interior design whiz.

Working with buyers

Buyers, as we discuss in Chapter 12, negotiate to get the most possible for the lowest reasonable price. This gives them a better chance at seeing some appreciation in their investment. By that same token, you're aiming for the greatest possible return on your property; negotiate with that aim in mind.

The two meet in mutual respect for the other's objectives. Specifically, focus your negotiations on the following:

- ✔ Price
- ✔ Conditions
- ✔ Benefits like chattels, upgrades, and goodwill

Pricing it right

A common strategy is to price a property slightly higher than what you hope to receive. This forces the buyer to meet your terms with an offer, usually less than your asking price, that should come near the real value of the property. A buyer willing to pay the asking price without questions is a sign you've either priced the property too low, or are extremely fortunate.

Buyers, especially in a *buyer's market* offering lots of choice to relatively few buyers, have a keen eye to pricing. You could defer a sale if the offers you're seeing aren't what you want, but you may not have the luxury of time.

To market, to market . . .

Marketing your property is a team effort between your real estate agent and you. Your property doesn't only need curb appeal, it needs exposure. Consider your property from the buyer's perspective: Where would you be likely to look for a listing for your property if you were buying it all over again?

Normally, your real estate agent sets up the marketing plan for your property, and does all the marketing for you. However, some agents simply list your property the Multiple Listing Service (www.mls.ca). Other Realtors offer a multifaceted 25-point marketing plan to promote your property. Here are some marketing avenues to consider:

✔ List through the Multiple Listing Service

✔ List through a brokerage's or real estate agent's Web site

✔ Promote in a real estate office window display

✔ Distribute a flyer by bulk mailing to people on the agent's distribution list or to homes in the surrounding neighbourhood announcing that the property is for sale

✔ Host an open house exclusively for real estate agents, to highlight the property and its features; each agent typically has an average of eight interested buyers at any one time, so the strategy multiplies your chance of finding an interested buyer

✔ Host a public open house for potential buyers

✔ Put up a lawn sign

✔ Advertise in daily and weekly community newspapers, as well as newspapers and magazines targeting property investors

---

To improve your chance of selling the property, gain as much exposure for the property as possible so that competition increases sufficiently to warrant a higher price. One of the key things you want to ask the real estate agent you select to market your property is what sort of marketing he can do for you. Write details of the marketing plan into the listing agreement. An effective plan may make a difference in how you optimize the curb appeal of your property, what price you ask, how quickly the property sells, and what you eventually sell for. We discuss the general process for selecting a real estate agent in Chapter 4.

Be sure to weigh the cost of a marketing blitz for your property against the higher value you hope to get from a property. Any exposure should have a payoff in the form of a faster sale, or greater sales proceeds.

Conditions: Clause for thought

A buyer's offer to purchase may include various subject clauses, points to be resolved before the deal goes firm and closes. Asking for a few clauses of your own gives you some leverage in the deal. These may include the following:

✔ **Removal of conditions in the event of a backup offer:** You may wish to keep your hands free in case a more attractive, competing bid emerges following receipt of an initial purchase offer. The standard time stated in such clauses is usually 72 hours. The clause stipulates the removal of conditions from the initial bid in the event a more favourable bid comes forward.

✔ **Legal review:** Your lawyer should review any real estate deal you enter, whether it's a purchase or sale. Ask for enough time to thoroughly review the purchaser's offer, and then in some cases follow up any specific concerns.

✔ **Timeline:** Set a time limit for the evaluation of the deal, usually a minimum of 24 hours but sometimes as much as four months. You want to be able to satisfy any outstanding issues and be able to close the deal properly. Once you accept a purchase offer, you'll also need to set a closing date. Requesting more time may give you greater opportunity to ensure a deal is the best one possible, but if the market is hot, you may opt to set a specific day and time for receiving offers. This creates an auction-like atmosphere, and prospective buyers know they need to offer their best price or risk losing the deal. A slower market allows for a more balanced approach and a longer time frame for reviewing offers and making counteroffers, sometimes up to two weeks.

We discuss subject clauses at greater length in Chapter 12.

Counting the benefits

Weaving a good story about a property is one way to support a relatively high asking price (note that by "weaving" we don't mean "making up"), but you can also point to several aspects of a property that support its claimed value:

✔ **Chattels:** The goods that are ancillary to the property itself are often assigned a value that is negotiable aside from any buildings and lands included in the deal. The greater the perceived value of these, the greater the price you can ask for the property.

✔ **Upgrades:** We discuss elsewhere in this chapter the importance of touting the improvements you've made to a property. The asking price should reflect these; highlight them as needed among the reasons why the property is worth the tremendous (yet very reasonable) amount you're seeking.

✔ **Goodwill:** Perhaps your property is a landmark apartment block on a prime corner. Perhaps the property has heritage status. You can sometimes assign a value to the importance of a property that pure market forces don't reflect. Knowledge of a property's history and importance boosts your chances of making a viable argument for its goodwill value.

Capitalizing on each of these elements allows you to boost the return a property delivers. You won't be able to claim each of them every time, but being familiar with their contribution to property value allows you to argue more effectively for a higher price.

Closing the deal

We discuss the legal requirements of closing a deal in Chapter 12. Yet from a vendor's point of view, closing costs are a primary consideration in completing a successful investment. Miscalculate the costs and years of hard work could suffer a significant blow.

A primary concern is *prepayment costs,* a penalty charged for pre-paying a *closed*, or locked-in, mortgage (we discuss closed mortgages and prepayment penalties in Chapters 6 and 7). The purchaser's assumption of your mortgage would save you from these charges, but you need to discuss any such arrangements during negotiations for the property.

For example, if five years are left on a mortgage's seven-year term and interest rates had decreased 3 percent from the rate on your mortgage, your decision to prepay the whole amount would leave the lender short in terms of lost interest revenue. The penalty in this scenario is normally the difference between your mortgage rate and the prevailing market rate for the balance of the term, or three months' interest (whichever is more). For an $800,000 locked-in mortgage bearing interest at a rate three percentage points above the rate when you decide to repay, you would find yourself paying a $24,000 penalty (that is, $800,000 x 0.03). But you could avoid the penalty if the buyer agreed to assume the mortgage.

When someone assumes the mortgage you originally secured, obtain a release from your lender in case the new buyer defaults on the mortgage. Otherwise, you could be held responsible for the balance of your original mortgage.

Make sure the proceeds from the deal are taxed as little as possible. Your accountant can advise you on potential tax mitigation strategies prior to closing the deal. In fact, such strategies should form part of your investment strategy, given their importance to your portfolio's bottom line.

Cutting losses

Sometimes it's not the neighbourhood that has entered a downturn, it's the property itself. Perhaps a number of unexpected maintenance issues have come up and the current circumstances in the neighbourhood prevent you from financing the kind of improvements you need to make. Perhaps the last tenants abused it and you can't get financing to renovate because of the kind of damage and the risk the neighbourhood poses.

For example, the neighbourhood may be known for marijuana grow-ops or other forms of illicit activity that make it highly undesirable. However, research indicates that new development is heading in the direction of this neighbourhood, and the municipality and police have decided to purge the area of undesirable elements by enforcing building and fire bylaws. These factors could influence your decision to buy and hold, even if you can't rent the house out, because of the depressed prices and elevated long-term hopes for the area.

Knowing when to cut losses in order to realize a property's full potential is important. We discuss strategies for dealing with the unexpected in Chapter 3, but a few further points are worth considering.

When a neighbourhood deteriorates and takes your rental property with it, you choose to refrain from renting it and simply hold it until the land value improves enough to deliver you a decent return. So long as the property isn't an eyesore or risk to the public, you can hold the property until such time as you find an economically viable use for it.

When you cease to rent a property, you'll probably face ongoing property taxes and other charges, so be sure you have the resources to handle these. You may be able to finance the charges with income from other investments, or it may simply make sense to swallow the charges rather than the charges as well as your ongoing losses.

You may not be able to address the downturn by yourself, but in cahoots with a partner (we discuss selecting partners in Chapter 5) you may be able to swing an arrangement that benefits everyone — you, a partner, and the neighbourhood! For example, you may be able to sell the property to an investor with greater means to finance a viable redevelopment of the property. Or you may consider a joint venture with another investor, or some other means of leveraging your property to see a gain.

Reinvesting the return

So, you've sold your property and ended up with a wad of cash. Now what?

Make the best of it!

We discuss several of your retirement-based options earlier in this chapter, but if that's not where you are in life then we hope you're looking at new real estate investment opportunities. Alternatively, you may want to consider committing the proceeds of your investment to a trust fund or annuity that can support you during your retirement years.

Having worked hard to develop a successful portfolio, you really deserve to enjoy the fruits of your labour.

Wills and (Real) Estate Planning

One occasion when you won't have to worry about selling . . . is when you buy the farm. But before you add that plot of earth to your portfolio, you should make arrangements that may make life easier for those you leave behind. That's right, you need a will — if only to preserve the good memories people have of you. Not having a will invites frustration for the administrators of your estate, and could result in your paying a lot more tax, essentially defeating your best efforts to be a successful real estate investor. A will ensures that your investments are efficiently and promptly distributed as you wish, not by a predetermined government formula.

A will isn't the only tool available to manage your estate. Powers of attorney also help facilitate the orderly management and transfer of your investments prior to your death.

Powers of attorney

Powers of attorney, either temporary or enduring, allow a trust company or trusted person to handle management of your assets in the event you're out of the country or otherwise incapable of managing your affairs personally. You must assign powers of attorney for each jurisdiction where you have assets, but one person may hold the power in every case. Powers of attorney are revocable at any time.

Powers of attorney are especially important for an investor in real estate. They facilitate the payment of bills and allow your representative to tackle legal issues that arise when you're mentally or physically unavailable. It gives them the authority to address tenants as you would were you able, and to sign contracts and agreements in your stead. All these can help facilitate the management of your properties should you suddenly become incapacitated.

Will

A will is a legal document best drawn up by a lawyer who can ensure it meets the requirements of your province or territory (wills aren't automatically transferable from province to province). Your will instructs your estate's *executor*, the person you entrust with carrying out your will, regarding the disposition of your estate. A will entrusts the executor with the following:

- ✔ Responsibility for paying outstanding bills and debts
- ✔ Authority to file your tax return and pay any taxes and fees owing against your properties
- ✔ Authority to sell your properties

Where there's a will, there's a way — to limit the involvement of government in the administration of your estate. Without a will, the provincial government effectively becomes executor of your estate through a court-appointed administrator. Should a family member not step forward to fulfill the role, it falls to the public trustee or some other representative of the government. Following an exhaustive inventory undertaken at the estate's expense, the estate is distributed according to provincial laws. This could result in your assets being sold on expedient but unfavourable terms, or your heirs may pay taxes that might have been deferred or reduced had an estate plan and will existed.

Unlike powers of attorney, a will valid in your place of residence at the time of your death is valid in all other jurisdictions. Assets in other jurisdiction, including the United States, would typically fall under the terms of that will. Two documents could actually confuse matters and expose your estate to litigation, so limit yourself to a single will. Obtain reliable legal advice for your specific circumstances.

Don't even think of writing your own will! It could be the kiss of death for your estate. The potential legal and tax risks could jeopardize your efforts to develop a successful real estate portfolio. Paying a lawyer who specializes in preparing wills and estate planning can save your heirs grief and prevent the government becoming a main beneficiary of your estate.

One of the best things you can do for those taking care of your estate is to leave a record of your investments. Although they might seem obvious to you, not everyone knows where to look for the information you take for granted. Statistically, one out of four people die suddenly, which gives no time to get your financial affairs in order. Take time to create, and regularly update, a list of your properties and investments — and make at least two copies. Keep one copy in a convenient location your executor knows, and the other with your will.

Dying to know more?

For advice regarding estate planning, consult a professional or organization that specializes in this area. Several have Web sites with basic tools that help you devise an estate and succession plan that suits your needs.

The Canadian Estate Planning Institute Inc. (www.estateplanning.ca), for instance, offers articles on financial and estate planning. It also provides several checklists and charts that give you a head start on drafting a succession plan for the real estate empire you've built.

The National Real Estate Institute Inc. (www.homebuyer.ca), with which Doug has an affiliation, is another excellent source of information.

And if you're looking for good old-fashioned print resources, pick up a copy of *Wills and Estates for Canadians for Dummies* by Margaret Kerr and JoAnn Kurtz (Wiley).

Part V
The Part of Tens

The 5th Wave   By Rich Tennant

"Evidently, he made millions flipping real estate in Japan."

In this part . . .

Do you need to contact a lawyer? Are you wondering how to increase the value of your property? Have a gander at this section for details on some of the many organizations qualified and willing to help you, lists of contacts for a variety of regional organizations, and some great ideas as to how you can boost your property's worth.

Chapter 17

Ten Resources for Reliable Information

In This Chapter

▶ Looking for help in all the right places

▶ Knowing whom — and when — to call

*T*hroughout this book, we mention various professionals and professional organizations that offer the skills, expertise, and basic information that can help you build a real estate investment portfolio that works.

Knowing that help is available is one thing — knowing when to call on help, and the best source of help in any given situation, is another. And, as always, you'll experience situations where a bit of cross-pollination will be more helpful than going straight to the one obvious choice.

This chapter highlights some of the resources available, the problems they can help you solve, and the ways you can make use of the expertise they offer to develop a successful portfolio.

Professional and Industry Organizations

Individual Realtors and property brokers are integral to the development of your real estate portfolio. But the professional and industry organizations that represent them and speak for the real estate trade as a whole can also be valuable resources as you research a market, build your portfolio, and deal with your broker.

Three types of organizations exist, each with distinct roles, and often with national, provincial, and local counterparts. These include

✔ **Boards** (the local body representing Realtors and the real estate industry in a given municipality or region, which in turn is a member of a provincial association): Nationally, the Canadian Real Estate Association (www.crea.ca) is the umbrella group that represents the various provincial real estate associations and local boards.

Real estate boards regularly produce reports on sales trends and market conditions. Using this information to gain a basic sense of local conditions, where the hot areas are, and the number of listings available for a given month can help you determine where a particular market is in a cycle.

✔ **Councils or commissions:** In most provinces and territories, councils regulate the activities of Realtors. Whether government or industry-run, councils typically set standards for the industry, handle complaints, and discipline members.

Suspicious about your Realtor's ethics, or a tactic the vendor's broker is pursuing? Your province's real estate council can tell you what's legal and what's not for Realtors in your area.

✔ **Institutes:** They educate and oversee the accreditation of Realtors. The national body is the Real Estate Institute of Canada (www.reic.ca); many provinces have a local counterpart.

Because real estate is a provincial responsibility, the structure of the industry and roles played by boards, associations, councils, and institutes varies from province to province. Visit the Web sites of the local organizations in your area to familiarize yourself with the roles of the various organizations, or give the organizations themselves a call to get more information, whether at the outset, or if the relationship with your broker goes sour. Here are the real estate associations for the various provinces and territories:

✔ Alberta Real Estate Association (www.abrea.ab.ca)

✔ B.C. Real Estate Association (www.bcrea.bc.ca)

✔ Manitoba Real Estate Association (www.realestatemanitoba.com)

✔ Newfoundland and Labrador Association of Realtors (www.homesplus.nf.net)

✔ New Brunswick Real Estate Association (www.nbrea.ca)

✔ Nova Scotia Association of Realtors (www.nsar.ns.ca)

✔ Ontario Real Estate Association (www.orea.com)

✔ Prince Edward Island Real Estate Association (www.peirea.com)

✔ Quebec Federation of Real Estate Boards (www.fciq.ca)

✔ Saskatchewan Real Estate Association (www.saskatchewanreal
estate.com)

✔ Yukon Real Estate Association (www.yrea.ca)

The councils and other bodies governing real estate board members in each province and territory include the following:

✔ Association des courtiers et agents immobiliers du Québec (www.
acaiq.com)

✔ Government of Newfoundland & Labrador, Government Service Centres
(www.gov.nf.ca/gsl/cca/tpl/realestate-licencing.STM)

✔ Government of Prince Edward Island, Corporate and Insurance Division
(www.gov.pe.ca/oag/ccaid-info/index.php3)

✔ Nova Scotia Real Estate Commission (www.nsrec.ns.ca)

✔ Real Estate Advisory Council (www.msc.gov.mb.ca/realestate)

✔ Real Estate Council of Alberta (www.reca.ab.ca)

✔ Real Estate Council of British Columbia (www.recbc.ca)

✔ Real Estate Council of Ontario (www.reco.on.ca)

✔ Saskatchewan Real Estate Commission (www.srec.sk.ca)

The councils for New Brunswick and the territories don't have Web sites, but you can still contact them at the following addresses:

Municipal & Community Affairs
Government of the Northwest Territories
Box 1320
Yellowknife, Northwest Territories
X1A 2L9
Tel: (867) 873-7118

Real Estate Council Of New Brunswick
PO Box 785
Fredericton, New Brunswick
E3B 5B4
Tel: (506) 455-9733

Yukon Government
PO Box 2703
Whitehorse, YK
Y1A 2C6
Tel: (800) 661-0408

Local Market Reports

The market reports that local real estate associations issue aren't the only sources of information about property sales and trends. Most private real estate companies also produce their own analyses of where markets are heading, and what's hot and what's not. Tapping into their knowledge as part of your basic market research (something we discuss in Chapters 3 and 4) will provide a more nuanced picture of what's going on in the market and may alert you to opportunities you otherwise wouldn't have considered.

Typical sources of market reports include

- **Banks and credit unions:** Because of their interest in the general state of the economy, banks and credit unions will often produce reports examining both general and sector-specific trends. The research typically takes a look at both national and provincial trends, and sometimes includes sections focusing on larger metropolitan areas. The reports sometimes have a direct connection to the investment trends, other times they highlight consumer issues such as housing affordability that may indicate where opportunities lie for investors. To access the reports, simply go to the publications section of the bank's Web sites and see what's available.

- **Brokerages:** Both residential and commercial brokerages issue quarterly and annual reports that examine sales and trends in particular areas, asset classes, and market segments. Get to know the firms dealing in the kind of property that interests you; regardless of the firm's size, it will likely produce a report that fills you in on what the firm and its agents are seeing. Most of these reports are available for the asking because they're a good way for the brokerage to keep its name in front of potential clients; you will often be able to access them online through the brokerage's Web site.

Some of the firms to contact for reports for residential properties include

- Royal LePage (www.royallepage.ca)
- Re/Max Canada (www.remax.ca)
- Century 21 Canada (www.century21.ca)
- Coldwell Banker Canada (www.coldwellbanker.ca)

For commercial offerings, contact

- Colliers International (www.colliers.com)
- CB Richard Ellis (www.cbre.com)
- Cushman & Wakefield LePage (www.cushmanwakefield.com)
- J.J. Barnicke Ltd. (www.jjb.com)

✔ **Government agencies:** Agencies such as Farm Credit Canada (www. fcc-fac.ca) and Statistics Canada (www.statcan.ca) generate reports that offer insights into property markets as well as economic issues that may affect demand for property, construction costs, and other facets of real estate. Many of these reports are available for free, and those that aren't are often available to consult through your local library.

A wealth of market reports is available for free, but specific information has a value! For a tailored report that addresses your specific interests or circumstances you may require the services of a consultant — and can expect to face a bill commensurate with the degree of information you're seeking. Have a look in the phone book for consultants in your area specializing in real estate or the specific facet of real estate that interests you. (See also the section in this chapter on appraisers.)

Canada Mortgage and Housing Corp.

The federally funded Canada Mortgage and Housing Corp. (www.cmhc.ca) is about more than mortgages and housing. It provides various forms of research, financing, and support services to the residential real estate sector that are worth investigating:

✔ **Financing:** Much of the federal government's investment in residential housing flows through CMHC, meaning a familiarity with the various programs and incentives it offers is key to tapping into cash that can make your property purchase or renovation project a bit more affordable (and a better investment). Typical forms of home financing from CMHC include funding for first-time home buyers, deals on mortgage insurance, and assistance for renovations (including those that add secondary suites or improve energy efficiency).

✔ **Research:** From housing starts to rental trends, building issues to business opportunities, CMHC has the lowdown on Canada's housing sector. Its annual housing outlook conference, held in major cities across Canada, provides an overview of the trends affecting residential real estate for the year ahead. Though not all CMHC's research is free of charge, it has much to offer. You'll be surprised at how much you can learn.

✔ **Support:** CMHC produces a variety of guides and reports to help you plan upgrades, full-scale renovations, or even new construction that will improve your property's value as an investment. Occasionally, CMHC hosts events that enable you to develop contacts within the real estate industry that could benefit your investment plans.

National Trade Associations

Owning a property involves more than plunking down the cash and waiting for a return. Our experience indicates that the range of services you'll need to access as an investor will always be more than you expect.

When something goes wrong, or you just need to talk to someone who possesses more specialized expertise than you have, contact a trade association that can put you in touch with someone with the knowledge and expertise to assist you.

Not all trade associations or not-for-profit groups are created equal. Some have better funding than others, some lack an efficient organizational structure, and others operate on a volunteer basis. Don't let frustration get the better of you! If you can't find the organization you need locally, or have trouble making contact, track down one in a neighbouring city or province, and see if they can help. They are usually happy to provide the advice you need, and may even be able to direct you to someone in your own area with the right answers or skills.

Assistance from trade organizations may include the following:

✔ **Advice:** Some trade organizations see a value in bridging the gap between their members and the public by providing advice that could generate business for their members. Provincial architectural associations, for example, may offer outreach programs that let homeowners know when to engage an architect and may even link homeowners with architects. Some groups educate homeowners about the best way to approach a project in the hope that property owners will use the services the group's members provide.

✔ **Supplier contacts:** No clue who is the best supplier of drywall in your area? Or where to find an antique radiator? Trade organizations can fill you in on sources and put you one step closer to finding contractors qualified to install specialized items. The Canadian Home Builders' Association (www.chba.ca), Mechanical Contractors' Association of Canada (www.mcac.ca), and similar organizations (most with provincial or municipal affiliates) are great resources to tap into.

✔ **Technical information:** For just about every component that goes into a building, a corresponding association exists. Consult these organizations to verify standards governing the following in your property:

 • Windows (Siding and Window Dealers Association of Canada, `www.sawdac.com`)

 • Electrical system (Electrical Contractors Association of Canada, `www.ceca.org`)

- Insulation (Thermal Insulation Association of Canada, www. tiac.ca)

- Flooring (North American Laminate Floor Association, www.nalfa.com; Concrete Floor Contractors Association of Canada, www.concretefloors.ca; Terrazzo, Tile and Marble Association of Canada, www.ttmac.com)

Discover how best to care for and maintain these elements of your property, and what to do with them once they reach the end of their useful life; often, industry organizations can suggest recycling or salvage alternatives.

Professional Appraisers

Appraisers are more than the people who tell you what your property's worth. An increasing number are branching out to provide services ranging from selecting sites for investors to studying the potential for developing specific properties in order to deliver the best return on an investor's dollar. These are people worth knowing!

The Appraisal Institute of Canada (www.aicanada.ca) is responsible for accrediting appraisers. The institute has chapters in each province that can connect you with institute members able to meet your needs.

Appraisers are familiar with property values, so they're ideal allies when it comes to appealing property taxes. They can build a case that may help you avoid a higher levy than you'd pay if you just sized up a property by itself. Similarly, they can also challenge the assessment of a property by a banker or insurer to ensure you're getting the best value for the property. Appraisers can also work in concert with financial planners to see that your portfolio is acquiring the right kinds of property to produce the maximum value in a given situation, or that properties are serving the right niche of the market to deliver the best possible return.

Given the growing reliance of lenders and insurers on automated valuation programs, we believe you'll get the most value by including an appraiser among your advisers (see Chapter 4). Tap their knowledge, not just their valuation skills,

The local chapters of the Appraisal Institute of Canada include the following:

- Alberta Association of the Appraisal Institute of Canada (www. appraisal.ab.ca)

- British Columbia Association Appraisal Institute of Canada (www. appraisal.bc.ca)

✔ L'Association du Québec de l'Institut canadien des évaluateurs (www.aqice.ca)

✔ Manitoba Association of the Appraisal Institute of Canada (www.aimanitoba.ca)

✔ New Brunswick Association of Real Estate Appraisers (www.nbarea.org)

✔ Nova Scotia Real Estate Appraisers Association (www.nsappraisal.ns.ca)

✔ Ontario Association of the Appraisal Institute of Canada (www.oaaic.on.ca)

✔ Saskatchewan Association of the Appraisal Institute of Canada (www.skaic.org)

Prince Edward Island and Newfoundland and Labrador's chapters don't have Web sites. Here are their addresses:

Newfoundland Provincial Association of the Appraisal Institute of Canada
PO Box 1571, Station C
St. John's, Newfoundland
A1C 5P3
Tel: (709) 753-7644

Prince Edward Island Provincial Association
PO Box 1796
Charlottetown, PEI
C1A 7N4
Tel: (902) 368-3355

Government-Run Sustainability Initiatives

Retrofitting properties to be more energy efficient, or constructing buildings to reflect so-called "green" or sustainable design elements, is a popular idea these days. Several organizations to help people develop sustainable homes and environment-friendly work spaces are out there:

✔ **Locally,** in the form of municipal sustainability programs and regional planning initiatives that encourage reductions in resource use, recycling programs, and responsible land use. Some communities have recycling centres where you can source salvaged or refurbished goods that reduce your requirements for new construction materials; centre staff are typically good sources of information on where to find out more about sustainable construction practices.

> ✔ **Nationally,** through groups such as the Canada Green Building Council (www.cagbc.org) that set standards and educate industry and the public about green building practices. The Canada Mortgage and Housing Corp. (www.cmhc.ca) also provides a number of guides that help homeowners understand how to create a more energy-efficient property.
>
> ✔ **Provincially,** through government programs and regional not-for-profit organizations that address issues relative to green building (check the Blue Pages in the phone book for references, if your local municipality is unable to point you in the right direction).

Be sure to consult your advisers and other professionals regarding the relative merits of pursuing green upgrades on your property. Renovations may add value to your property, but if you stand little chance of seeing a payback from the green features, they may not be that sustainable within your portfolio.

National and Provincial Law Societies

Staying on the right side of the law is important for any investor. You should also know who to contact if you encounter difficulties with your lawyer.

Nationally, the Federation of Law Societies of Canada (www.flsc.ca) represents the common interests of the individual provincial and territorial law societies. The 14 provincial and territorial law societies across Canada are responsible for making sure lawyers respect their obligations to clients. Most provide some form of information on issues the legal profession is facing, including with respect to real estate. Common issues worth discussing with the law society in your region include

> ✔ Concerns about potential conflict of interest or other unprofessional conduct
>
> ✔ Suspected cases of real estate fraud involving a lawyer
>
> ✔ Suspected wrongdoing or misconduct by a lawyer

Law societies are not the appropriate bodies to approach about excessive fees, or differences of opinion with a lawyer — for that, you're on your own and you have to sort things out yourself.

Here are the Web sites for the provincial and territorial law societies include the following:

- Barreau du Quebec (www.barreau.qc.ca)
- Chambre des notaires du Québec (www.cdnq.org)
- Law Society of Alberta (www.lawsocietyalberta.com)
- Law Society of British Columbia (www.lawsociety.bc.ca)
- Law Society of Manitoba (www.lawsociety.mb.ca)
- Law Society of Newfoundland and Labrador (www.lawsociety.nf.ca)
- Law Society of New Brunswick (www.lawsociety-barreau.nb.ca)
- Law Society of the Northwest Territories (www.lawsociety.nt.ca)
- Law Society of Nunavut (www.lawsociety.nu.ca)
- Law Society of Prince Edward Island (www.lspei.pe.ca)
- Law Society of Upper Canada (www.lsuc.on.ca)
- Law Society of Yukon (www.lawsocietyyukon.com)
- Nova Scotia Barristers' Society (www.nsbs.ns.ca)
- The Law Society of Saskatchewan (www.lawsociety.sk.ca)

Fundraising Networks

Networking with the goal of becoming a respected — even if small-scale — player in your industry is critical to the overall success of your investment career. It's not just real estate organizations you can network with, however. Fundraising networks can also be important to your success.

Financial networking involves more than, say, having lunch with your banker. It often means meeting other entrepreneurs and fellow investors in your community. Major centres often have organizations that can link you with sources of capital. Common places to find financial connections include the following:

- **Angel financing networks:** Match-making organizations are set up to connect people with money to investment opportunities. Angel investment networks often cover sectors beyond just real estate, but knowing who the players are, and even making known your own investment interests through these networks, may yield benefits.
- **Economic development offices of local, regional, and provincial governments:** You may not want to tap government funding to buy property, but knowing the movers and shakers in your community may connect you with private investors willing to do business with you. Often, municipal economic development offices create the environment for investors like you to do business.

Owners' Associations

Not surprisingly, given the large number of property investors in Canada and the range of issues they face, organizations exist that can help property owners with just about anything they might face. Owner organizations allow property investors to speak with a common voice on important issues ranging from property taxes to major development projects having an impact on a region. Some major organizations in Canada include the following:

- ✔ **Apartment owners' associations,** most of which operate on a provincial basis with local divisions. Membership may be most appealing to large property owners, but smaller investors with just a handful of properties are not barred from joining. In fact, if you've got plans to build your portfolio, hooking up with an association like this may allow you to develop relationships that make further investments possible.

- ✔ **Building Owners and Managers Association** (www.bomacanada.ca) is a national organization representing commercial property owners. Consider joining if you own several commercial properties and would like to meet others responsible for their management.

- ✔ **National Association of Industrial and Office Properties** (www.naiop.org), which represents industrial and office property owners in Canada's major cities. Membership typically includes larger investors and suppliers to the industrial and office sector.

Some organizations for investment property owners across the country include the following:

- ✔ B.C. Apartment Owners and Managers Association (www.bcapartmentowners.com)

- ✔ BOMA British Columbia (www.boma.bc.ca)

- ✔ BOMA Calgary (www.boma.ca)

- ✔ BOMA Canada (www.bomacanada.ca)

- ✔ BOMA Edmonton (www.bomaedmonton.org)

- ✔ BOMA Greater Toronto (www.bomatoronto.org)

- ✔ BOMA Ottawa (www.bomaottawa.org)

- ✔ BOMA Manitoba (www.bomamanitoba.ca)

- ✔ BOMA Quebec (www.boma-quebec.org)

- ✔ BOMA Regina (www.bomaregina.ca)

- ✔ Canadian Federation of Apartment Associations (www.cfaa-fcapi.org)

- ✔ Corporation des Propriétaires Immobiliers du Québec (CORPIQ) (www.corpiq.com)

- ✔ Federation of Rental-housing Providers of Ontario (www.frpo.org)

- ✔ Investment Property Owners' Association of Nova Scotia (www.ipoans.ns.ca)

- ✔ Saskatchewan Rental Housing Industry Association (www.srhia.ca)

The cost of an annual membership in any one organization may outweigh the benefits of membership. Many of the events the organizations host are open to non-members for a slightly higher fee than members pay. Even if you aren't a member, you can benefit from the organization's services and events.

Builders' Associations

Renovating your property may boost its value as an investment, but make sure you get the proper advice! Several organizations that may not at first glance seem to have a connection to investment property may have the tips to help you make the most of your investment.

Swapping stories with friends who've done projects similar to yours may be a great way to gain tips, but approaching the right organizations can put you in touch with workers who have unique skills, granting agencies willing to support your project, and resource people with guides that can bring you up to speed on current best practices for your type of building.

These organizations include the following:

- ✔ **Canadian Home Builders' Association** (www.chba.ca), and local counterparts, which can refer you to companies that have the skills, experience, and credibility that will make sure your job gets done properly.

- ✔ The **Canada Mortgage and Housing Corp.** (www.cmhc.ca), whose interest in fostering energy-efficient housing makes it an ideal resource for background information, tips, and forms of financing that can facilitate your renovation project.

- ✔ **Local heritage organizations**, many of which provide not only resources that can help you complete a renovation that reflects a home's history and architecture, but also access to funds from various levels of government. Allowing an older property to express its age may make it a more valuable asset to potential purchasers. Moreover, knowing its history may allow you to tap grants for part or all of the renovation.

An appraiser or financial planner can also advise you on the potential value a renovation could add to your property, making these and other professionals equally important sources of information regarding a renovation. In addition, municipal staff may have advice regarding the project you're considering.

Here are some regional home builders' associations:

- ✔ Canadian Home Builders Association — Alberta (www.chbaalberta.ca)
- ✔ Canadian Home Builders Association — British Columbia (www.chbabc.org)
- ✔ Canadian Home Builders' Association — Eastern Newfoundland (www.nfbuilders.com)
- ✔ Manitoba Home Builders' Association (www.homebuilders.mb.ca)
- ✔ New Brunswick Home Builders' Association (www.nbhome.nb.ca)
- ✔ Nova Scotia Home Builders' Association (www.nshba.ns.ca)
- ✔ Ontario Home Builders' Association (www.homesontario.com)
- ✔ Saskatchewan Home Builders' Association (www.saskhomebuilders.ca)

Chapter 18

Ten Ways to Build Property Value

*I*n this chapter, we outline steps you can take to maximize the value of your property. Chances are, considering such strategies will help your property to give a better return in the long run. For each point, we discuss why it's important, suggest approaches you can take to implement changes to your current practices, and flag organizations that can help you.

Warm Up to Energy Efficiency

Energy efficiency is about more than saving money! Just because you need less energy to heat and operate a building doesn't mean it has to be less comfortable. Often, it can create a more pleasant environment in which to live and work, with an interior temperature that's more even. A stable interior climate makes a building a desirable place for tenants or other users. The payback to you, as the building owner, comes in lower operating costs and a more stable cash flow from satisfied users who want to stick around.

On the other hand, you may need to invest in upgrading the building. Some consultants advise against going for an energy-efficient retrofit unless you're renovating the entire building. The changes necessary may require you to gut most of the structure, so incorporating energy enhancements as part of a general upgrade makes sense.

Before you begin, work with a consultant to identify the most critical areas for upgrading. Which parts of your property deliver the most bang for your renovation buck? And how many bucks do you need? Establishing a budget helps you set priorities for the project.

Several local and national organizations offer resources to get you started on a retrofit. The federal Office of Energy Efficiency (oee.nrcan.gc.ca) provides information on saving energy, links to retrofit incentive programs, and directories of consultants who can provide evaluations of the energy efficiency of your building. Many of the incentives for homeowners are through the Canada Mortgage and Housing Corp. (www.cmhc.ca).

Locally, utility providers across the country provide information on energy efficiency. Though these often have to do with electricity use, many also encourage homeowners to save on heating costs.

Sustain Interest with Retrofits

The *replacement cost* of a building is the cost of building from scratch at some point in the future. The longer a building's life span, the lower its effective replacement cost. Take the example of a light bulb: A cheap light bulb that burns out in 1,000 hours may be more expensive in the long-run — that is, incur a higher replacement cost — than an expensive bulb that lasts 2,000 hours because it will need replacing twice as often. To cut your replacement cost, go with the more expensive bulb that offers better value for your money in the long-term.

Sustainable building practices work the same way, with several studies now showing that environment-friendly design not only reduces the long-term replacement cost but also increases the value of a property. Sustainable features often reduce the wear-and-tear on a building by reducing energy demands, resource consumption, and the general stress on a building. Many so-called sustainable projects are built from scratch, but retrofit programs allow you to create a more valuable property from the shell of an older one (some would even say the retrofit is an example of sustainable practice).

Sustainable buildings are also healthy buildings with limited negative health impacts on users. Here are some key indicators of sustainable components in a building:

- ✔ Carpets and glues with limited or no *off-gassing,* the release of volatile organic compounds (VOCs) responsible for the new home or new car smell

- ✔ Low VOC paints

- ✔ Low-flow toilets

- ✔ Air filtration systems that capture and limit circulation of dust, mould, and other particulates

Canada Mortgage and Housing Corp. (www.cmhc.ca) is one resource for information on sustainable and healthy buildings. The Ottawa-based Healthy Indoors Partnership is another group whose mandate is to foster healthy indoor environments (www.healthyindoors.com).

A number of local organizations operated by local municipalities or oriented toward specific issues are also able to support you in the planning and implementation of a sustainable building retrofit.

Consider Your Investment Ongoing

Full-on retrofits aren't the only way to boost the value of your property. The habit of making ongoing investments in your property can also help build value. Think of it as pyramiding (something we discuss in Chapter 1) on the micro level. Rather than buying properties in sequence and developing a portfolio by constantly trading up, you build the value of a property by making regular improvements.

The improvements could be as simple as investing in new fixtures one year, or steadily upgrading the appliances or carpets as tenants move on. The slow but steady pace should allow you to make the investments on cash flow rather than having to make a single investment that requires outside financing.

Regular investments require planning, however. A strategy allows you to transform the property somewhat regularly, so you aren't left with all new appliances in half the suites and vintage appliances steadily growing more unreliable in the rest. (That kind of a scenario would probably require you to ditch the appliances in one go: Negotiate a discount for buying in bulk, and get rid of your maintenance headaches all at once!)

Making ongoing investments is a matter of personal choice, so we really can't point you to a support organization. Your best bet is to sit down with your accountant or property manager, take stock of your property, and identify various aspects of the building you could possibly improve. Points to consider in each case include

- Current age
- Style
- Operating cost
- Maintenance cost
- Expected life span and depreciation outstanding, if any
- Replacement cost

A quick tally and analysis of the costs and cachet of the various elements should highlight the areas where you need to focus your attention. Tenants will find that vintage green range and yellowing melamine countertop fashionably retro for only so long.

Discover Alternative Uses

Whether you're thinking *dépanneur*-turned-residence in Montreal or an artist's studio in a former corner store at the base of an old rooming house in Vancouver, just a little imagination can go a long way to turning your dud of a property into a desirable location.

Changing the target market for your property can help you secure higher rents with minimal investment. A new use can also provide cash flow where once there was none, as in the case of a finished basement that becomes student accommodation.

The bylaws and policies of your municipality determine what alternatives you can explore for your property. If you require a rezoning to change the use, the change may not be cost-effective and could narrow your market significantly. Even an all-purpose retail space may not be suited for all types of businesses.

As with any new venture, research the market in the surrounding area to determine the uses that would best serve the market and command higher-than-average rates for the area. The last thing some streets need is another coffee shop. But a dental office might be just the thing.

To research the market, consult relevant research reports or a knowledgeable real estate broker. If you envision a commercial use for the property, you could consult a broker who may also be willing to market the property for you.

Secure Tenants

Be kind to your tenants: That's one of the best ways to ensure they stay with you for as long as possible. We discuss landlord–tenant relations in Chapters 13 and 14, but we would be remiss here if we didn't mention fostering good tenant relations as one of the ways you can build property value.

To put things in perspective, let's consider the opposite scenario — how tenant turnover diminishes property value:

- ✔ **Greater vacancies, less income:** Sure, a tenant who gives notice and leaves may gift you with her deposit, but how quickly are you going to be able to rent out the unit she's vacated? A good unit may rent out quickly, but you may face significant delays depending on market conditions, the time of year, and other factors. The less income you have to show for it, the less valuable your investment is as an income-producing property.

  Potential purchasers aren't the only ones who want to know your property's income and performance. Lenders' perceptions are also influenced by a poor performance, and affect how much they're willing to give you to finance other projects.

- ✔ **Tenant replacement costs:** As with any business, income isn't the only measure of performance. Margins are also an important indicator of how good an investment your business is. Tenant turnover not only threatens income, it narrows your margins by forcing you to advertise and spend on other expenses you wouldn't have faced had the tenant stayed.

- ✔ **Word of mouth:** Just as positive tenant experiences can be good advertising for you, bad experiences may get around and reduce demand for your property. Disgruntled tenants warn friends not to rent from you, and you may end up with only the most desperate or unaware tenants — not the class you want, because they put your investment at greater risk of damage. (We may exaggerate just a tad, but Peter's seen it happen.)

- ✔ **Bad will:** Just as goodwill figures into the price purchasers are willing to pay for your property, *bad will* reduces the premium the property commands. Bad will accounts for detractions like poor location, or in the case of tenant turnover, undesirability, low demand, and generally bad karma. You may never know the extent of the property's bad reputation, but it could be playing a role in making your property difficult to lease out and, ultimately, to sell.

Convinced? We thought so. Respect your tenants, and a stable cash flow follows. Don't respect them, and not only might you lose income, but also the value of your property might suffer.

Encourage Referrals

Having a stable tenant base is important to a stable cash flow from your investment property. Many tenants find a property where camaraderie between neighbours is part of the dynamic an attractive feature.

To encourage this, and reduce the frequency with which you may otherwise need to advertise for new tenants, you may wish to offer existing tenants a finder's fee when vacancies arise. They may have friends or colleagues interested in the space, and rewarding them for reducing your hassles is a nice touch.

Although it's great to have a close-knit group of tenants, the last thing you want to create is a situation in which a mob mentality develops, especially one in which your property isn't respected. A group of difficult tenants that's too close can, in some situations, create an obstacle to effective property management.

Careful judgment of character helps you weed out unsuitable or unsavoury tenants or sets of tenants before they become a problem to their neighbours — and to your precious investment.

Undertake Upgrades Between Tenants

Rather than undertaking a complete makeover or regular maintenance (after all, you don't always have access to a tenant's suite), you can focus on simple upgrades between leases. A few touches like a new paint job, flooring, and the like allow you to justify increased rents to subsequent tenants.

The challenge, of course, is knowing which improvements to make and the level of rent the market is willing to accept for them. Refinishing a hardwood floor without cleaning up the cracked walls doesn't make sense, and none of the above pays off if tenants don't see a value in it. (Positioning a property toward tenants who see a value in such things is part of the trick too.)

Here are some key aspects of a unit that deserve regular attention and review:

- Carpets and flooring
- Walls and wall coverings
- Lighting and fixtures
- Kitchen area
- Bathroom area

Generally, you may be able to charge a rent 10 to 15 percent above what you charged prior to the upgrade, enough above the maximum rent increase allowed during a given tenancy to make the upgrade worthwhile.

Apartment owners' associations can provide guidance regarding upgrades most likely to pay off in your area, or can direct you to consultants able to advise you on changes you could make. Many apartment owners face similar situations, so connecting with others helps you decide what works best for your property.

Having an improvement strategy and maintenance schedule for your property allows you to effectively combine regular maintenance and major upgrades into the management of a property.

Raise the Rent

The greater the rent you can obtain for a property, the more valuable the property can be. But legislation limits rent increases in most areas, a protection for cash-strapped tenants as well as a moderating factor for landlords.

Tenants should receive what they pay for, but you also want rents to reflect the value of a property. And unfortunately, increases in operating costs such as heating bills and ongoing maintenance require that rents keep pace with economic realities. Raising rents on existing tenants leasing from month-to-month is just one means of ratcheting up returns. You may prefer to renegotiate leases at specific intervals to have greater control over rents. Some residential landlords, for example, offer leases annually rather than for a one-year term that continues on a month-to-month basis thereafter. The formal renegotiation of the lease doesn't preclude the existing tenant from continuing to occupy the premises, but the landlord has an opportunity to redefine the relationship and increase rents as needed.

Alternatively, you may wish to assess the average stay of tenants, gauge where rents and operating costs are going for your area, and charge new tenants a rent that reflects the future rental environment. It's an aggressive tactic but the advantage is that tenants know how much they'll be paying — and you are assured of a reputation as a landlord disinclined to raise rents.

Rents that reflect your call of future trends are inherently risky, yet they can work if the property rented justifies the rent asked. After all, we're not suggesting you charge something completely out of line with the market!

Be sure you check the restrictions that the landlord-tenancy legislation in your province imposes on rent increases. A rent increase in excess of the legal limits could result in a challenge that not only brings you bad publicity but also penalties.

Consider Paid Parking

The real estate you're trading on in a revenue-generating property isn't just the units you rent out. Most apartments and commercial developments come with parking areas that can be lucrative little revenue generators. In large urban centres where parking is in short supply, many tenants opt to rent their parking spots to commuters.

Don't let your tenants have all the fun! Suites with parking spots should fetch a premium from tenants. Whether the fee is part of a tenant's monthly rent or a separate fee charged to users who may or may not be tenants, you should take advantage of demand for parking to maximize the property's value to users of all kinds.

To determine how much you should charge for parking, check what the local municipality is charging for on-street parking and charge at least double that rate. You're factoring in the convenience and security to users of a dedicated parking spot.

Trade Up

We didn't say anywhere in this chapter that building property value had to take place at the same property. Sometimes, the best option lies in selling (something we discuss in Chapter 16) and reinvesting the proceeds in a property with greater potential. It's natural, as your portfolio grows, to want to trade up to properties that promise a better return.

Some of the circumstances in which trading up may make sense include the following:

- ✔ You have made all the improvements to the property you wish to make.
- ✔ Rents for the property show little potential to appreciate.
- ✔ Equity in your existing property is sufficient to allow you to purchase in an area with greater potential for price appreciation.
- ✔ You're ready for a change.

Ideally, the value you've built in your original property continues to grow in the new investment property. You won't have sold out, you have bought in to a new, more lucrative venture!

Whatever the reason for trading up, consult your advisers to ensure market circumstances are favourable and that the sale and reinvestment meshes with your overall investment strategy.

Glossary

● ●

*T*his glossary provides plenty of plain-language definitions for terms we've used in this book, and others you may come across in the course of buying, selling, and managing your properties.

ACB: See *Adjusted cost base*.

Acceleration clause: Usually written into a mortgage to allow the lender to accelerate or call the entire principal balance of the mortgage, plus accrued interest, when the payments become delinquent.

Adjusted cost base (ACB): The value of the real property established for tax purposes. It is the original cost plus any allowable capital improvements, plus certain acquisition costs, plus any mortgage interest costs, less any depreciation.

Agreement of purchase and sale: A written agreement between the owner and a purchaser for the purchase of real estate for a predetermined price and terms.

Amenities: Generally, those parts of the condominium or apartment building that are intended to beautify the premises and that are for the enjoyment of occupants rather than for utility.

Amortization: The reduction of a loan through periodic payments in which interest is charged only on the unpaid balance.

Amortization period: The actual number of years it will take to repay a mortgage loan in full. This can be well in excess of the loan's term. For example, mortgages often have five-year terms but 25-year amortization periods.

Analysis of property: The systematic method of determining the performance of investment real estate using a property analysis form.

Appraised value: An estimate of the fair market value of the property, usually performed by an appraiser.

Assessment fee: Also referred to as the maintenance fee. A monthly fee that condominium owners must pay, usually including management fees, costs of common property upkeep, heating costs, garbage-removal costs, the owner's contribution to the contingency reserve fund, and so on. In the case of time-shares, the fee is normally levied annually.

Assumption agreement: A legal document signed by a home buyer that requires the buyer to assume responsibility for the obligations of a mortgage made by a former owner.

Balance sheet: A financial statement that indicates the financial status of a condominium corporation or apartment building, or other revenue property, at a specific point in time by listing its assets and liabilities.

Base rent: The fixed rent paid by a tenant. This is separate from any rent paid as a result of extra charges or percentage rents.

Blended payments: Equal payments consisting of both a principal and an interest component, paid each month during the term of the mortgage. The principal portion increases each month, while the interest portion decreases, but the total monthly payment does not change.

Budget: An annual estimate of a condominium corporation or apartment building's expenses and the revenues needed to balance those expenses. There are operating budgets and capital budgets. (See also *Capital budget.*)

Canada Mortgage and Housing Corporation (CMHC): The federal Crown corporation that administers the National Housing Act. CMHC services include providing housing information and assistance, financing, and insuring home-purchase loans for lenders.

Canadian Real Estate Association (CREA): An association of members of the real estate industry, principally real estate agents and brokers.

Capital budget: An estimate of costs to cover replacements and improvements, and the corresponding revenues needed to balance them, usually for a 12-month period. Different from an operating budget.

Capital gain: Profit on the sale of an asset that is subject to taxation.

Capital improvements: Major improvements made to a property that are written off over several years rather than expensed off in the year in which they are made.

Capitalization rate (CAP): The percentage of return on an investment when purchased on a free-and-clear or all-cash basis.

Charge: A document registered against a property, stating that someone has or believes he or she has a claim on the property.

Closing: The actual completion of the transaction acknowledging satisfaction of all legal and financial obligations between buyer and seller, and acknowledging the deed or transfer of title and disbursement of funds to appropriate parties.

Closing costs: The expenses over and above the purchase price of buying and selling real estate.

Closing date: The date on which the sale of a property becomes final and the new owner takes possession.

Collateral mortgage: A loan backed up by a promissory note and the security of a mortgage on a property. The money borrowed may be used for the purchase of a property or for another purpose, such as home renovations or a vacation.

Common area: The area in a condominium project that is shared by all of the condominium owners, such as elevators, hallways, and parking lots.

Common area maintenance: The charge to owners to maintain the common areas, normally due on a monthly basis.

Condominium: A housing unit to which the owner has title and of which the owner also owns a share in the common area (such as elevators, hallways, swimming pool, land, et cetera).

Condominium corporation: The condominium association of unit owners incorporated under some provincial condominium legislation, automatically at the time of registration of the project. It is called a strata corporation in British Columbia. Under each of the provincial statutes, it will differ from an ordinary corporation in many respects. The condominium corporation, unlike a private business corporation, usually does not enjoy limited liability, and any judgment against the corporation for the payment of money is usually a judgment against each owner. The objects of the corporation are to manage the property and any assets of the corporation, and its duties include effecting compliance by the owners with the requirements of the Act, the declaration, the bylaws, and the rules.

Condominium council: The governing body of the condominium corporation, elected at the annual general meeting of the corporation.

Conventional mortgage: A mortgage loan that does not exceed 75 percent of the appraised value or of the purchase price of the property, whichever is the less. Mortgages that exceed this limit generally must be insured by mortgage insurance, such as that provided by CMHC and GEM.

Conversion: The changing of a structure from some other use, such as a rental apartment to a condominium apartment.

Conveyancing: The transfer of property, or title to property, from one party to another.

Debt service: Cost of paying interest for use of mortgage money.

Deductions: The expenses that the Canada Revenue Agency allows one to deduct from gross income.

Deed: This document conveys the title of the property to the purchaser. Different terminology may be used in different provincial jurisdictions.

Depreciation: The amount by which a property owner writes off the value of a real estate investment over the useful life of the investment. Does not include the value of the land.

Down payment: An initial amount of money (in the form of cash) put forward by the purchaser. Usually it represents the difference between the purchase price and the amount of the mortgage loan.

Encumbrance: See *Charge.*

Equity: The difference between the price for which a property could be sold and the total debts registered against it.

Equity return: The percentage ratio between an owner's equity in the property and the total of cash flow plus mortgage principal reduction.

Escrow: The holding of a deed or contract by a third party until fulfillment of certain stipulated conditions between the contracting parties.

Estate: The title or interest one has in property such as real estate and personal property that can, if desired, be passed on to survivors at the time of one's death.

Fair market value: The value established on real property that is determined to be one that a buyer is willing to pay and for which a seller is willing to sell.

Fee simple: A manner of owning land, in one's own name and free of any conditions, limitations, or restrictions.

Financial statements: Documents that show the financial status of the condominium corporation, apartment building, or other revenue property at a given point in time. Generally includes income and expense statement and balance sheet.

Fiscal year: The 12-month period in which financial affairs are calculated.

Floating-rate mortgage: Another term for variable-rate mortgage.

Foreclosure: A legal procedure whereby the lender obtains ownership of, or the right to sell, the property following default by the borrower.

GE Mortgage Insurance Canada (GEM): A private company providing mortgage insurance in Canada.

GEM: The initials for GE Mortgage Insurance Canada. See *GE Mortgage Insurance Canada.*

High-ratio mortgage: A conventional mortgage loan that exceeds 75 percent of the appraised value or purchase price of the property. Such a mortgage must be insured.

Income, gross: Income or cash flow before expenses.

Income, net: Income or cash flow after expenses (but generally before income tax).

Interest averaging: The method of determining the overall average interest rate being paid when more than one mortgage is involved.

Interim financing: The temporary financing by a lender during the construction of real property for resale, or while awaiting other funds.

Leases, sub: Contract by which the lessee leases part of his or her premises to another user.

Legal description: Identification of a property that is recognized by law, that identifies that property from all others.

Lessee: The tenant in rental space.

Lessor: The owner of the rental space.

Letter of intent: Used in place of a formal written contract with a deposit. The prospective purchaser informs the seller, in writing, that he or she is willing to enter into a formal purchase contract upon certain terms and conditions if they are acceptable to the seller.

Leverage: The use of financing or other people's money to control large pieces of real property with a small amount of invested capital.

Limited partnership: An investment group in which one partner serves as the general partner and the others as limited partners. The general partner bears all of the financial responsibility and management of the investment. The limited partners are obligated only to the extent of their original investment plus possible personal guarantees.

Listings, exclusive agency: A signed agreement by a seller in which he or she agrees to co-operate with one broker. All other brokers must go through the listing broker.

Listings, multiple: (See also *Multiple Listing Service.*) A system of agency/ sub-agency relationships. If Broker A lists the property for sale, "A" is the vendor's agent. If Broker B sees the MLS listing and offers it for sale, "B" is the vendor's sub-agent.

Listings, open: A listing given to one or more brokers, none of whom have any exclusive rights or control over the sale, by other brokers or the owner of the property.

Marginal tax rate: That point in income at which any additional income will be taxed at a higher tax rate.

MLS: See *Multiple Listing Service.*

Mortgage: The document that pledges real property as collateral for an indebtedness.

Mortgage, balloon: A mortgage amortized over a number of years, but that requires the entire principal balance to be paid at a certain time, short of the full amortization period.

Mortgage, constant: The interest rate charged on a mortgage consisting of both the rate being charged by the lender and the rate that represents the amount of principal reduction each period.

Mortgage, deferred payment: A mortgage allowing for payments to be made on a deferred or delayed basis. Usually used where present income is not sufficient to make the payments.

Mortgage, discounted: The selling of a mortgage to another party at a discount or an amount less than the face value of the mortgage.

Mortgage, first: A mortgage placed on a property in first position.

Mortgage, fixed: This is a conventional mortgage, with payments of interest and principal. Fixed terms with a fixed rate can vary from six months to ten years or more.

Mortgage, insurance: Insurance provided by the lender as an option for the borrower. It would pay out the balance outstanding on the mortgage, in the event of the borrower's death.

Mortgage, interest only: Payments are made only to interest. There is no principal reduction in the payment.

Mortgage, points: The interest rate charged by the lender.

Mortgage, second: A mortgage placed on a property in second position to an already existing first mortgage.

Mortgage, variable: A mortgage with an interest rate that fluctuates with the Bank of Canada interest rate. The mortgagee just pays the interest, with optional pay-down on the principal. Different from a fixed-rate mortgage (see *Mortgage, fixed*).

Mortgage wraparound: Sometimes called an all-inclusive mortgage. A mortgage that includes any existing mortgages on the property. The buyer makes one large payment on the wraparound and the seller continues making the existing mortgage payments out of that payment.

Mortgagee: The lender.

Mortgagor: The borrower.

Multiple Listing Service (MLS): A service licensed to member real estate boards by the Canadian Real Estate Association. Used to compile and disseminate information by publication and computer concerning a given property to a large number of agents and brokers.

National Housing Act (NHA) Loan: A mortgage loan that is insured by Canada Mortgage and Housing Corp. to certain maximums.

Offer to purchase: The document that sets forth all the terms and conditions under which a purchaser offers to purchase property. This offer, when accepted by the seller, becomes a binding agreement of purchase and sale once all conditions have been removed.

Operating budget: An estimate of costs to operate a building or condominium complex and corresponding revenues needed to balance them, usually for a 12-month period. Different from a capital budget.

Operating costs: Those expenses required to operate an investment property, generally excluding mortgage payments.

Option agreement: A contract, with consideration, given to a purchaser of a property, giving him or her the right to purchase at a future date. If the individual chooses not to purchase, the deposit is forfeited to the seller.

Personal property: Property in an investment property, such as carpeting, draperies, refrigerators, et cetera, that can be depreciated over a shorter useful life than the structure itself.

PI: Principal and interest due on a mortgage.

PIT: Principal, interest, and taxes due on a mortgage.

Prepayment penalty: A penalty charge written into many mortgages that must be paid if the mortgage is paid off ahead of schedule.

Principal: The amount the purchaser actually borrowed, or the portion of it still owing on the original loan.

Property manager: A manager or management company hired to run an investment property for the owner.

Purchase-and-sale agreement: See *Agreement of purchase and sale*.

Pyramiding: The process of building real estate wealth by allowing appreciation and mortgage principal reduction to increase the investors' equity in a series of ever larger properties.

Resident manager: An individual, usually living in the building, who handles all of the day-to-day problems therein.

Sale/lease-back: The tenant in a building sells it to an investor and leases it back for a period of years.

Tax shelter: The tax write-off possible through the depreciation benefits available on investment real estate ownership.

Title: Generally, the evidence of right that a person has to the possession of property.

Title insurance: This insurance covers the purchaser or vendor, in case of any defects in the property or title, that existed at the time of sale but were not known until after the sale.

Trust account: The separate account in which a lawyer or real estate broker holds funds until the real estate closing takes place or other legal disbursement is made.

Trust funds: Funds held in trust, either as a deposit for the purchase of real property or to pay taxes and insurance.

Unit: Normally refers to the rental suite or that part of a condominium owned and occupied or rented by the owner.

Useful life: The term during which an asset is expected to have useful value.

Vacancy allowance: A projected deduction from the scheduled gross income of a building to allow for loss of income due to vacant apartments or other rental units.

Value, assessed: The property value as determined by local, regional, or provincial assessment authority.

Vendor: A person selling a piece of property.

Vendor take-back: A procedure wherein the seller (vendor) of a property provides some or all of the mortgage financing in order to sell the property. Also referred to as vendor financing.

Zoning: Rules for land use established by local governments.

Index

• C •

• *M* •

Notes

Notes

Notes

Notes

Notes

Notes

BUSINESS & PERSONAL FINANCE

0-470-83768-3

0-470-83740-3

Also available:

- Accounting For Dummies
  0-7645-7836-7
- Business Plans Kit For Dummies
  0-7645-9794-9
- Canadian Small Business Kit For
  Dummies 0-470-83818-3
- Investing For Canadians For
  Dummies 0-470-83361-0
- Leadership For Dummies
  0-7645-5176-0

- Managing For Dummies
  0-7645-1771-6
- Marketing For Dummies
  0-7645-5600-2
- Money Management All-in-One Desk
  Reference For Canadians For
  Dummies 0-470-83360-2
- Stock Investing For Canadians For
  Dummies 0-470-83342-4

HOME & BUSINESS COMPUTER BASICS

0-7645-7326-8   0-7645-8849-4

Also available:

- Blogging For Dummies
  0-471-77084-1
- Excel 2003 All-in-One Desk Reference
  For Dummies 0-7645-3758-x
- Macs For Dummies 0-7645-5656-8

- Office 2003 All-in-One Desk
  Reference For Dummies
  0-7645-3883-7
- Outlook 2003 For Dummies
  0-7645-3759-8
- PCs For Dummies 0-7645-8958-x
- Upgrading & Fixing PCs For
  Dummies 0-7645-1665-5

FOOD, HOME, GARDEN, HOBBIES, MUSIC & PETS

0-7645-9904-6   0-7645-5232-5

Also available:
- Diabetes Cookbook For Dummies
  0-7645-5130-2
- Gardening For Canadians For
  Dummies 1-894413-37-7
- Holiday Decorating For Dummies
  0-7645-2570-0
- Home Improvement All-in-One
  Desk Reference For Dummies
  0-7645-5680-0
- Knitting For Dummies
  0-7645-5395-x-
- Piano For Dummies 0-7645-5105-1

- Puppies For Dummies
  0-7645-5255-4
- Scrapbooking For Dummies
  0-7645-7208-3
- Sudoku For Dummies
  0-470-01892-5
- Dog Training For Dummies
  0-7645-8418-9
- 30-Minute Meals For Dummies
  0-7645-2589-1

INTERNET & DIGITAL MEDIA

0-7645-9802-3   0-471-74739-4

Also available:
- CD & DVD Recording For Dummies
  0-7645-5956-7
- eBay For Dummies 0-7645-5654-1
- Electronics For Dummies
  0-7645-7660-7
- Fighting Spam For Dummies
  0-7645-5965-6
- Genealogy Online For Dummies
  0-7645-5964-8

- Google For Dummies
  0-7645-4420-9
- Home Recording For Musicians For
  Dummies 0-7645-8884-2
- The Internet For Dummies
  0-7645-8996-2
- Podcasting For Dummies
  0-471-74898-6

SPORTS, FITNESS, PARENTING, RELIGION & SPIRITUALITY

0-471-76871-5   0-7645-5418-2

Also available:
- The Bible For Dummies
  0-7645-5296-1
- Catholicism For Dummies
  0-7645-5391-7
- Coaching Hockey For Dummies
  0-470-83685-7
- Curling For Dummies
  0-47083828-0

- Fitness For Dummies
  0-7645-7851-0
- Pilates For Dummies
  0-7645-5397-6
- Teaching Kids to Read For
  Dummies 0-7645-4043-2
- Weight Training For Dummies
  0-7645-76845-6

TRAVEL

0-470-83398-X   0-7645-7386-1

Also available:
- Alaska For Dummies 0-7645-7746-8
- Cancun and the Yucatan For Dummies 0-7645-7828-6
- Cruise Vacations For Dummies 0-7645-9830-9
- Europe For Dummies 0-7645-7529-5
- Ireland For Dummies 0-7645-7749-2
- Las Vegas For Dummies 0-7645-7382-9
- London For Dummies 0-471-74870-6
- New York City For Dummies 0-7645-6945-7
- Nova Scotia, New Brunswick & Prince Edward Island For Dummies 0-470-836739-x
- Paris For Dummies 0-7645-7630-5
- Vancouver & Victoria For Dummies 0-470-83684-9
- Walt Disney World & Orlando For Dummies 0-471-78250-5

NETWORKING, SECURITY, PROGRAMMING & DATABASES

0-7645-3910-8   0-7645-5784-X

Also available:
- Ajax For Dummies 0-471-78597-0
- Access 2003 All-in-One Desk Reference For Dummies 0-7645-3988-4
- Beginning Programming For Dummies 0-7645-4997-9
- C++ For Dummies 0-7645-6852-3
- Firewalls For Dummies 0-7645-4048-3
- Network Security For Dummies 0-7645-1679-5
- Networking For Dummies 0-7645-7583-x
- TCP/IP For Dummies 0-7645-1760-0
- XML For Dummies 0-7645-8845-1
- Wireless All-in-One Desk Reference For Dummies 0-7645-7496-5

HEALTH & SELF-HELP

0-470-83370-X   0-7645-4149-8

Also available:
- Arthritis For Dummies 0-7645-7074-9
- Asthma For Dummies 0-7645-4233-8
- Breast Cancer For Dummies 0-7645-2482-8
- Controlling Cholesterol For Dummies 0-7645-5440-9
- Depression For Dummies 0-7645-3900-0
- Fertility For Dummies 0-7645-2549-2
- Fibromyalgia For Dummies 0-7645-5441-7
- Improving Your Memory For Dummies 0-7645-5435-2
- Menopause For Dummies 0-7645-5458-1
- Pregnancy For Dummies 0-7645-4483-7
- Relationships For Dummies 0-7645-5384-4
- Thyroid For Dummies 0-471-78755-8

EDUCATION, HISTORY & REFERENCE

0-470-83656-3   0-7645-2498-4

Also available: